Collect

PREWAR
LIONEL
TRAINS
1900-1942

David Doyle

©2007 David Doyle

Published by

krause publications
An Imprint of F+W Publications

700 East State Street • Iola, WI 54990-0001
715-445-2214 • 888-457-2873
www.krausebooks.com

Our toll-free number to place an order or obtain
a free catalog is (800) 258-0929.
All rights reserved. No portion of this publication may be reproduced or transmitted in any form or by any means, electronic or mechanical, including photocopy, recording, or any information storage and retrieval system, without permission in writing from the publisher, except by a reviewer who may quote brief passages in a critical article or review to be printed in a magazine or newspaper, or electronically transmitted on radio, television, or the Internet.

Library of Congress Catalog Number: 2006935438
ISBN 13-digit: 978-0-89689-462-4

Designed by Kay Sanders
Edited by Justin Moen

Printed in China

Acknowledgments

When I worked on my first Lionel-related book, "The Standard Catalog of® Lionel Trains, 1945-1969," I had the assistance of a number of friends I had made through my years of collecting trains from that era. When I undertook this book, however, I realized that I would need to reach out for help to an even wider circle of collectors. As a result, not only has my knowledge been broadened, but so too has the circle of people that I call friends.

Many collectors and businesses shared photographs with me or allowed me to make my own images of rare and important pieces in their collections. Many knowledgeable collectors and dealers graciously reviewed the manuscript and offered corrections, criticism and commentary, and provided valuable insight on values for the items listed. Every effort has been made to present complete and accurate information here, and any errors are purely my own.

The late Gary Lavinous and his team of dedicated volunteers stayed until nearly midnight at the National Toy Train Museum helping me photograph many of the rarest pieces shown in this volume. Though their day was nearing 18 hours long, they dismantled display cases to allow access, not only without complaining, but with genuine enthusiasm.

Jan Athey, reference librarian for the Train Collector's Association, graciously located and allowed us to photograph many of Lionel's prewar catalogs. Former TCA president Dr. Paul Wassermann supplied additional images for that, and other chapters as well.

After long work days, Bill Blystone then worked well into the evening photographing items from his extensive prewar collection. Jim Nicholson allowed our photographer to spend two days in his home taking photos, then lent additional items for studio photography. With the date of the world's largest train show, the Eastern Division TCA meet in York, Pa., just around the corner–a show he runs as a volunteer–Clem Clement allowed us to photograph his wonderful Standard Gauge collection.

Barb Jones lent not only her photographic skills, but also her wonderful prewar collection and vast knowledge to this effort. Scott Douglas, another respected prewar collector, also provided photographs and information critical to this work.

The chapter on Lionel's smallest trains, and perhaps the smallest niche in prewar collecting, 00, would not have been possible without the help of Ken Shirey.

My old friend, Jeff Kane at www.ttender.com, not only sent individual items from his extensive inventory of prewar Lionel repair parts, but also many scarce 00 trains.

Dave McEntarfer contributed many photos, and much enthusiasm and experience, to this project. Joe Mania, who produces exquisite reproductions of some of Lionel's earliest, rarest and most valuable trains, provided photographs of these products as an aid in differentiating authentic pieces from reproductions. His integrity is to be commended.

Parts with Character shared much knowledge and experience with me, as well as allowing needed photos to be taken.

Barry Gilmore, who once gave the sage collecting advice, "Never buy a train you feel you should apologize for," opened his collection to our camera. Dennis Waldron answered many questions about Lionel's scale and semiscale production.

Train collecting is a passion for the entire Tschopp family, and they all pitched in on this project. Brothers Bob and John opened their collection for photography and shared their knowledge. Their sister, Mary Burns and her husband Terry put in a long, long day helping photograph the couple's fabulous prewar collection. Bob Senior provided several rare Standard Gauge pieces, and teen-ager Bobby, the newest collector of the family, tireless located trains for photography.

James D. Julia auctions provided photos of a few key pieces from their past sales.

Greg Stout of Stout Auctions, who arguably handles the largest train collections in the country, granted us unlimited access for photography, and as a result, saved many, many hours of work and miles of driving. His phenomenal knowledge and amazing memory were tremendous assets in this project.

A handful of collectors chose to remain anonymous. Their anonymity, however, does not lessen the value of their contributions of photographs and information to this work. Thank you.

CONTENTS

LIONEL TRAINS AND THE COLLECTING HOBBY	6
HOW TO USE THIS COLLECTOR'S GUIDE	12
2-7/8-INCH GAUGE AND STANDARD GAUGE	20
O-GAUGE	78
OO-GAUGE	146
ACCESSORIES, TOYS AND NOVELTIES	158
LIONEL CATALOGS AND PAPER PRODUCTS	232
APPENDIX I Awakening Sleeping Toys	252
APPENDIX II Setting Up Your Train	257
GLOSSARY	265

No. 2 TROLLEY

Lionel Trains and the

Lionel—few brand names have the instantaneous recognition that Lionel enjoys in its second century. Young or old, male or female, it seems almost everyone identifies the name with toy trains—in fact, to many people the two are synonymous.

The firm bears the middle name of its founder, Joshua Lionel Cohen, the son of immigrants, born Aug. 25, 1877. Young Cohen, a clever inventor and shameless self-promoter with a clear head for business, formed the company with Harry Grant on Sept. 5, 1900. Their first business was with the U.S. Navy, producing fuses for mines.

The Navy work completed, Cohen began tinkering, trying to find a product to keep him and his partner busy and his new firm afloat. A motor he developed for a less-than-successful fan was installed under a gondola car. The car was placed on a circle of steel rails connected to dry cell batteries and, in 1900, the age of Lionel Electric Trains began.

As originally conceived, the "train"—still only a motorized gondola car—was to be an animated window display for shopkeepers to use promoting other products. Immediately, though, it was apparent that there

Collecting Hobby

was more interest in the displays than the goods they held and the transition from merchandising aid to retail product was made.

In 1902, in addition to the gondola car, Lionel offered a miniature trolley, the first step towards realism. Like the gondola, the trolley ran on two-rail 2-7/8-inch gauge track. The first catalog was produced in 1900 and an American icon was born. Unfortunately, Cohen's partner Grant, though also a gifted inventor, was not a capable administrator. This led to a man joining the payroll whom was arguably as influential to the company, and its trains, as Cohen himself; an Italian immigrant named Mario Caruso. Hired at age 18 as a laborer, Caruso rose to secretary-treasurer, managing the company's factories, first in New York, then New Haven, followed by Newark—and ultimately the massive 15-acre Irvington plant—in a no-nonsense manner. Quality, production and cost-control were always of great concern and skillfully balanced by Caruso.

In 1906, Lionel began producing trains that rolled on "Standard Gauge" track, and, in 1915, this was supplemented by the smaller "O-Gauge" trains. Though Lionel made forays into other sizes, namely OO in 1938, and, after World War II, three attempts at HO, it was to be O-Gauge where Lionel ultimately rose to notoriety. It is also the predominate size of trains produced after World War II.

In 1909, Lionel first used the slogan "Standard of the World," but it would be many years before the bold statement would become fact.

In 1910, for reasons unknown today, Cohen changed his last name to the one he is remembered by today, Cowen. A few years later, in 1918, the firm would change names as well, as the Lionel Manufacturing Co. became The Lionel Corp.

While toy train production continued in Lionel's plant during the first World War, alongside were defense products—after all, that is how the company was born—primarily signaling and navigational devices. This type of relationship would continue as long as The Lionel Corp. was in the manufacturing business, during both wartime and peacetime.

In 1923, Lionel revamped its Standard Gauge offerings, replacing the somewhat realistic but dingy colors used previously with a veritable kaleidoscope of blues, greens, yellows and oranges...all augmented with bright brass, copper and nickel trim. These later trains constitute what is considered the classic era of Standard Gauge production.

The Great Depression was hard on Lionel, but harder on its competition. During the recession that preceded the Great Depression, Lionel, along with American Flyer, took over its bankrupt competitor Ives. In 1930, Lionel became the sole owner of Ives. Thirty-six years later Lionel would take over American Flyer as well.

World War II would bring a halt to Lionel's toy production, with toy train production ending in June 1942. The Lionel plant, like countless

50 WARTIME FREIGHT TRAIN, 1943

others throughout the country, became totally devoted to manufacturing military products.

The complete cessation of train production for three years provided Lionel the opportunity to revamp its line. When production resumed in the fall of 1945, not only was Standard Gauge not mentioned, but the O-Gauge trains had newly designed trucks and couplers that were incompatible with the previous models and a newly designed plastic-bodied gondola car. Over the next few years, plastics would increasingly replace the previously used metals in Lionel's products.

Joshua Cowen resigned as Chairman of the Board at the end of 1958 and less than a year later sold his stock in the firm to a syndicate headed by his eccentric and controversial great-nephew, Roy Cohn.

Ultimately, in 1969, The Lionel Toy Corp. (as it had become known in 1965) exited the toy train business by licensing the name and selling the tooling to the Fundimensions Division of General Mills. Some production was moved immediately and by the mid-1970s, Lionel trains were no longer a presence in the huge Hillside plant.

With the exception of 1967, Lionel Trains have been, and are still, in production since 1945, and trains were available even in the bleak 1967. Today's Lionel trains have elaborate paint schemes and sophisticated electronics undreamed of at the dawn of the 20th century. Despite these advances, they lack the mystique of the originals. Many of today's trains are manufactured as a collectible, to be displayed or operated. Rarely are they played with, as Josh Cowen urged his young patrons. Perhaps it is memories of a small child remembering expectations of Christmases long ago, or sneaking the new catalog to school hidden in a tablet, hoping to one day own that special item, that fuels today's interest in yesterday's toys. Counter to what one may think by glancing at the prices in vintage catalogs, Lionel trains were always expensive, high-quality toys. They were built to last a lifetime and many have. Now that the baby boomers have reached adulthood, many of childhood's financial constraints are lifted—the toys of youthful dreams are at last within grasp.

COLLECTING

Toy train collectors are their own fraternity, eagerly welcoming new buffs with a sincere interest in toy trains. Avail yourself of this knowledge base and friendship. No matter if you are an experienced collector or a rookie, something can always be learned. There is no substitute for experience in this hobby, as in any other. No book, no matter how complete, contains all the answers. Thousands of words and the best illustrations cannot equal the experience gained by holding a piece in your own hands. There is no finer place than in the home of a friend and fellow collector. The piece that is not for sale can be examined unhurried and questions can be answered honestly, an excellent preparation for seeking an item in the marketplace.

The advent of Internet auctions has been a boon for collectors in remote areas. But for those in more populous areas, there is no substitute for shopping in the company of fellow collectors at hobby shops and train shows, especially for the neophyte. Examining an item personally, with the counsel of more experienced collectors, is especially urged when purchasing expensive, often repaired or forged items.

However, after gaining some experience, working with a trusted and reputable train auction company can provide access to trains that may take years, or even decades, to acquire.

Enthusiasts have been collecting toy trains perhaps as long as they have been produced. In the United States, the largest and oldest collectors group is the Train Collector's Association, or TCA. Founded in 1954 in Yardley, Pa., the group has grown to more than 31,000 members. An annual convention is held at various locations around the country each summer. Smaller, regional groups called Divisions and Chapters dot the nation. Twice each year, one such group, the Eastern Division, hosts the largest toy train show in the world. The York Fairgrounds, in York, Pa., becomes a veritable Mecca for the toy train buff with several buildings encompassing more than 100,000 square feet of toy trains for sale,

100 ELECTRIC LOCOMOTIVE

Collecting

display or trade. Members of the TCA agree to abide by a code of conduct, assuring fair and honest dealings between members. The nationally recognized grading standards were developed by the TCA.

The TCA National Headquarters and the associated National Toy Train Museum is located in Strasburg, Pa. The Train Collector's Association can be reached at its Web site, www.traincollectors.org, or by writing to:

Train Collector's Association, P.O. Box 248, 300 Paradise Lane, Strasburg, PA 17579. Phone (717) 687-8623.

The second-oldest organization is the Toy Train Operating Society, formed on the West Coast in 1966. Similar in style and purpose to the TCA, traditionally the bulk of the TTOS members and events have been in the west, but have been gradually spreading eastward. The TTOS can be contacted at:

Toy Train Operating Society, 25 W. Walnut Street, Suite 308, Pasadena, CA 91103. Phone (626) 578-0673.

One of the first, and certainly the largest Lionel-specific clubs is the Lionel Collector's Club of America. Founded Aug. 1, 1970, by Jim Gates of Des Moines, Iowa, the organization has grown steadily since. The club was founded on the idea that collectors and operators of Lionel trains need an organization of their own. The club's mailing address is:

LCCA Business Office, P.O. Box 479 La Salle, IL 61301-0479.

The youngster of these groups is the Lionel Operating Train Society, or LOTS. Founded in 1979 by Larry Keller of Cincinnati, this club's purpose is providing a national train club for operators of Lionel trains and accessories. Like the others, it publishes magazines, swap-lists and a membership directory. LOTS can be reached at:

LOTS Business Office, 6376 West Fork Road, Cincinnati, OH 45247-5.

390E 2-4-2 STEAM LOCOMOTIVE

How to Use This

This book is intended to aid both the novice and the experienced collector of Lionel products. The subject matter is broken down into groups by gauge: Standard Gauge, O-Gauge and OO Gauge. Within these subcategories, the items are arranged numerically by stock number. The stock number on the vast majority of Lionel's products was stamped either on the side or underside of the item.

Thus, if you pick up a Standard Gauge gondola car that is numbered 212, you can turn to the Standard Gauge chapter and move through the listings until you reach the number 212. You will then find that this car was a Standard Gauge car produced from 1926 through 1940, and it was made in at least three distinct colors. Near many listings, you will find a photo of the item described.

For items produced over a period of years, several details must be studied to accurately date each piece. Most of these dating clues involve the trucks and couplers on the cars, or boxes they were packaged in.

There are also chapters on toys and accessories, as well as catalogs and paper products.

Lionel trains were built to provide a "lifetime of happiness" to quote one of the company's later advertising slogans. With proper care, they will do that and more.

2 TROLLEY

Collector's Guide

CONDITION AND RARITY

To the collector, condition is everything. The Train Collector's Association, the world's oldest and largest train collector group, established precise language for describing the condition of collectible trains in order to protect both the buyer and the seller. These standards have been used for so long by reputable dealers and collectors that their meaning is common knowledge in the hobby.

These grading standards are as follows:

Fair, or C4: Well-scratched, chipped, dented, rusted, warped.

Good, or C5: Small dents, scratches, dirty.

Very Good, or C6: Few scratches, exceptionally clean, no major dents or rust.

Excellent, or C7: Minute scratches or nicks, no dents or rust, all original, less than average wear.

Like New, or C8: Only the slightest signs of handling and wheel wear, brilliant colors and crisp markings; literally like new. As a rule, Like New trains must have their original boxes in comparable condition to realize the prices listed in this guide.

Mint, or C10: Brand new, absolutely unmarred, all original and unused. Items dusty or faded from display, or with fingerprints from handling, cannot be considered mint. Although Lionel test ran their locomotives briefly at the factory, items "test run" by consumers cannot be considered mint. Most collectors expect mint items to come with all associated packaging with which they were originally supplied.

As one can imagine, mint pieces command premium prices. The supply is extremely limited and the demand among collectors is great, so often the billfold of the buyer, rather than a more natural supply and demand situation, limits the price of such pieces.

In addition to the categories stated above, two other classifications are important in the toy train hobby: restored and reproduction.

Restored: A number of the trains found in the marketplace have been restored. The rugged steel construction of many of the items has insured that the item itself has survived, even if its brilliant enamel coating did not. Fortunately, many of these worn and scuffed items have been rescued from the trash bin, disassembled, stripped of their old finish and a new finish applied. Coupled with mechanical repairs and polished or replaced brightwork, these trains now shine with all their previous glory. Unfortunately, some of the more larcenous types of our society choose to represent these restored items as excellent condition originals—often painting them in the more desirable color combinations to boot. Under those circumstances, remember, it is not the train that is cheating, it's the seller.

No values are assigned in this book for restored items. The quality of restorations vary widely, ranging from spectroscopically matched paints applied to carefully stripped cars to "close enough" off the rack spray paints applied sometimes even directly over the old paint. Also, some collectors loath restored items, no matter how well done, or how honestly marked as restored. These factors combine to make assigning values to restored items virtually impossible. Use your own judgment, and remember, no matter how scarce an original is in a given color, the value of a restored item is not affected by color.

Further, collecting prewar trains is becoming an old enough hobby that some early restorations are 50 years old and have acquired a patina of their own. For neophytes contemplating a major purchase, it is extremely important that you have absolute confidence in the seller, and hopefully the assistance of an experienced collector as well. If you are looking to add a specific item to your collection, it is extremely helpful to visit other collectors and carefully examine an original in advance. This will help you, much more than photos in this or any other book, to know what an item should look like.

Reproduction: Reproductions allow enthusiasts to enjoy operating trains that otherwise they could not locate, could not afford or would feel too risky to operate. A number of firms, including Joe Mania Trains, Williams Reproductions, Kramer Reproductions, MTH and even Lionel itself, have built excellent reproductions of items from Lionel's prewar era. Their products are clearly, but discretely marked as reproductions. Unfortunately, other firms and individuals have reproduced items, particularly from Lionel's early years, without any indication that they are not of Lionel manufacture. These items are much more akin to being forgeries intended to deceive for great financial gain, rather than a reproduction built to permit enjoyment. None of the national train collecting organizations knowingly allows these items into their shows or meets, but occasionally they do slip in, as they often do at independent shows. Be especially wary of 2-7/8-inch items and early Standard Gauge—both prime areas for forgeries.

Condition and Rarity

Values for forgeries are not given in this volume, as they are worthless on the legitimate market.

Demand is one of the key factors influencing values. The postwar Santa Fe F-3 diesel was the most produced locomotive in Lionel's history, yet clean examples still command premium prices due to demand.

Rarity, or scarcity, is also a factor influencing the value of trains. Low production quantities or extreme fragility cause some items to be substantially more difficult to find than others. When scarcity is coupled with demand, the result is a premium price, while other items, extremely scarce, command only moderate prices due to lack of demand or appreciation on the part of collectors. In this guide, we have rated each item on a scale of one to eight for rarity. One represents the most common items, such as the UTC Lockon, while eight is assigned to those items hardest to find, such as the wooden 200 Electric Express gondola with Cowen's initials. It is hoped that this rarity rating will help the collector when having to choose which of similar priced items to buy by answering the proverbial "How likely am I to get this chance again?" question.

Supply, as a short-term extension of rarity, whether actual or temporary, also affects price. If only one sought after item is at a given show, the seller is unlikely to negotiate or reduce his price. If however multiple sellers at a given event have identical items, no matter how rare, the temporary market glut can bring about temporarily reduced prices.

Lastly, the **buyer's intent** will affect what he or she is willing to pay. A collector who intends to add a piece to a permanent collection will obviously pay more for an item than a dealer who is intending to resell the item will pay for the same item.

Prices are given in this guide for trains in Good, Very Good and Excellent condition. Trains in less than Very Good condition are not generally considered collectible, and as mentioned earlier, Mint condition trains are too uncommon to establish pricing on, as is the case for many prewar trains in Like New condition.

The prices listed are what a group of collectors would consider a reasonable market value when dealing at a train show or meet. Listed is a price they would be willing to pay to add that piece to their collections. When buying at a specialized train auction with Internet access, one can expect to pay more, as the pool of potential buyers is greater. The savings in fuel often offsets this increased cost, by reducing lodging and time that would otherwise be spent tracking a given item down over time by searching from show to show.

When contemplating a sale to a dealer, you should expect to receive 30 to 50 percent less than the value listed, with the poorer condition the trains the greater the amount of discount, due to the greater difficulty the dealer will have selling them. Remember that these prices are only a guideline. You are spending your money. What an item is worth to you is of greater importance than what it is worth to the author. Conversely, the publisher does not sell trains, this is not a mail-order catalog and you should not expect a dealer or collector to "price match."

LIONEL BOXES

Lionel, like other manufacturers, boxed its products to ease handling and protect the trains en route and once at the market. The boxes were strictly utilitarian and throughout much of the prewar era, no thought was given to eye appeal. It was intended that the trains be sold by attentive, trained salespeople. Self-service, and thus consumer-oriented packaging, was not in Lionel's marketing plan.

The box that most often comes to the mind's eye when thinking of Lionel trains is the traditional orange and blue box introduced just prior to World War II. However, from 1900 through 1942, Lionel used several types of boxes for its rolling stock. Most of these were comparatively drab. Scattered throughout this book are photos of selected pieces with their original packaging. Items produced over an extended period of time sometimes used a variety of boxes during their production run, so boxes for a given piece can legitimately vary from those shown in this book. Beware, however, that many unknowing (or uncaring) collectors and dealers often place items in the improper vintage box in an effort to "upgrade" the packaging.

One reason for this is that, relatively speaking, few boxes survived. The boxes, being pasteboard, were more fragile than the sturdy trains and inherently would have a lower survival rate. Plus, people were buying TRAINS, not boxes, so many of the boxes went out with the trash on Christmas morning. Even in the early days of collecting, boxes, especially set boxes and outer master cartons, were considered bulky nuisances and were thrown away. Today, any given box is scarcer than its intended contents, and clean trains in their original boxes command a premium price in the marketplace. Even the boxes themselves have developed a collector market. But remember, to be proper, the box must be not only the same stock number, but also the same vintage as the train inside.

AIDS TO DATING TRAINS

Unlike certain other collectibles, the age of a Lionel train is not a factor in its value. That is, an older train is not inherently more valuable than a newer train. It is rather the variations in construction throughout an item's production run that affect its scarcity, and thus value. Some Lionel trains are marked on the sides with "New" or "Built" dates. These dates are totally irrelevant to when a piece was actually produced and are decorative only.

Although a few collectors specialize in a specific year or two of Lionel production, they are the exception as opposed to the rule. Rather, establishing the production date of these trains is done more as a curiosity by most collectors, or when they are trying to properly and precisely recreate a given train set.

Among the key aids to dating trains are the construction techniques used in the manufacture of the trucks and couplers, and the type of original packaging used, if still present.

TRACK

Track forms the foundation of real and toy railroad systems, so it is fitting that it also forms the basis for the principle sections of this book.

During the prewar era, Lionel produced four broad types of track systems: 2-7/8-inch Gauge, Standard Gauge, O-Gauge and OO-Gauge. This book is divided accordingly.

The earliest was the 2-7/8-inch Gauge two-rail track which is described in the same-named chapter of this book. The other "odd" sized trackage was OO-Gauge, which came in both two and three-rail versions. Both are described in detail in the OO chapter of this book.

The balance of Lionel's products operated on track with either 2-1/8-inch spacing between the rails or track with a 1-1/8-inch rail-to-rail spacing. The broader track, introduced to the product line in 1906, was dubbed Standard Gauge by Lionel.

The narrower track, referred to as O-Gauge, was first produced by Lionel in 1915, came in a variety of styles. Initially eight curved sections could be joined to form a circle 28-1/2 inches in diameter. In 1919 the radius of the track was increased, with a circle, still requiring eight sections, to now be 31-1/2 inches in diameter. Straight sections were 10-1/2 inches long.

When Lionel assimilated the former Ives product line into theirs, with it came a smaller cross-sectioned, lighter weight track with a 27-inch diameter circle. Known alternately as Lionel-Ives, Winner or Lionel Junior track, ultimately the moniker was bestowed by which it is still known today—027. This size was even made in two-rail form for use with windup sets. Like the O-Gauge track, 027 track sections were connected by inserting steel pins protruding from one section into the hollow rails of the adjacent section.

In 1934, a wider-radius version of O-Gauge track was introduced. Known as 072, its broad curves leant themselves to the large streamlined passenger trains and scale-proportioned freight cars and locomotives that Lionel produced in the late 1930s and early 1940s. Sixteen of these curved sections were required to form a circle. Matching turnouts were produced, as well as 14-inch long straight sections for use with this track system.

The following year Lionel introduced what was to be its finest trackage of the prewar era. Known as "T-rail," rather than the tubular cross section of the 0 and 027 tracks, which were formed from sheet metal, T-rail had solid steel rails that more closely resembled real railroad track, and were joined in a similar manner, with tiny fishplates being bolted to adjoining sections. T-rail straight and 72-inch diameter curved tracks, as well as turnouts, were offered through 1942. At that time, production was interrupted by World War II, along with the rest of Lionel's train line. After the war, production of T-rail was not resumed.

HOW TO USE THIS COLLECTOR'S GUIDE

REFERENCE EXAMPLE

1. →
2. → **9E (Type II)**: The orange 0-B-0 was also produced with the
3. → Bild-A-Loco motor, which was retained by two quick-release levers.
4. →

VG	EX	LN	RARITY
600	850	1200	6
↑ A.	↑ B.	↑ C.	↑ D.

1.) **Photo:** In some listings, photos are supplied to better help identify and verify what Model and Type you possess.

2.) **Listing Name/Type:** Items will be listed by Model number and Variation number (Type).

3.) **Listing Description:** Located directly after the Listing Name/Type is a brief description of the listing, giving vital information to better help identification.

4.) **Values Table:** Below the Listing Description is the Values Table. Values for each condition are in U.S. Dollars.

   A.) **VG=*Very Good:*** Few scratches, exceptionally clean, no major dents or rust.

   B.) **EX=*Excellent:*** Minute scratches or nicks, no dents or rust, all original, less than average wear.

   C.) **LN=*Like New:*** Only the slightest signs of handling and wheel wear, brilliant colors and crisp markings; literally like new. As a rule, Like New trains must have their original boxes in comparable condition to realize the prices listed in this guide.

   D.) **Rarity:** On a scale of 1-8, this system will assess the accessibility and rarity of the particular listing. On occasion, an item may be so rare that there is not enough reference to place a price or rarity.

2-7/8-Inch Gauge

2-7/8-INCH GAUGE

When Lionel entered production of electric trains in 1901, it chose a track system with 2-7/8-inch spacing between the rails. Though bulky and crude by later standards, these trains were the foundation upon which the miniature railroad dynasty was built.

The track itself was made up of individual wooden crossties, routed to accept bands of steel that acted as the rails. Setup was considerably more time-consuming and awkward than that of later sectional track systems such as Standard and O-Gauges. This was due not only to the infancy of Lionel's toy train production, but also to its original market—store window displays in retailers of other wares. Rather than a toy, the trains were to be merchandising aids—attention getters—for other products such as jewelry. Thus, they were expected to be set up and remain in place for some time, with the assembly done by adults.

By 1905, Lionel trains were becoming firmly entrenched as toys, and this was the final year 2-7/8-inch gauge trains were offered. Today, the early trains listed in this chapter are among the most difficult to find and the most valuable trains of the prewar era. This has led to not only reproductions, but in some cases outright forgeries.

2-7/8-inch Gauge and Standard Gauge

STANDARD GAUGE

Introduced in 1906, Standard Gauge offered two considerable advantages over the previously offered 2-7/8-inch gauge. Foremost was sectional track. This allowed the train display to be quickly and easily assembled and disassembled without tools, and by children. The second advantage was in its more compact size, measuring 2-1/8 inches between the rails. Perhaps the most obvious change, however, was the addition of the center third rail, which would remain a hallmark of Lionel trains to this day.

This third rail, while in most instances unrealistic, greatly simplified the operation of the trains, and permitted the creation of elaborate track layouts without the additional polarity reversing circuitry required of two-rail electric trains. First dubbed two-inch Gauge in Lionel literature, in 1909, in a stroke of marketing genius, the new trackage began to be referred to as "Standard Gauge" —creating in the mind of the public the impression that anything else was substandard, or abnormal.

In time, both Ives and Chicago (later American Flyer) built trains that ran on 2-1/8-inch gauge track, but trademark law prevented the makers from referring to them as Standard Gauge. Lionel ceased producing Standard Gauge trains in 1940.

2-7/8-inch Gauge and Standard Gauge

2 TROLLEY, 1906-1916

2 TRAILER, 1906-1916

5 0-4-0 STEAM, 1906-1909

5 SPECIAL 0-4-0 STEAM, 1906-11

2-7/8-inch Gauge and Standard Gauge

	VG	EX	LN	RARITY
1 TROLLEY: 1906-14; cream body, orange band, orange roof, five windows.	$2,000	$3,500	$5,000	7
White body, blue or olive band and roof, five windows.	1,800	3,300	4,800	6
Blue body, cream band, blue roof, six windows.	1,500	2,500	4,000	5
1 TRAILER: Companion item to the 1 Trolley, later cataloged as 111.	1,000	1,900	2,800	7
2 TROLLEY: 1906-1916, "No. 2 ELECTRIC RAPID TRANSIT No. 2," yellow or red.	1,200	1,600	2,200	7
2 TRAILER: Companion item to the 2 Trolley, later cataloged as 200.	1,000	1,500	2,000	8
3 TROLLEY: 1906-13, cream or dark green body.	1,500	2,500	3,500	8
3 TRAILER: Non-powered trailer matching 3 trolley.	1,200	2,200	3,200	8
4 TROLLEY: 1906-12, cream or green body.	2,500	4,000	5,500	8
5 0-4-0 STEAM: 1906-1909, blued steel boiler with turned wood boiler fronts, domes and smokestacks, did not come with a tender.				
Lettered "N.Y.C. & H.R.R.," thin-rimmed drive wheels.	800	1,000	1,200	5
Lettered "N.Y.C. & H.R.R.R.," thin-rimmed drive wheels.	1,000	1,200	1,500	6
Lettered "B. & O. R.R.," thin-rimmed drive wheels.	1,500	1,900	2,500	8
Lettered "PENNSYLVANIA," thin-rimmed drive wheels.	1,400	1,800	2,300	8
Lettered "N.Y.C. & H.R.R.R.," thick-rimmed drive wheels.	700	900	1,100	6
5 SPECIAL 0-4-0 STEAM: 1906-11. Identical to the 5 but for the addition of a small tender. Rubber-stamped "N.Y.C. & H.R.R.R." Single truck tender.	1,100	1,300	1,600	7

2-7/8-INCH GAUGE AND STANDARD GAUGE

6 4-4-0 STEAM, 1906-23

7 STEAM, 1910-12

7 STEAM, 1912-23

8 TROLLEY, 1908-14

2-7/8-inch Gauge and Standard Gauge

	VG	EX	LN	RARITY
Single-truck tender rubber stamped "B. & O. R.R.," locomotive lettered "N.Y.C. & H.R.R.R."	$1,100	$1,300	$1,600	7
Two-truck tender and loco lettered "N.Y.C. & H.R.R.R."	1,100	1,300	1,600	7
Two-truck tender and loco lettered "PENNSYLVANIA."	1,100	1,300	1,600	7
6 4-4-0 STEAM: 1906-23, steel boiler and cab, thin-rimmed drivers lettered "N.Y.C. & H.R.R.R."	600	1,000	1,600	6
Steel boiler and cab, thin-rimmed drivers lettered "PENNSYLVANIA."	900	1,400	1,900	7
Steel boiler and cab, thin-rimmed drivers lettered "B. & O. R.R."	900	1,400	1,900	7
Steel boiler and cab, thin-rimmed drivers, lettered "B. & M. R.R."	900	1,400	1,900	7
Steel boiler and cab, thin-rimmed drivers, provision for train lighting, lettered "N.Y.C. & H.R.R.R."	600	1,000	1,600	6
Steel boiler and cab, thick-rimmed drivers, provision for train lighting, lettered "N.Y.C. & H.R.R.R."	500	800	1,200	5
Steel boiler and cab, thick-rimmed drivers, provision for train lighting, lettered "N.Y.C. & H.R.R.R." and "4351."	500	800	1,200	5
6 SPECIAL STEAM: 1908-09, 4-4-0, brass, with nickel trim.	2,000	2,400	3,000	7
7 STEAM: 1910-12, 4-4-0 brass and nickel, thin rims.	2,000	2,400	3,000	7
1912-23, 4-4-0 brass and nickel, thick rims.	1,800	2,000	2,400	6
8 TROLLEY: 1908-14, nine or 11 windows, cream or dark green body, orange band and roof.	3,000	4,200	6,000	8

2-7/8-INCH GAUGE AND STANDARD GAUGE

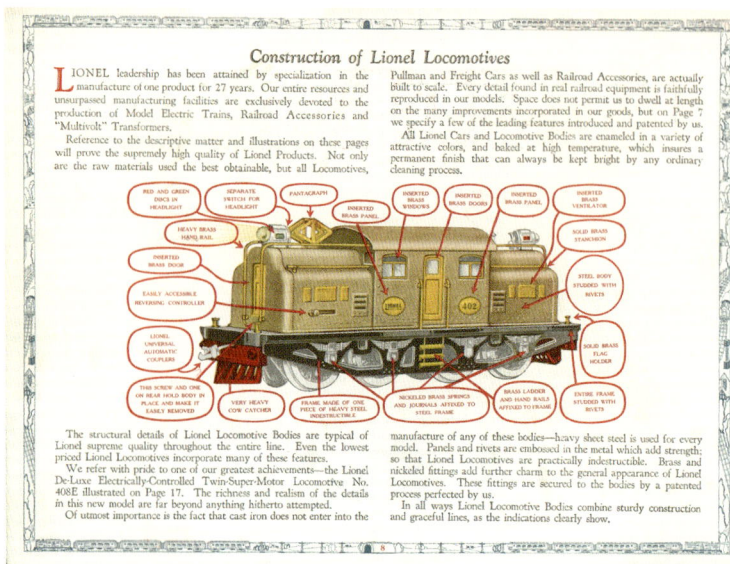

1927 LIONEL CATALOG

1927 LIONEL CATALOG

Twin-Super-Motor Locomotives

FOR "LIONEL STANDARD" TRACK—2¼ INCHES WIDE

AS the American boy expects Lionel to introduce model railroad equipment that is in keeping with electric railroad development, we offer the new Electrically-Controlled Locomotives, made in six different types as illustrated on these pages. They are the result of years of experiment and research by Lionel engineers.

The locomotives shown on this page are for use with Passenger Cars Nos. 428, 429, 430, 431, 418, 419 and 490, illustrated on Page 31; also with Freight Cars Nos. 211 to 219, illustrated on Pages 27 and 28.

The new Electrically-Controlled Locomotives are the only ones made that will operate on direct current as well as on alternating current, dry cells or storage batteries. A patented electrical device makes it possible to operate or reverse these locomotives without using more current than models that are reversed by hand. When the Electrically-Controlled Locomotive is running forward, front headlight is illuminated—when it is reversed, rear one shines brilliantly and forward one is automatically cut out.

All "Lionel Standard" Locomotives are made either with hand reversing controller, or with electrically-controlled reversing mechanism that also can be operated by hand.

We are proud to show the De-Luxe Locomotive No. 408E illustrated on this page. It is one of Lionel's greatest achievements. The illustration clearly shows the great amount of realistic detail incorporated in it. In addition to the details of construction indicated on Page 8, this locomotive includes two operating pantagraphs, two illuminated signal lanterns on front of locomotive, two flags, and an enormous amount of extra special detail in the superstructure. It is indeed a triumph of model engineering skill.

No. 408E—De-Luxe Twin-Super-Motor Electrically-Controlled Locomotive—the world's finest model.

No. 408E "Lionel Standard" De-Luxe Twin-Super-Motor Electrically-Controlled Locomotive—17 inches long, 8½ inches high to top of pantagraph. This locomotive can be started, stopped, reversed and operated at any speed at any distance from the track by means of No. 81 controlling rheostat supplied with it. Complete with lamps for headlights and front lanterns. Price $44.00

Code Word "EAST"

Nos. 402 and 402E

No. 402 "Lionel Standard" Twin-Super-Motor Reversible Locomotive—17 inches long, 6½ inches high. Complete with 2 lamps for electric headlights. Price $32.25

Code Word "HAVEN"

No. 402E "Lionel Standard" Electrically-Controlled Twin-Super-Motor Locomotive — Same as No. 402, but equipped with electrically-controlled mechanism which starts, stops, reverses and operates it at any speed at any distance from the track by means of No. 81 controlling rheostat supplied with it. Price $40.00

Code Word "YORK"

17

1927 LIONEL CATALOG

Construction of Lionel "O" Gauge Motors

DRIVING GEARS ("A")—They are made of heavy steel blanks, machine-cut. They mesh without friction and are far superior to gears with punched teeth.

Field ("B")—The field is made of a number of specially prepared transformer steel laminations. This construction represents a much stronger field than if a single piece of steel were used.

Third Rail Shoe Support ("C")—Made of heavy fibre to which the third rail contact rollers are attached. Our construction protects rollers from injury, for the brackets can be bent against the fibre without disturbing the arc of the spring that gives them the correct tension against the third rail.

Wheels ("D")—Lionel was first to introduce die-cast wheels. They are absolutely balanced. A nickel-plated steel rim is forced over the tread of the wheel to insure long wear.

Collecting Shoes ("E")—They collect current from the third rail. Made of solid brass turnings and revolve on steel shafts which pass through phosphor bronze supports. They insure perfect contact with the third rail at all times so that locomotives will run at uniform speed.

Frame ("F")—Made of very heavy steel punchings, embodying great detail. Will withstand more than the ordinary amount of wear and tear.

Journals ("G")—Made of heavy brass, nickel-plated. Attached to the frames by mechanical means. They add greatly to the appearance of the structure.

Cowcatchers ("H")—The construction of the cowcatchers varies with the type of locomotive on which they are used. Many of them are part of the steel frame which is made in one piece, and others are heavy castings rigidly attached to the frame.

Flag Posts ("J")—All our locomotives are equipped with four flag posts, two at each end of the frame; a very realistic detail.

Tanks ("K")—These tanks are made of brass, nickel-plated, and are separable pieces attached to the frame, which further accentuates the great detail.

Lionel Automatic Couplers ("L")—Made of heavy steel, nickel-plated and polished. They are scientifically constructed so that cars cannot become detached when in motion, but are easily taken apart when desired. The new improved Lionel Coupler with invisible spring arrangement is a great advance over any similar device ever made.

Illustration shows the type of motor used in "O" Gauge Locomotives Nos. 248, 252 and 253.

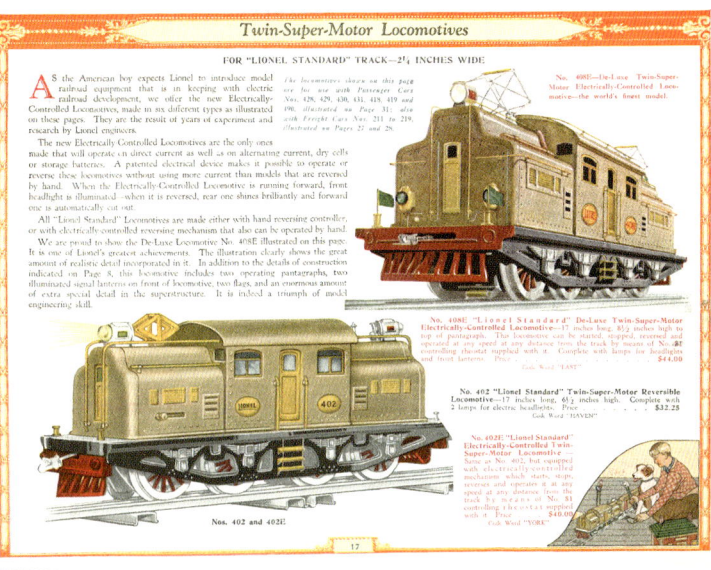

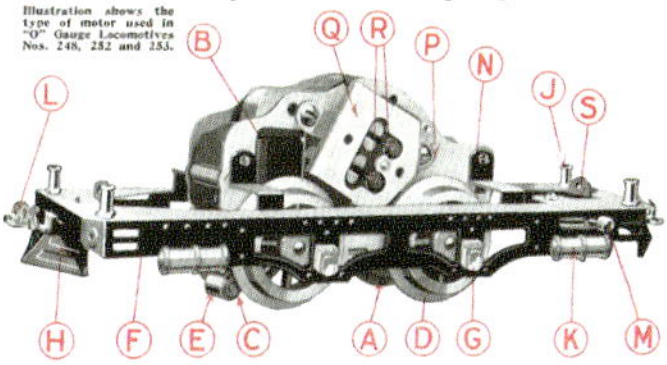

THE NEW LIONEL "O" GAUGE ELECTRICALLY-CONTROLLED SUPER-MOTOR

This marvelous new motor will haul twice as many cars as any other "O" Gauge Motor now on sale. The illustration below shows some of the remarkable features that make this possible. Notice the new system of gearing which gives maximum hauling power with minimum current consumption.

The electric-controlling mechanism is built right into the motor, and is completely protected against injury. This new "O" Gauge Super-Motor, a triumph of engineering skill, is one of Lionel's greatest achievements.

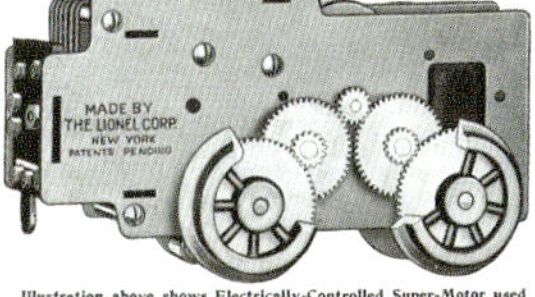

Illustration above shows Electrically-Controlled Super-Motor used in "O" Gauge Locomotives Nos. 254E and 251E.

The same Super-Motor with hand reversing mechanism is used in "O" Gauge Locomotives Nos. 254, 251 and in Twin-Super-Motor No. 256.

Reversing Controllers ("M")—Lionel Reversing Controllers have been in use for many years during which time they have given thorough satisfaction. They are the only controllers in use that cannot get out of order. They operate very easily and due to the brass cups and spring tension, the electrical contact is always permanent.

Frame Support ("N")—The frame is supported to the motor with only four screws. This simple method of construction was originally introduced by us in 1913. All parts of Lionel Locomotives can be easily reached for cleaning.

Side Plates ("P")—Made of heavy gauge steel and support all working parts. All bearing holes are reinforced with phosphor bronze bushings. The alignment of these holes is absolutely perfect so that gears work with minimum friction. All holes are drilled and reamed to proper diameter. The accuracy of these plates compares with the frame work of a very fine clock.

Brush Plate ("Q")—The unique construction permits rapid change of brushes after motor has been in use for a considerable period. The brushes fit in brass cups. Two properly tempered steel springs give the correct pressure of the brush on the commutator until brushes are worn down to the end. Brushes are replaced by simply raising the springs, lifting up worn-out brushes and dropping in new ones.

Brushes ("R")—We were the first manufacturers of model trains to equip our motors with combination gauze and graphite brushes that wear long and are self-lubricating.

Removable Locomotive Body ("S")—The bodies of all Lionel Locomotives are held in place on the frame with only two screws, one at each end of the locomotive. Supporting members are placed at several points of the frame that rigidly hold the body in place.

Commutator—Made of bronze, and perfectly turned when connected to armature so that it is absolutely parallel with brushes. Commutator surface is polished so as to reduce all friction when in contact with brushes.

Armature—Made of specially prepared electrical sheets mounted on a drill rod shaft. It is perfectly insulated and wound with the correct amount of triple insulated wire.

4

1927 LIONEL CATALOG

2-7/8-INCH GAUGE AND STANDARD GAUGE

8 ELECTRIC, 1925-32

10 INTERURBAN, 1910

10 ELECTRIC, 1925-29

11 FLATCAR 1906-26

2-7/8-inch Gauge and Standard Gauge

	VG	EX	LN	RARITY
8/8E ELECTRIC: 1925-32, 0-B-0, dark olive or Mojave.	$150	$175	$200	2
Olive, maroon or red.	175	215	250	3
Peacock or pea green.	350	350	600	6
9 MOTOR CAR: 1909, used the same smaller body as the 1908-09 number 8. Painted cream and orange.	3,000	4,200	6,000	8
1910-12, larger green and cream body.	3,000	4,200	6,000	8
9E ELECTRIC: 1928-35, 0-B-0, orange, gray or two-tone green.	800	1,000	1,300	6
9U ELECTRIC: 1928-29, 0-B-0, orange loco kit. Assembled examples without box are worth about 50 percent less.	1,500	2,200	3,000	7
10 INTERURBAN: 1910, maroon with three soldered-on roof vents.	2,000	3,100	4,200	8
Maroon, green and gold trim, stamped "10 INTERURBAN 10."	1,000	1,600	2,200	7
Dark olive green.	1,000	1,600	2,200	7
10 ELECTRIC: 1925-29, 0-B-0, Mojave, gray, peacock.	150	175	200	2
Red "Macy's."	600	750	900	7
10E ELECTRIC: 1926-30, 0-B-0, gray.	150	175	200	2
Peacock with a black frame.	125	160	180	1
Peacock with dark green frame or State Brown.	350	425	500	6
Red.	600	750	900	7
11 FLATCAR: 1906-26, maroon, orange, red, brown or gray.	50	75	100	8
12 GONDOLA: 1906-26, red, dark olive, brown or gray.	40	65	100	6
13 CATTLE CAR: 1906-26, green.	50	75	100	3-5
14 BOXCAR: 1906-26, red or orange.	50	75	100	3

2-7/8-inch Gauge and Standard Gauge

15 OIL CAR, 1906-26

16 BALLAST CAR, 1906-26

19 COMBINE, 1910-12

29 DAY COACH, 1907-1914

2-7/8-INCH GAUGE AND STANDARD GAUGE

	VG	EX	LN	RARITY
Yellow-orange.	$200	$325	$450	6
Dark green "Harmony Creamery."	Too rarely traded to value.			
15 OIL CAR: 1906-26, tank car, red, maroon, brown.	50	70	100	3
16 BALLAST CAR: 1906-26, maroon, brown or green.	90	125	175	3
17 CABOOSE: 1906-25, red, maroon or brown.	40	60	90	3
18 PULLMAN: 1910-12, dark olive over red primer.	800	1,500	2,400	8
1913-26, dark olive, with or without illumination.	100	150	200	5
Yellow-orange or Mojave.	300	550	900	7
19 COMBINE: 1910-12, dark olive over red primer.	800	1,500	2,400	8
1913-26, dark olive, with or without illumination.	100	150	200	5
Yellow-orange.	300	550	900	7
29 DAY COACH: 1907-1909, 13-7/8" long.	1,200	2,000	3,100	8
1910-14, 15-1/4" long, olive or maroon.	550	750	1,000	6
31 COMBINE: 1921-25, dark olive, orange, brown or maroon. Matches the 35 Pullman and 36 Observation.	60.	70	80	3
32 MAIL CAR: 1921-25, dark olive, orange, brown or maroon. Matches the 35 Pullman and 36 Observation.	60	70	80	3

2-7/8-INCH GAUGE AND STANDARD GAUGE

	VG	EX	LN	RARITY
33 ELECTRIC LOCOMOTIVE: 1913-24.				
0-C-0, dark olive, rubber-stamped "NEW YORK - CENTRAL - LINES."	$400	$600	$900	4
0-C-0, black, rubber-stamped "NEW YORK - CENTRAL – LINES."	500	750	1,000	5
0-C-0, dark olive, rubber-stamped "PENN R.R."	700	1,000	1,300	7
0-B-0, midnight blue.	750	1,200	1,600	7
0-B-0, black, dark olive, dark green or gray.	100	125	150	3
Factory repaint, colors include: red, maroon, peacock and red with cream stripe.	300	450	600	7

The 33 Electric Locomotive was produced in many colors from 1913 to 1924.

LIONEL ELECTRIC TOY TRAINS & Multivolt Transformers

Electric and Steam-Type Trains for Standard Guage Track, 2⅛ Inches Wide

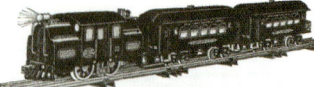

ELECTRIC PULLMAN OUTFIT No. 34.
Outfit No. 34—Comprises No. 33 Locomotive, 1 No. 35 Pullman Car, 1 No. 36 Observation Car, 8 curved and 2 straight sections of track, making an oval 4 ft. 8 in. long by 3½ ft. wide. Length of train 34 in. Price, packed in strong box with full directions for operating................$14.50

ELECTRIC FREIGHT TRAIN OUTFIT No. 37.
Outfit No. 37—Comprises No. 33 Locomotive, 1 No. 112 Gondola Car, 1 No. 117 Caboose, and 8 sections curved track, making a circle 3½ ft. in diameter. Length of train, 31 in. Price, packed in strong box with full directions for operating...............$12.00

ELECTRIC FREIGHT TRAIN OUTFIT No. 39.
Outfit No. 39—Comprises No. 38 Locomotive, 1 No. 116 Coal Car, 1 No. 117 Caboose and 8 sections curved track, making a circle 3½ ft. in diameter. Length of train 32 in. Price, packed in strong box with full directions for operating...............$13.00

ELECTRIC PULLMAN OUTFIT No. 40.
Outfit No. 40—Comprises No. 38 Locomotive, 2 No. 35 Pullman Cars, 1 No. 36 Observation Car, 8 curved and 4 straight sections of track, making an oval 5 ft. 9 in. long and 3½ ft. wide. Length of train, 4 ft. Price, packed in strong box with full directions for operating...............$20.00

ELECTRIC FREIGHT OUTFIT No. 41.
Outfit No. 41—Comprises No. 38 Locomotive, and 1 each Nos. 112 Gondola, 113 Cattle Car, 114 Box Car, 116 Coal Car, 117 Caboose, 8 curved and 4 straight sections of track, making an oval 5 ft. 9 in. long by 3½ ft. wide. Length of train, 5 ft. 4 in. Price, packed in strong box with full directions for operating...$18.00

ELECTRIC PASSENGER OUTFIT No. 44.
Outfit No. 44—Comprises No. 42 Locomotive, 1 No. 29 Day Coaches, 8 curved and 4 straight sections of track, making an oval 5 ft. 9 in. long. Length of train, 52 in. Price, packed in strong box with full directions for operating...............$25.00

OUTFITS No. 420 AND 421—PULLMAN TRAINS DE LUXE

Outfit No. 420—Passenger Train De Luxe. Comprises No. 42 Locomotive, 1 each Nos. 18 Pullman Car, 19 Pullman and Baggage Car, 190 Observation Car, 8 curved and 8 straight sections of track, making an oval 3½ ft. wide by 8 ft. 2 in. long. The outfit also includes a series of 3 lights complete with cords for interior illumination of cars.
This train outfit is the most beautiful one made and considering the finish and the liberal equipment is big value for the price. The locomotive body and the cars are finished in handsome non-chipping enamel. All the wheels are nickeled and polished. The cars have seats in the interior, upon which miniature figures can be placed. The transoms in the roofs of the cars are fitted with imitation stained glass, as are also the windows; and the lights shining through them are wonderfully realistic. Length of train, 63 in. Price, packed in strong box with full directions for operating...............$35.00

Outfit No. 421—Similar in every respect to Outfit No. 420 above, but equipped with Locomotive No. 54, finished in nickel and brass. No better toy train can be obtained for the money. Price, packed in strong box and full directions for operating...............$42.50

STEAM-TYPE ELECTRIC PASSENGER OUTFIT No. 43.
Outfit No. 43—Comprises 1 No. 51 Locomotive and Tender, 2 No. 29 Day Coaches, 8 curved and 4 straight sections of track, making an oval 3½ ft. wide by 5 ft. 9 in. long. Length of train, 53 in. Price, packed in strong box with full directions for operating...............$21.00

ELECTRIC PULLMAN OUTFIT No. 52.
Outfit No. 52—Comprises No. 53 Locomotive, 1 each Nos. 180 Pullman Car, 181 Pullman and Baggage Car, 182 Observation Car, 8 curved and 4 straight sections of track, making an oval 3½ ft. wide by 5 ft. 9 in. long. Length of train, 54 in. Price, packed in strong box with full directions for operating...$25.00

STEAM-TYPE ELECTRIC PULLMAN OUTFIT No. 50.
Outfit No. 50—Comprises No. 51 Locomotive and Tender, 1 each Nos. 180 Pullman Car, 181 Pullman and Baggage Car, 182 Observation Car, 8 curved and 4 straight sections of track, making an oval 3½ ft. wide by 5 ft. 9 in. long. Length of train, 5 ft. Price, packed in strong box with full directions for operating $27.00

STEAM-TYPE ELECTRIC PULLMAN OUTFITS No. 620 and 621.
Outfit No. 620—Equipment and cars are same as described in Outfit No. 420, but has steam-type Locomotive No. 6 instead of the electric-type No. 42. A very handsome outfit, and represents very big value. Price, packed in strong box with full directions for operating...............$40.00

Outfit No. 621—Similar to Outfit No. 620 described above, but has steam-type Locomotive No. 7, finished in nickel and brass; a strong, beautiful outfit. Price, packed in strong box with full directions for operating...............$57.50

DE LUXE FREIGHT TRAIN OUTFITS.
Outfit No. 422—Comprises No. 42 Locomotive and the complete line of Freight Cars numbered 11 to 17 illustrated on another page of this pamphlet, together with 8 curved and 10 straight sections of track, making an oval 3½ ft. wide and 3 ft. 5 in. long. Complete train is 7 ft. in length. Price, complete, packed in strong box...............$35.00

Outfit No. 423—Similar to the above, but includes Locomotive No. 54, finished in nickel and brass. Price, complete, packed in strong box...............$45.00

Outfit No. 622—Same equipment as above outfit, but includes steam-type Locomotive No. 6, with Tender, as described on another page of this pamphlet. Price, complete, packed in strong box...............$40.00

Outfit No. 623—Same equipment as above outfit, but includes steam-type Locomotive No. 7 and Tender, finished in nickel and brass. Price, complete, packed in strong box...............$50.00

LOCOMOTIVE No. 33. LOCOMOTIVE No. 38. LOCOMOTIVE Nos. 42 & 54
No. 33—Length 11 in., width 3 in., height 4½ in. Outfit includes 8 sections curved track, making a circle 3½ ft. in diameter. Has Electric Headlight and connection for lighting interior of passenger cars. Price...............$10.00

No. 38—Length 12 in., width 3½ in., height 5 in. Outfit includes 8 sections curved track, making an oval 3½ ft. in diameter. Has Electric Headlight, Reversing Controller and connection for lighting interior of passenger cars. Price...............$12.00

No. 53—Length 13 in., width 3½ in., height 5 in. Outfit includes 8 curved and 4 straight sections of track, making an oval 5 ft. 9 in. long. Has Electric Headlight, Reversing Controller and connection for lighting interior of passenger cars. Price...............$13.50

No. 42—Length 13½ in., width 4 in., height 6 in. Outfit includes 8 curved and 4 straight sections of track, making an oval 3½ ft. wide by 5 ft. 9 in. long. Has Electric Headlight, Reversing Controller, and connection for lighting interior of passenger cars. Has 8 driving wheels, connected in pairs. Price...............$17.50

No. 54—Dimensions same as No. 42. Locomotive of nickel and brass, beautifully finished. Most elaborate electric-type locomotive we make. Price...$27.50

2-7/8-INCH GAUGE AND STANDARD GAUGE

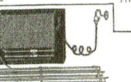

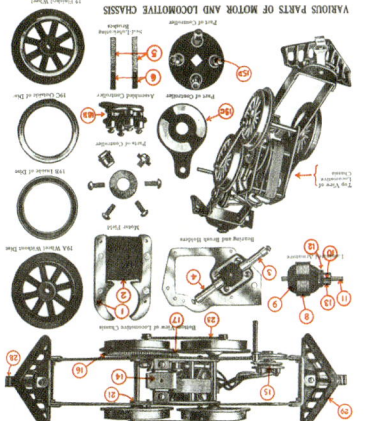

1917 LIONEL CATALOG

During 1913-24, the 33 Electric Locomotive was produced in both 0-B-0 and 0-C-0 versions and in a variety of colors.

36 OBSERVATION, 1912-26

2-7/8-INCH GAUGE AND STANDARD GAUGE

	VG	EX	LN	RARITY
34 ELECTRIC LOCOMOTIVE: 1912, 0-C-0 dark olive.	$400	$600	$800	7
34 ELECTRIC LOCOMOTIVE: 1913, 0-B-0 dark olive.	200	285	400	5
35 PULLMAN: 1912-26, dark olive, orange, brown or maroon. Matches the 36 Observation.	60	70	80	5
Midnight-blue.	450	700	1,000	8
36 OBSERVATION: 1912-26, dark olive, orange, brown or maroon. Matches the 35 Pullman.	60	70	80	5
Midnight-blue.	450	700	1,000	8

36 OBSERVATION, 1912-26

The 38 0-B-0 Electric was offered 1913-24 in many colors.

2-7/8-INCH GAUGE AND STANDARD GAUGE

	VG	EX	LN	RARITY
38 ELECTRIC: 1913-24, 0-B-0, painted dark olive and rubber stamped with "PENN R.R." lettering.	$400	$500	$600	7
"NEW YORK - CENTRAL – LINES," turned handrail stanchions, painted black or gray.	100	120	150	4
"NEW YORK - CENTRAL – LINES," maroon.	150	210	275	5
"NEW YORK - CENTRAL – LINES," dark green.	250	300	350	5
Gray, green, maroon or black.	100	120	150	
Brown.	250	280	325	4
Red, Mojave, pea green, or peacock and red with cream trim.	400	500	600	7

The 38 0-B-0 Electric was offered 1913-24 in many colors.

The 0-B+B-0 42 Electric was sold in various colors during 1912-13.

2-7/8-inch Gauge and Standard Gauge

	VG	EX	LN	RARITY
42 ELECTRIC: 1912; 0-B+B-0, square hoods, dark green.	$700	$1,000	$1,500	7
42 ELECTRIC: 1913, 0-B+B-0, round hoods, gray, dark gray, black, olive green, dark green or Mojave.	275	375	500	4
Maroon and peacock.	1,100	1,500	2,000	7

The 0-B+B-0 42 Electric was sold in various colors during 1912-13.

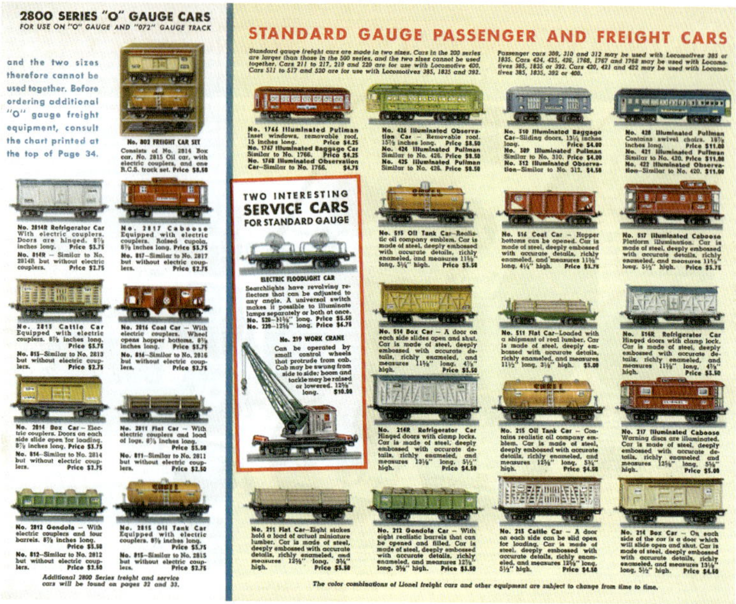

2800 SERIES "O" GAUGE CARS

FOR USE ON "O" GAUGE AND "072" GAUGE TRACK

and the two sizes therefore cannot be used together. Before ordering additional "O" gauge freight equipment, consult the chart printed at the top of Page 34.

No. 802 FREIGHT CAR SET Consists of No. 2814 Box car, No. 2815 Oil car, with electric couplers, and one R.C.S. track set. Price $8.50

No. 2814R Refrigerator Car With electric couplers. Doors are hinged. 8⅞ inches long. Price $3.75
No. 814R – Similar to No. 2814R but without electric couplers. Price $2.75

No. 2817 Caboose Equipped with electric couplers. Raised cupola. 8⅞ inches long. Price $3.75
No. 817–Similar to No. 2817 but without electric couplers. Price $2.75

No. 2813 Cattle Car Equipped with electric couplers. 8⅞ inches long. Price $3.75
No. 813–Similar to No. 2813 but without electric couplers. Price $2.75

No. 2816 Coal Car – With electric couplers. Wheel opens hopper bottoms. 8⅞ inches long. Price $3.75
No. 816–Similar to No. 2816 but without electric couplers. Price $2.75

No. 2814 Box Car – Electric couplers. Doors on each side slide open for loading. 8⅞ inches long. Price $3.75
No. 814–Similar to No. 2814 but without electric couplers. Price $2.75

No. 2811 Flat Car – With electric couplers and load of logs. 8⅞ inches long. Price $3.50
No. 811–Similar to No. 2811 but without electric couplers. Price $2.50

No. 2812 Gondola – With electric couplers and four barrels. 8⅞ inches long. Price $3.50
No. 812–Similar to No. 2812 but without electric couplers. Price $2.50

No. 2815 Oil Tank Car Equipped with electric couplers. 8⅞ inches long. Price $3.75
No. 815–Similar to No. 2815 but without electric couplers. Price $2.75

Additional 2800 Series freight and service cars will be found on pages 32 and 33.

STANDARD GAUGE PASSENGER AND FREIGHT CARS

Standard gauge freight cars are made in two sizes. Cars in the 200 series are larger than those in the 500 series, and the two sizes cannot be used together. Cars 211 to 217, 219 and 220 are for use with Locomotive 400. Cars 511 to 517 and 520 are for use with Locomotives 385, 1835 and 392.

Passenger cars 309, 310 and 312 may be used with Locomotives 385 or 1835. Cars 424, 425, 426, 1766, 1767 and 1768 may be used with Locomotives 385, 1835 or 392. Cars 420, 421 and 422 may be used with Locomotives 385, 1835, 392 or 400.

No. 1766 Illuminated Pullman Inset windows, removable roof. 15 inches long. Price $4.25
No. 1767 Illuminated Baggage Car Similar to No. 1766. Price $4.25
No. 1768 Illuminated Observation Car–Similar to No. 1766. $4.75

No. 426 Illuminated Observation Car – Removable roof. 15⅞ inches long. Price $8.50
No. 424 Illuminated Pullman Similar to No. 426. Price $8.50
No. 425 Illuminated Pullman Similar to No. 426. Price $8.50

No. 310 Illuminated Baggage Car–Sliding doors. 13¼ inches long. Price $4.00
No. 309 Illuminated Pullman Similar to No. 310. Price $4.00
No. 312 Illuminated Observation–Similar to No. 312. $4.50

No. 420 Illuminated Pullman Contains swivel chairs. 18⅞ inches long. Price $11.00
No. 421 Illuminated Pullman Similar to No. 420. Price $11.00
No. 422 Illuminated Observation–Similar to No. 420. $11.00

TWO INTERESTING SERVICE CARS FOR STANDARD GAUGE

ELECTRIC FLOODLIGHT CAR Searchlights have revolving reflectors that can be adjusted to any angle. A universal switch makes it possible to illuminate lamps separately or both at once.
No. 520–11⅜" long. Price $5.50
No. 220–12⅝" long. Price $6.75

No. 219 WORK CRANE Can be operated by small control wheels that protrude from cab. Cab may be swung from side to side; boom and tackle may be raised or lowered. 12⅝" long. $10.00

No. 515 Oil Tank Car–Realistic oil company emblem. Car is made of steel, deeply embossed with accurate details, richly enameled, and measures 11⅜" long, 5¼" high. Price $3.50

No. 516 Coal Car – Hopper bottoms can be opened. Car is made of steel, deeply embossed with accurate details, richly enameled, and measures 11⅜" long, 4¼" high. Price $3.75

No. 517 Illuminated Caboose Platform illumination. Car is made of steel, deeply embossed with accurate details, richly enameled, and measures 11⅜" long, 5½" high. Price $3.75

No. 514 Box Car – A door on each side slides open and shut. Car is made of steel, deeply embossed with accurate details, richly enameled, and measures 11⅜" long, 4⅞" high. Price $3.50

No. 511 Flat Car–Loaded with a shipment of real lumber. Car is made of steel, deeply embossed with accurate details, richly enameled, and measures 11½" long, 3⅛" high. $3.00

No. 514R Refrigerator Car Hinged doors with clamp lock. Car is made of steel, deeply embossed with accurate details, richly enameled, and measures 11⅜" long, 4⅞" high. Price $3.50

No. 214R Refrigerator Car Hinged doors with clamp locks. Car is made of steel, deeply embossed with accurate details, richly enameled, and measures 13⅛" long, 5½" high. Price $4.50

No. 215 Oil Tank Car – Contains realistic oil company emblem. Car is made of steel, deeply embossed with accurate details, richly enameled, and measures 12⅝" long, 5¾" high. Price $4.50

No. 217 Illuminated Caboose Warning discs are illuminated. Car is made of steel, deeply embossed with accurate details, richly enameled and measures 12⅝" long, 5⅛" high. Price $5.00

No. 211 Flat Car–Eight stakes hold a load of actual miniature lumber. Car is made of steel, deeply embossed with accurate details, richly enameled, and measures 12⅝" long, 3¾" high. Price $3.50

No. 212 Gondola Car – With eight realistic barrels that can be opened and filled. Car is made of steel, deeply embossed with accurate details, richly enameled, and measures 12⅞" long, 3⅝" high. Price $3.50

No. 213 Cattle Car – A door on each side can be slid open for loading. Car is made of steel, deeply embossed with accurate details, richly enameled, and measures 12⅝" long, 5½" high. Price $4.50

No. 214 Box Car – On each side of the car is a door which will slide open and shut. Car is made of steel, deeply embossed with accurate details, richly enameled, and measures 13⅛" long, 5½" high. Price $4.50

The color combinations of Lionel freight cars and other equipment are subject to change from time to time.

1939 LIONEL CATALOG

STANDARD GAUGE FREIGHT CARS

Freight Cars Nos. 211 to 217 are for use with Locomotive No. 400E. Nos. 511 to 517 are for Nos. 385E, 1835E and 392E. Lionel reserves the right to change colors of cars from time to time.

No. 511 Standard Gauge Flat Car–Loaded with a shipment of real lumber. 11½ inches long, 3⅛ inches high. Price $3.00

No. 512 Standard Gauge Gondola Car–With 8 barrels that can be opened and filled. 11⅜ inches long, 3⅛ inches high. Price $3.00

No. 513 Standard Gauge Cattle Car–Door on each side slides open for loading. 11⅜ inches long, 5 inches high. Price $3.50

No. 514R Standard Gauge Refrigerator Car – Hinged doors with clamp lock. 11⅜ inches long, 4⅞ inches high. Price $3.50

No. 514 Standard Gauge Box Car–A door on each side slides open and shut. 11⅜ inches long, 4⅞ inches high. Price $3.50

No. 515 Standard Gauge Oil Car – Aluminum finish. Realistic oil company emblem. 11⅜ inches long, 5¼ inches high. Price $3.50

No. 516 Standard Gauge Coal Car – Hopper bottoms can be opened and closed. 11⅜ inches long, 4¼ inches high. Price $3.75

No. 517 Standard Gauge Illuminated Caboose – Raised cupola. Platform illumination. 11⅜ inches long, 5½ inches high. Price $3.75

No. 211 Standard Gauge Flat Car–Eight stakes hold a load of lumber. 12⅝ inches long, 3¾ inches high. Price $3.50

No. 212 Standard Gauge Gondola Car–With 8 barrels that can be opened and filled. 12⅞ inches long, 3⅝ inches high. Price $3.50

No. 213 Standard Gauge Cattle Car–Door on each side slides open for loading. 12⅝ inches long, 5½ inches high. Price $4.50

No. 214 Standard Gauge Box Car–Doors slide open and shut. 13⅛ inches long, 5½ inches high. Price $4.50

No. 214R Standard Gauge Refrigerator Car–Hinged doors with clamp locks. Embellished with inset name and number plates. 13⅛ inches long, 5½ inches high. Price $4.50

No. 215 Standard Gauge Oil Car–Tank is finished in gleaming aluminum. Contains realistic Sun Oil Company emblem. 12⅝ inches long, 5¾ inches high. Price $4.50

No. 216 Standard Gauge Coal Car – Hopper bottoms can be opened and closed by means of a wheel on the top of car. 13 inches long, 4⅞ inches high. Price $4.50

No. 217 Standard Gauge Illuminated Caboose –Richly enameled finish. Rear warning discs are illuminated by platform light. 12⅝ inches long, 5⅛ inches high. Price $5.00

43

1938 LIONEL CATALOG

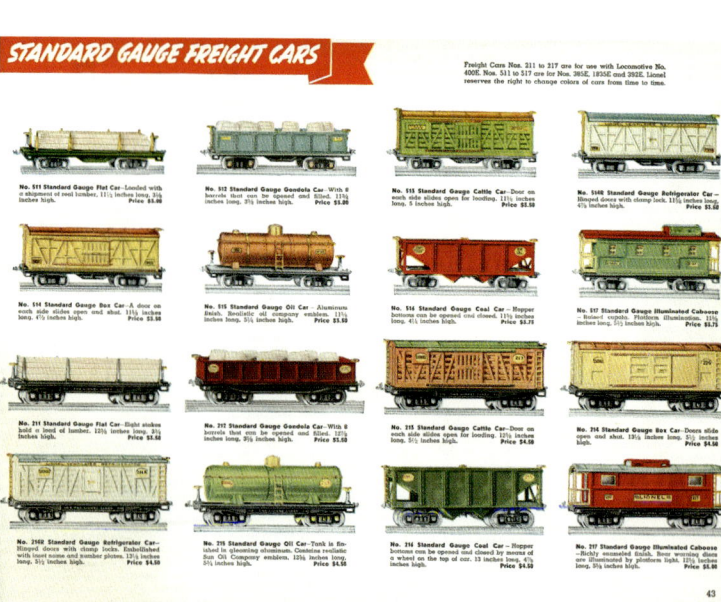

2-7/8-INCH GAUGE AND STANDARD GAUGE

STANDARD GAUGE ★ Track Width, Between Running Rails, 2⅛"

1938 LIONEL CATALOG

STANDARD GAUGE ★ Track Width, Between Running Rails, 2⅛"

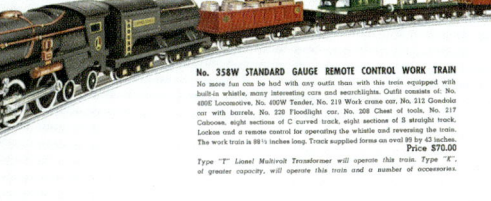

1938 LIONEL CATALOG

2-7/8-INCH GAUGE AND STANDARD GAUGE

50 0-B-0 ELECTRIC, 1924

53 ELECTRIC

The 1913-20 version of 54 Electric was an 0-B+B-0 with rounded hoods.

100 TROLLEY, 1910-16

2-7/8-Inch Gauge and Standard Gauge

	VG	EX	LN	RARITY
50 ELECTRIC: 1924, 0-B-0, painted dark green.	$110	$150	$225	4
Painted maroon.	300	450	600	7
Painted dark gray.	110	150	225	4
Painted Mojave.	150	210	300	5
51 STEAM: 1912-23, 4-4-0, black.	500	700	1,000	5
53 ELECTRIC: 1911, 0-C-0.	Too infrequently traded to establish pricing.			
1912, 0-B+B-0, maroon, round hood.	1,100	1,600	2,500	6
1915-19, 0-B-0, maroon, square hood.	450	650	850	3
1915-19, 0-B-0, 12-1/2" long, Mojave or dark olive.	650	1,000	1,400	6
1920-21, 0-B-0, 11-1/8" long, maroon or orange.	200	325	500	6
54 ELECTRIC: 1912, 0-B+B-0, 15-1/2" long, square-top hoods, unlettered brass body.	2,500	3,200	4,000	8
54 ELECTRIC: 1913-20, 0-B+B-0, 15-1/2" long, round-top hoods, unlettered brass body.	1,800	2,300	2,800	6
60 ELECTRIC: Mid-1910s, 0-B-0, same as 33 marked for F.A.O. Schwartz.	Too rarely, if ever, traded to establish pricing.			
61 ELECTRIC: Mid-1910s, 0-B+B-0, same as 42 marked for F.A.O. Schwartz.	Too rarely, if ever, traded to establish pricing.			
62: Mid-1910s, 0-B-0, same as 38 marked for F.A.O. Schwartz.	Too rarely, if ever, traded to establish pricing.			
100 TROLLEY: 1910-16, assorted variations, equally valued.	1,100	1,800	2,600	6

100 ELECTRIC LOCOMOTIVE, 1903-05

190 OBSERVATION, 1910-27

The 1901-02 200 MOTORIZED GONDOLA had a wooden body.

The 1903-05 version of the 200 MOTORIZED GONDOLA had a steel body.

2-7/8-inch Gauge and Standard Gauge

	VG	EX	LN	RARITY
100 ELECTRIC LOCOMOTIVE: 1903-05, had "No. 5" stamped on its sides and ends.	$7,000	21,000	35,000	8
101 SUMMER TROLLEY: 1910-13.	1,200	1,900	2,600	7
112 GONDOLA: 1910-26, dark olive green or gray, 6-1/2" long.	200	275	375	7
Red, brown, dark or light gray, 9-1/2" long.	50	60	75	4
113 CATTLE CAR: 1912-26, green.	40	50	60	4
114 BOXCAR: 1912-26, red, yellow-orange or orange.	40	50	60	6
116 BALLAST CAR: 1910-26, maroon, brown, dark green or dark gray.	60	80	110	3
117 CABOOSE: 1912-26, dark red, brown, maroon or Tuscan.	30	40	60	4
180 PULLMAN: 1911-21, maroon or brown.	75	100	125	4
181 COMBINE: 1911-21, maroon or brown.	75	100	125	4
182 OBSERVATION: 1911-21, maroon or brown.	75	100	125	4
190 OBSERVATION: 1910-27, dark olive or yellow-orange, with or without illumination.	100	150	200	4
200 MOTORIZED GONDOLA: 1901-02, wooden-bodied motorized gondola.	15,000	21,000	35,000	8
200 MOTORIZED GONDOLA: 1903-05, steel body.	8,000	10,000	15,000	8
202 SUMMER TROLLEY: 1910-13.	1,200	2,100	3,200	8
211 FLATCAR: 1926-40, black.	100	150	225	3
212 GONDOLA: 1926-40, gray, maroon or light green.	75	115	150	4

213 CATTLE CAR, 1926-35

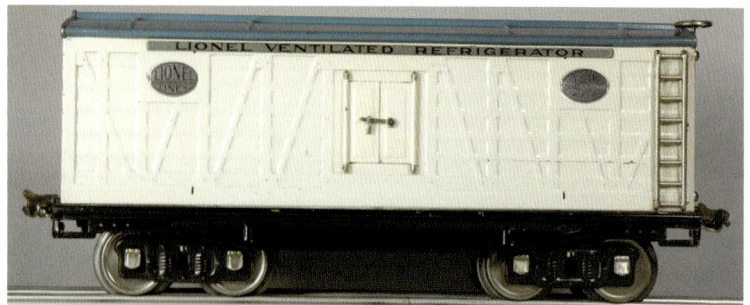
214R REFRIGERATOR CAR, 1929-40

219 CRANE CAR, 1926-40

300 ELECTRIC TROLLEY CAR, 1901-05

2-7/8-inch Gauge and Standard Gauge

	VG	EX	LN	RARITY
213 CATTLE CAR: 1926-35, mojave, terracotta or pea green.	$125	$200	$300	5
1935-40, cream.	200	350	600	8
214 BOXCAR: 1926-40, terracotta.	175	225	300	6
Cream.	125	175	250	4
Yellow.	300	400	525	6
214R REFRIGERATOR CAR: 1929-40, pearl or white body.	250	375	500	6
215 OIL CAR: 1926-29, pea green, ivory or buff.	150	200	250	2
Aluminum-colored with Sunoco decal.	325	400	525	7
216 HOPPER CAR: 1926-38, dark green.	200	275	375	5
217 CABOOSE: orange, olive or pea green.	250	400	550	7
1927-36, red.	125	175	250	3
218 DUMP CAR: 1926-38, commonly with Mojave-painted dump bin, rarely with pea green or gray dump bin.	200	275	350	3
219 CRANE CAR: 1926-40, peacock cab.	150	200	250	4
White cab.	200	375	625	7
Yellow cab.	250	350	475	5
220 SEARCHLIGHT CAR: 1931-36, terracotta light base.	225	300	375	4
Green light base.	350	425	550	6
300 ELECTRIC TROLLEY CAR: 1901-05.	5,000	6,500	10,000	8
303 SUMMER TROLLEY: 1910-13.	1,500	2,500	3,500	8
309 ELECTRIC TROLLEY TRAILER: 1904-05, non-motorized companion to the 300.	8,000	10,000	15,000	8

2-7/8-INCH GAUGE AND STANDARD GAUGE

309 ELECTRIC TROLLEY TRAILER, 1904-05

310 BAGGAGE, 1926-39

312 OBSERVATION, 1926-39

318E ELECTRIC, 1924-32

2-7/8-INCH GAUGE AND STANDARD GAUGE

	VG	EX	LN	RARITY
309 PULLMAN: 1926-39, 13-1/4" long illuminated passenger car painted Mojave.	$100	$125	$150	3
Pea green.	50	75	100	1
State brown.	125	160	200	6
Light blue.	100	125	150	3
Medium blue.	125	160	200	6
Stephen Girard green.	150	200	275	7
Maroon with terracotta roof.	150	200	275	7
310 BAGGAGE: 1926-39, 13-1/4" long companion to the 309 and 312 painted Mojave.	100	125	150	3
Pea green.	50	75	100	1
State brown.	125	160	200	6
Light blue.	100	125	150	3
Medium blue.	125	160	200	6
Stephen Girard green.	150	200	275	7
312 OBSERVATION: 1926-39, 13-1/4" long companion to the 309 and 312 painted Mojave.	100	125	150	3
Pea green.	50	75	100	1
State brown.	125	160	200	6
Light blue.	100	125	150	3
Medium blue.	125	160	200	6
Stephen Girard green.	150	200	275	7
318/318E ELECTRIC: 1924-32, 0-B-0, pea green, dark gray, Mojave, light gray.	150	200	250	3
State brown.	250	325	425	6
Black, 318E.	600	775	1,050	8
319 PULLMAN: 1924-30, maroon body and roof "New York Central."	95	120	160	3
"LIONEL LINES."	175	250	350	5

2-7/8-INCH GAUGE AND STANDARD GAUGE

320 BAGGAGE, 1925-29

332 BAGGAGE, 1926-33

337 PULLMAN, 1925-32

338 OBSERVATION, 1925-32

2-7/8-INCH GAUGE AND STANDARD GAUGE

	VG	EX	LN	RARITY
320 BAGGAGE: 1925-29, maroon body and roof "New York Central."	$95	$120	$160	3
"LIONEL ELECTRIC RAILROAD."	95	120	160	3
"LIONEL ELECTRIC RAILROAD," 500-series trucks.	175	250	350	5
"Illinois Central" markings.	175	250	350	5
322 OBSERVATION: 1924-30, maroon body and roof, "New York Central."	95	120	160	3
"THE LIONEL LINES."	95	120	160	3
"THE LIONEL LINES," 500-series trucks.	175	250	350	5
332 BAGGAGE: 1926-33, Mojave, olive green or peacock with decal lettering.	100	140	190	6
Gray, red or peacock.	70	95	125	3
State brown.	175	275	300	8
337 PULLMAN: 1925-32, "THE LIONEL LINES," "NEW YORK CENTRAL LINES," Mojave.	80	100	125	3
Olive green with red trim.	100	140	190	3
Olive green with maroon trim.	80	100	125	2
Pea green or red with cream trim.	125	175	225	5
Olive green with maroon trim, "Illinois Central" markings.		Too infrequently traded to establish accurate pricing.		
338 OBSERVATION: 1925-32, "THE LIONEL LINES," "NEW YORK CENTRAL LINES," Mojave.	80	100	125	3
Olive green with red trim.	100	140	190	3
Olive green with maroon trim.	80	100	125	2
Pea green or red with cream trim.	125	175	225	5
Olive green with maroon trim, "Illinois Central" markings.		Too infrequently traded to establish accurate pricing.		

2-7/8-INCH GAUGE AND STANDARD GAUGE

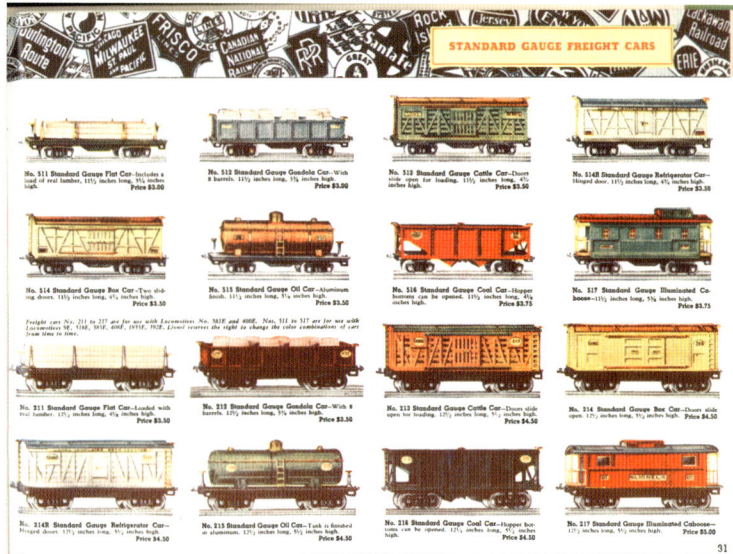

1936 LIONEL CATALOG

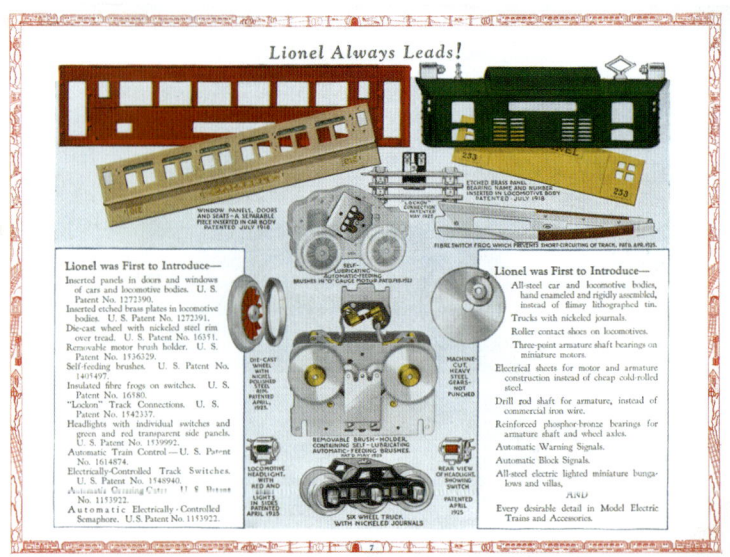

1927 LIONEL CATALOG

2-7/8-INCH GAUGE AND STANDARD GAUGE

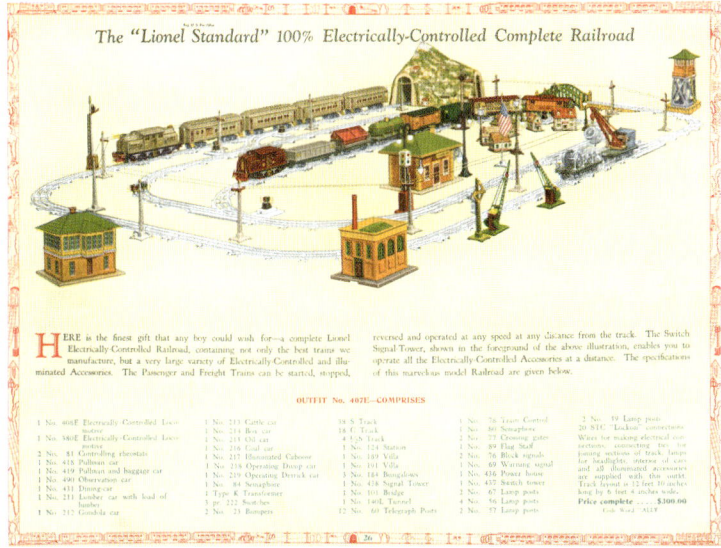

1927 LIONEL CATALOG

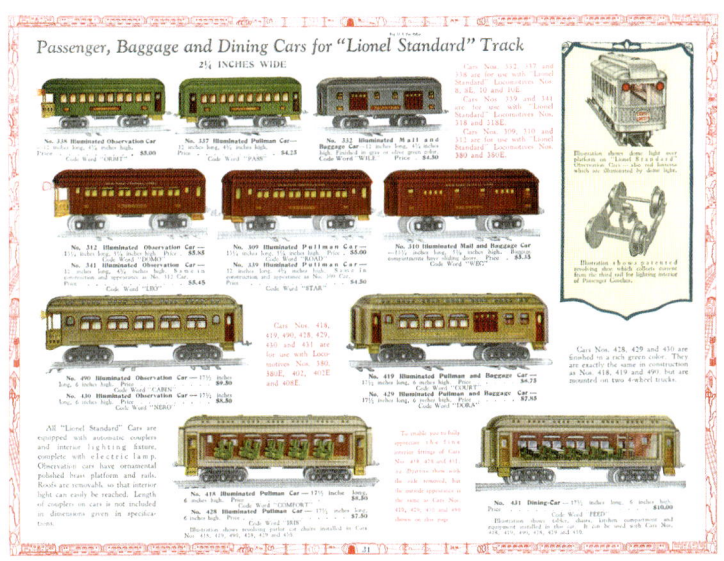

1927 LIONEL CATALOG

2-7/8-INCH GAUGE AND STANDARD GAUGE

339 PULLMAN, 1925-33

341 OBSERVATION, 1925-33

380E ELECTRIC, 1926-29

381E ELECTRIC, 1928-29

2-7/8-inch Gauge and Standard Gauge

	VG	EX	LN	RARITY
339 PULLMAN: 1925-33, gray; peacock with peacock roof.	$40	$60	$90	1
Peacock with dark green roof.	60	90	125	2
Peacock with Ives decal lettering.	100	140	190	6
State brown.	175	275	300	8
341 OBSERVATION: 1925-33, gray; peacock with peacock roof.	40	60	90	1
Peacock with dark green roof.	60	90	125	2
Peacock with Ives decal lettering.	100	140	190	6
State brown.	175	275	300	8
380 ELECTRIC: 1923-27, 0-B-0, 13-1/2" long 0-B-0, Mojave.	450	550	650	6
Maroon.	300	350	400	3
Dark green.	375	425	475	5
380E ELECTRIC: 1926-29, 0-B-0, maroon.	300	350	400	3
Dark green.	375	425	475	5
Mojave.	450	550	650	6
381 ELECTRIC: 1928-29, 2-B-2, 18" long, State green body.	1,600	1,900	2,200	6
381E ELECTRIC: 1928-36, 2-B-2, 18" long, State green body.	1,500	2,100	2,700	6

381U ELECTRIC: 1928-29, 2-B-2, assembly kit in 1928-29. Much of the value of this item is predicated on the presence of the original box and tools. Inclusion of these items can increase the value up to 50 percent.

	VG	EX	LN	RARITY
Number plates marked 381U.	1,800	2,800	4,000	8
Number plates marked 381.	1,400	2,400	3,400	7
384/384E STEAM: 1930-32, 2-4-0, black with 384T or 390T tender.	350	475	650	2
With orange-striped 390T tender.	400	525	700	5

2-7/8-INCH GAUGE AND STANDARD GAUGE

385E 2-4-2 STEAM, 1933-39

390E 2-4-2 STEAM, 1929-31

390E 2-4-2 STEAM, 1929-31

390E 2-4-2 STEAM, 1929-31

2-7/8-inch Gauge and Standard Gauge

	VG	EX	LN	RARITY
385E STEAM: 1933-39, gunmetal, came with a 384T, 385TW or 385W tender.	$400	$550	$750	5
390 STEAM: 1929, 2-4-2, black, with 390T tender.	500	625	850	7
390E STEAM: 1929-31, 2-4-2 with 390T tender, black.	400	550	750	5
Two-tone green.	1,000	1,450	2,000	8
Two-tone blue.	600	900	1,300	7
392E STEAM: 1932-39, black.	700	900	1,200	4
Gunmetal.	1,000	1,400	2,000	6
400 EXPRESS TRAILER CAR: 1903-05, non-motorized version of the 200 Electric Express gondola.	5,000	7,000	12,000	8

A blue-painted 400E was used to tow Lionel's Blue Comet passenger train.

392E STEAM

2-7/8-INCH GAUGE AND STANDARD GAUGE

1937 LIONEL CATALOG

1937 LIONEL CATALOG

2-7/8-INCH GAUGE AND STANDARD GAUGE

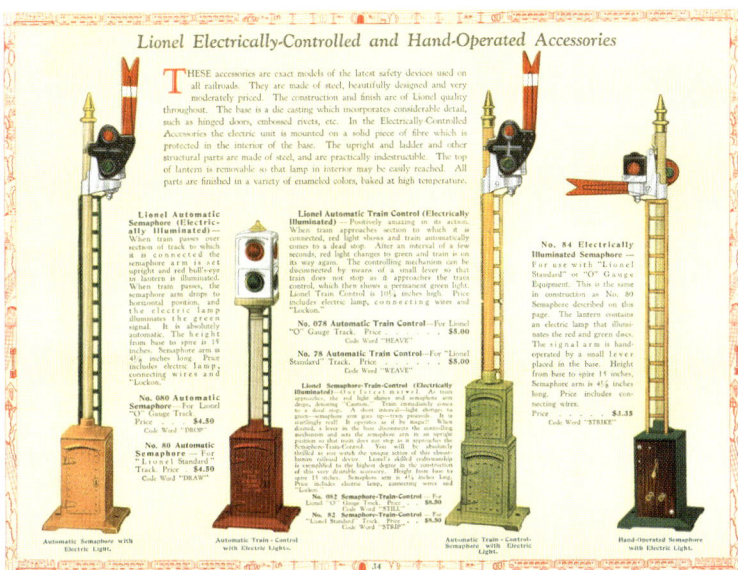

1927 LIONEL CATALOG

1927 LIONEL CATALOG

2-7/8-INCH GAUGE AND STANDARD GAUGE

The 400E 4-4-2 was Lionel's best Standard Gauge steamer from 1931-1939. Some of the 400E locomotives had nickel trim.

BLUE 400E, 1931-1939

402 0-B+B-0 ELECTRIC, 1923-29

2-7/8-INCH GAUGE AND STANDARD GAUGE

	VG	EX	LN	RARITY
400E STEAM: 1931-39, 4-4-2 with 400T tender, black.	$1,500	$1,750	$2,100	4
Black with crackle finish.	3,000	4,200	6,000	8
Gunmetal.	1,800	2,300	2,800	4
Blue.	2,000	2,500	3,100	5
402/402E ELECTRIC: 1923-29, 0-B+B-0, Mojave.	350	425	550	6
408E ELECTRIC: 1927, 0-B+B-0, Mojave or apple green.	700	900	1,200	5
State brown.	2,100	2,400	2,700	7
State green.	2,000	2,700	3,500	7

402E 0-B+B-0 ELECTRIC, 1923-29

408E 0-B+B-0 ELECTRIC, 1927

2-7/8-INCH GAUGE AND STANDARD GAUGE

412 CALIFORNIA PULLMAN, 1929-35

413 COLORADO PULLMAN, 1929-35

414 ILLINOIS PULLMAN, 1929-35

2-7/8-INCH GAUGE AND STANDARD GAUGE

	VG	EX	LN	RARITY
412 PULLMAN, CALIFORNIA: 1929-35, 21-1/2" long, State green or State brown. Lionel's largest, most elaborate and most expensive Standard Gauge passenger cars.	$800	$1,250	$1,800	7
413 PULLMAN, COLORADO: 1929-35, matches the 412.	800	1,250	1,800	7
414 PULLMAN, ILLINOIS: 1929-35, green.	1,000	1,500	2,000	7
Brown.	1,200	1,700	2,300	8
416 OBSERVATION, NEW YORK: 1929-35, matches the 412.	800	1,250	1,800	7

414 ILLINOIS PULLMAN, 1929-35

416 NEW YORK OBSERVATION, 1929-35

2-7/8-inch Gauge and Standard Gauge

418 PULLMAN, 1923-32

419 COMBINATION, 1923-32

419 COMBINATION, 1923-32

420 PULLMAN, FAYE

2-7/8-INCH GAUGE AND STANDARD GAUGE

	VG	EX	LN	RARITY
418 PULLMAN: 1923-32, four- or six-wheel trucks, Mojave.	$175	$250	$350	4
Apple green.	300	400	500	7

(Illinois Central cars bring a substantial premium, but are too rarely traded to establish accurate pricing.)

	VG	EX	LN	RARITY
419 COMBINATION: 1923-32, four- or six-wheel trucks, Mojave.	175	250	350	4
Apple green.	300	400	500	7

(Illinois Central cars bring a substantial premium, but are too rarely traded to establish accurate pricing.)

	VG	EX	LN	RARITY
420 PULLMAN, FAYE: 1930s, 18-3/4" long, two-tone blue, six-wheel trucks and complete interiors.	600	800	1,000	6
421 PULLMAN, WESTPHAL: 1930s, 18-3/4" long, two-tone blue, six-wheel trucks and complete interiors.	600	800	1,000	6
422 OBSERVATION, TEMPEL: 1930s, 18-3/4" long, two-tone blue, six-wheel trucks and complete interiors.	600	800	1,000	6

421 PULLMAN, WESTPHAL

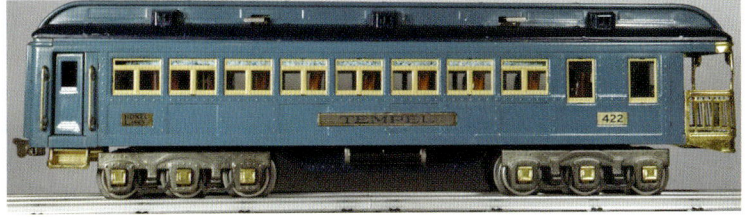

422 OBSERVATION, TEMPEL

2-7/8-INCH GAUGE AND STANDARD GAUGE

424 PULLMAN, LIBERTY BELL, 1931-40

425 PULLMAN, STEPHEN GIRARD, 1931-40

426 OBSERVATION, CORAL ISLE, 1931-40

428 PULLMAN, 1926-30

2-7/8-INCH GAUGE AND STANDARD GAUGE

	VG	EX	LN	RARITY
424 PULLMAN, LIBERTY BELL: 1931-40, two-tone Stephen Girard green and dark green.	$450	$550	$675	6
425 PULLMAN, STEPHEN GIRARD: 1931-40, two-tone Stephen Girard green and dark green.	450	550	675	6
426 OBSERVATION, CORAL ISLE: 1931-40, two-tone Stephen Girard green and dark green.	450	550	675	6
428 PULLMAN: 1926-30, dark green.	225	280	350	4
Orange.	575	675	800	6
429 COMBINATION: 1926-30, dark green.	225	280	350	4
Orange.	575	675	800	6
430 OBSERVATION: 1926-30, dark green.	225	280	350	4
Orange.	575	675	800	6
431 DINING CAR: 1927-32, matches 418, 419 and 490, six-wheel trucks, Mojave.	400	500	600	6
Apple green, dark green or orange.	450	575	750	8
Four-wheel trucks, dark green.	450	575	750	8
490 OBSERVATION: 1923-32, companion to the 418 Pullman and 419, four- or six-wheel trucks, Mojave.	175	250	350	4
Apple green.	300	400	500	7
500 ELECTRIC DERRICK CAR: Motorized flatcar with manually operated derrick.	10,000	13,000	15,000	8
511 FLATCAR: 1927-40, green, with simulated lumber load.	50	70	100	3
512 GONDOLA: 1927-39, peacock, or light green.	30	40	50	2
513 CATTLE CAR: 1927-38, olive green.	75	110	150	5
Orange.	50	75	100	3

2-7/8-INCH GAUGE AND STANDARD GAUGE

514R REFRIGERATOR CAR, 1929-40

515 TANK CAR, 1927-40

517 CABOOSE, 1927-40

600 DERRICK TRAILER, 1903-04

2-7/8-INCH GAUGE AND STANDARD GAUGE

	VG	EX	LN	RARITY
Cream.	$80	$115	$150	6
514 BOXCAR: 1929-40, cream.	100	125	150	3
Yellow.	125	200	300	6
514 REFRIGERATOR CAR: 1927-28, pearl, with peacock roof and long plate reading "LIONEL VENTILATED REFRIGERATOR."	200	300	400	5
514R REFRIGERATOR CAR: 1929-40, pearl with peacock roof.	100	200	300	4
White with peacock roof.	100	200	300	4
White with blue roof.	350	450	600	6
515 TANK CAR: 1927-40, terracotta, cream or silver.	80	125	175	3
Ivory.	100	150	225	4
Orange.	350	525	725	6
516 HOPPER CAR: 1928-40, painted red.	150	225	275	4
With rubber-stamped lettering.	200	275	375	5
517 CABOOSE: 1927-40, pea green.	50	75	100	2
Red, black roof, red cupola, orange windows.	350	500	800	8
Apple green.	Too rarely traded to establish accurate pricing.			
All red.	100	125	150	2
520 SEARCHLIGHT CAR: 1931-36, terracotta or green light platform.	100	150	200	3
600 DERRICK TRAILER: 1903-04, 2-7/8-inch gauge, non-motorized version of the 500. Apple green or maroon and black.	7,500	10,000	15,000	8
800 BOXCAR: 1904-05, Sometimes referred to by collectors as "jail cars," 14-1/2" long motorized boxcar lettered "METROPOLITAN EXPRESS."	5,000	8,000	10,000	8

2-7/8-INCH GAUGE AND STANDARD GAUGE

800 BOXCAR, 1904-05

1000 TROLLEY, 1905

1050 PASSENGER CAR TRAILER, 1905

1910 0-C-0 ELECTRIC, 1910-11

2-7/8-inch Gauge and Standard Gauge

	VG	EX	LN	RARITY
900 BOX TRAIL CAR: 1904-05, non-powered companion to the 800.	$4,000	$7,000	$9,000	8
1000 TROLLEY: 1905, 2-7/8-inch gauge 14-3/4" long trolley, maroon with a black roof and frame.	8,000	11,000	15,000	8
1050 PASSENGER CAR TRAILER: 1905, non-powered matching companion to the 1000.	9,000	12,000	16,500	8
1766 PULLMAN: 1934-40, terracotta or red sides and maroon roofs.	350	500	700	6
1767 PULLMAN: 1934-40, terracotta or red sides and maroon roofs. Matches 1766 Pullman.	350	500	700	6
1768 OBSERVATION: 1934-40, terracotta or red sides and maroon roofs. Matches 1766 and 1767 Pullmans.	350	500	700	6
1835E STEAM: 1934-39, black, with 384T, 1835TW or 1835W tender.	500	650	900	4
1910 ELECTRIC: 1910-11, 0-C-0, 9-3/4" long.	800	1,300	1,900	6
1912, 10-3/8" long, dark olive green lettered "New York - New Haven - and Hartford" or "New York Central LINES."	500	950	1,400	5
1910 PULLMAN: Circa 1910, uncataloged dark olive passenger car.	900	1,250	1,700	8
1911 ELECTRIC: 1910-12, squared hood tops, olive green.	900	1,200	1,800	6
1910-12, squared hood tops, maroon.	1,000	1,400	2,000	7
1913-on, rounded hood tops, 0-B-0 dark olive.	700	950	1,200	5

2-7/8-INCH GAUGE AND STANDARD GAUGE

1911 0-B-0 ELECTRIC, 1910-12

1912 0-B+B-0 ELECTRIC, 1910-12

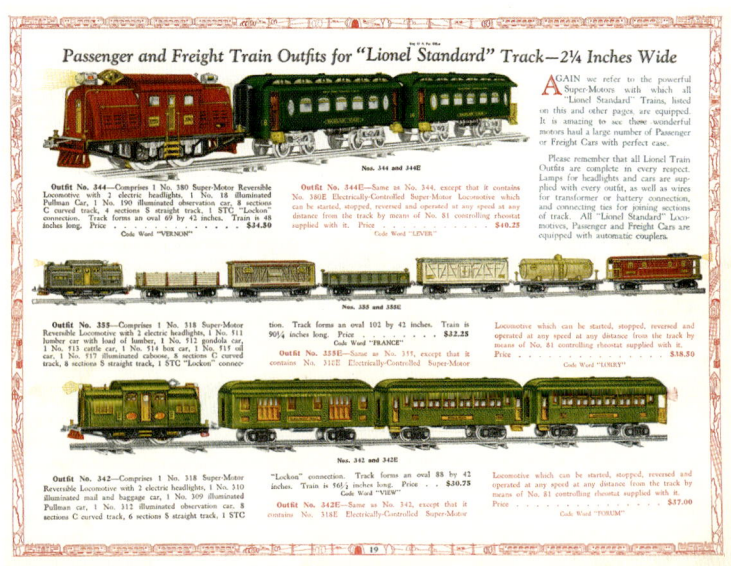

1927 LIONEL CATALOG

2-7/8-inch Gauge and Standard Gauge

	VG	EX	LN	RARITY
1911 ELECTRIC SPECIAL: 1911-12, jumbo size version of the 1911 with 0-B+B-0 wheel arrangement, maroon "New York - New Haven - and Hartford" or "NEW YORK - CENTRAL – LINES" lettering.	$1,000	$1,600	$2,500	7
1912 ELECTRIC: 1910-12, 15-1/2" long 0-B+B-0, dark green, "New York - New Haven and Hartford" or "NEW YORK - CENTRAL – LINES" lettering.	1,200	1,900	2,600	7
1912 SPECIAL: 1911, same as the normal 1912, but with a polished brass body.	2,300	3,500	4,500	6
2200 TRAILER: A matching non-powered trailer was made to pair with the 202 trolley.	1,100	2,000	3,000	8
3300 TRAILER: A matching non-powered trailer was made to pair with the 303.	1,200	1,900	2,600	7

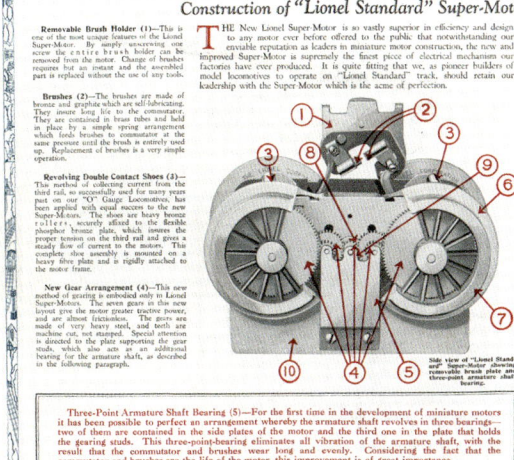

1927 LIONEL CATALOG

2-7/8-INCH GAUGE AND STANDARD GAUGE

1936 LIONEL CATALOG

1936 LIONEL CATALOG

2-7/8-INCH GAUGE AND STANDARD GAUGE

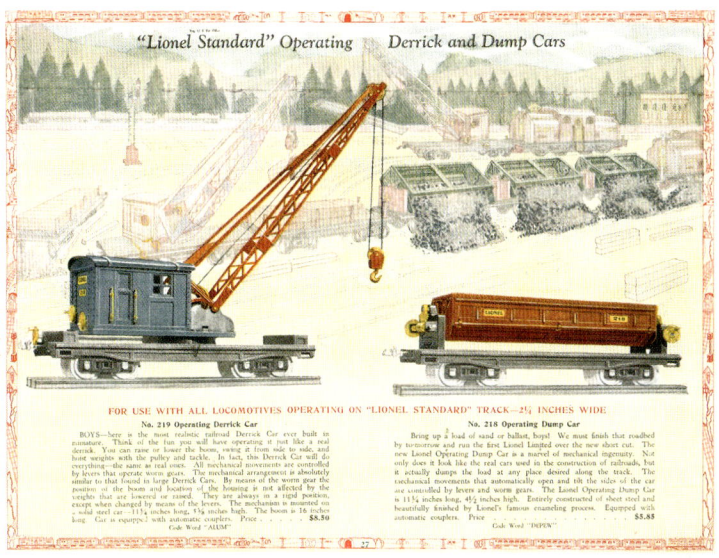

1927 LIONEL CATALOG

1927 LIONEL CATALOG

O-Gauge

In 1915, a new size of trains appeared in the catalog. Unlike the 1906 replacement of 2-7/8-inch trains with Standard Gauge, the new line, known as O-Gauge, was an addition to the then-current Standard Gauge line.

Riding on rails spaced 1-1/4 inches apart, the purpose of the new size was similar to the purpose of Standard Gauge nine years before—to offer a more compact train, thus appealing to a broader market. The smaller size also allowed another benefit—lower cost. The track itself was

O-Gauge

constructed much like its Standard Gauge counterpart—even the rails themselves had the same cross section—with three rails permanently attached to steel crossties.

Lionel was not the first to make trains in this size, but in time the name "Lionel" would become virtually synonymous with "O-Gauge train." In a mere two decades, this newcomer would totally eclipse Standard Gauge in sales and, even today, is the most popular size of trains made by Lionel.

O-Gauge

4U ELECTRIC, 1928-29

150 ELECTRIC, 1917-25

154 ELECTRIC, 1917-23

158 ELECTRIC, 1919-23

O-Gauge

	VG	EX	LN	RARITY
4 ELECTRIC: 1928-32, 1-B-1 electric locomotive.				
Orange.	$450	$650	$900	6
Gray.	600	900	1,300	7
4U ELECTRIC: 1928-29, 1-B-1 electric locomotive, kit of orange 4. To attain the values listed, the kit must be unassembled and complete with all packaging.	1,200	2,000	4,000	8
150 ELECTRIC: 1917-25, 0-B-0, two different body styles.				
Dark green, dark olive, brown or maroon.	115	150	200	6
Peacock, gray or Mojave.	100	200	300	7-8
152 ELECTRIC: 1917-29, 0-B-0.				
Dark green, dark olive, dark gray, light gray or pea green.	50	75	110	3
Mojave.	300	400	550	6
Peacock.	400	550	700	8
153 ELECTRIC: 1924-25, 0-B-0.				
Dark green, dark olive, gray, maroon or peacock.	80	110	150	4
Mojave.	115	150	200	6
154 ELECTRIC: 1917-23.	80	110	150	5
156 ELECTRIC: 1917-23, 2-B-2.				
Dark green.	400	550	725	7
Olive green.	550	700	875	7
Gray.	750	900	1,100	8
Maroon.	400	550	725	7
Mojave.	750	900	1,100	8
156X: 1923-24, less expensive 0-B-0 version of the 156, olive green, gray, maroon, mojave or brown.	350	425	550	5
158 ELECTRIC: 1919-23, 0-B-0, dark green, gray, black.	80	125	175	3
201 STEAM: 1940-42, 0-6-0 switcher, with or without bell-ringing 2201 tender.	375	525	725	6

203 ARMORED LOCOMOTIVE, 1917-21

203 0-6-0 STEAM SWITCHER, 1940-41

225E 2-6-2 STEAM, 1938-41

226E 2-6-4 STEAM, 1938-41

O-Gauge

	VG	EX	LN	RARITY
203 ARMORED LOCOMOTIVE: 1917-21.	$1,100	$1,600	$2,500	8
203 STEAM: 1940-41, 0-6-0 switcher, with or without bell-ringing 2203 tender.	375	450	550	5
204 STEAM: 1940-41 2-4-2, with 1689T or 2689T tender.				
Gunmetal.	75	110	150	5
Black.	50	70	100	3
224 or 224E STEAM: 1938-41, 2-6-2, with die-cast or plastic 2224 tender, 2689W sheet metal tender.				
Black.	100	150	200	3
Gunmetal.	500	850	1,200	7
225 or 225E STEAM: 1938-41, 2-6-2, with die-cast or plastic-bodied 2235 tender, or 2225 or 2265 sheet-metal tender.				
Black.	200	280	400	4
Gunmetal.	200	280	400	4
226 or 226E STEAM: 1938-41, 2-6-4, with 2226W tender.	350	475	650	5
227 STEAM: 1939-42, 0-6-0 with 2227T or 2227B tender. Catalog number on boiler front, "8976" under cab window.	550	750	975	5
228 STEAM: 1939-42, 0-6-0 with 2228T or 2228B tender. Catalog number on boiler front, "8976" under cab window.	550	750	975	4
229 or 229E STEAM: 1939-42, 2-4-2 with 2689T, 2689W, 2666T or 2666W tender. Black or gunmetal.	100	130	175	3
230 STEAM: 1939, 0-6-0 with 2230T or 2230B tender. Catalog number on boiler front, "8976" under cab window.	800	1,300	1,900	6
231 STEAM: 1939, 0-6-0 with 2231T or 2231B tender. Catalog number on boiler front, "8976" under cab window.	650	1,200	1,800	5

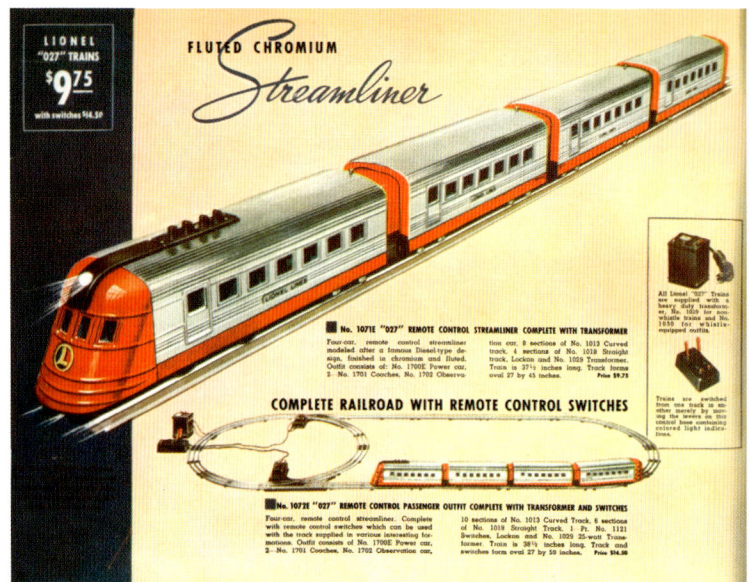

1937 LIONEL CATALOG

1937 LIONEL CATALOG

O-Gauge

1936 LIONEL CATALOG

1936 LIONEL CATALOG

O-Gauge

238 4-4-2 STEAM, 1936-40

249E 2-4-2 STEAM, 1936-39

250E 4-4-2 STEAM, 1935

252 0-B-0, ELECTRIC, 1926-35

253 0-B-0, ELECTRIC, 1924-36

O-GAUGE

	VG	EX	LN	RARITY
232 STEAM: 1940-41, 0-6-0 with 2232B tender. Catalog number on boiler front, "8976" under cab window.	$650	1,200	1,800	5
233 STEAM: 1940-42, 0-6-0 with 2233B tender. Catalog number on boiler front, "8976" under cab window.	650	1,200	1,800	5
238/238E STEAM: 1936-40, 4-4-2, gunmetal or black, with 265T, 265W, 2265W or 2225W.	250	300	375	3
248 ELECTRIC: 1927-32, 0-B-0.				
Dark green.	100	140	200	5
Peacock, orange or red.	50	90	140	2
Terracotta.	150	225	325	5
249/249E STEAM: 1936-39, 2-4-2, gunmetal or black, with 265T or 265W tender.	75	125	200	3
250 ELECTRIC: 1926, 1934, 0-B-0, dark green, peacock, terracotta or orange.	150	190	250	5
250E STEAM: 1931-1936, 4-4-2, gloss orange, black and gray. Came with 250W, 250WX, 250T, 2250W or 2250T tender.	600	1,000	1,600	5
251/251E ELECTRIC: 1925-32, 0-B-0, gray, red.	275	325	400	4
252/252E ELECTRIC: 1926-35, 0-B-0 peacock or olive.	75	110	150	3
Maroon.	300	450	650	8
Terracotta.	100	140	200	4
Yellow-orange.	100	140	200	4
253/253E ELECTRIC: 1924-36, 0-B-0, mojave, peacock or Stephen Girard green.	100	150	225	3
Maroon or gray.	175	300	450	6
Terracotta or dark green.	200	300	400	5
Pea green or red.	225	325	475	6

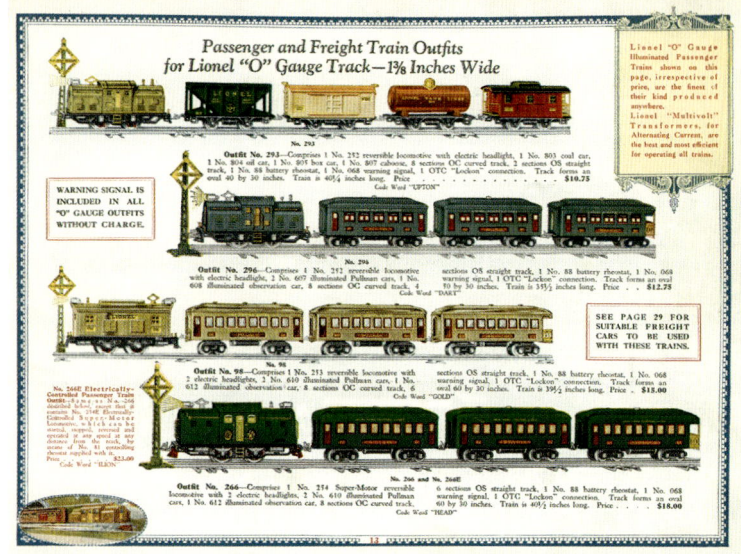

1927 LIONEL CATALOG

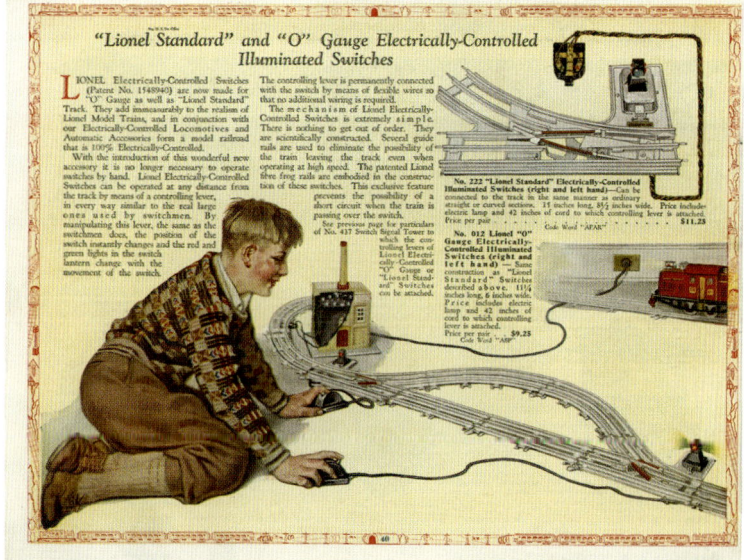

1927 LIONEL CATALOG

O-GAUGE

A LIONEL STANDS THE HARDEST WEAR AND GIVES THE LONGEST SERVICE

1934 LIONEL CATALOG

LIONEL ELECTRIC TYPES ARE THE FINEST EVER BUILT

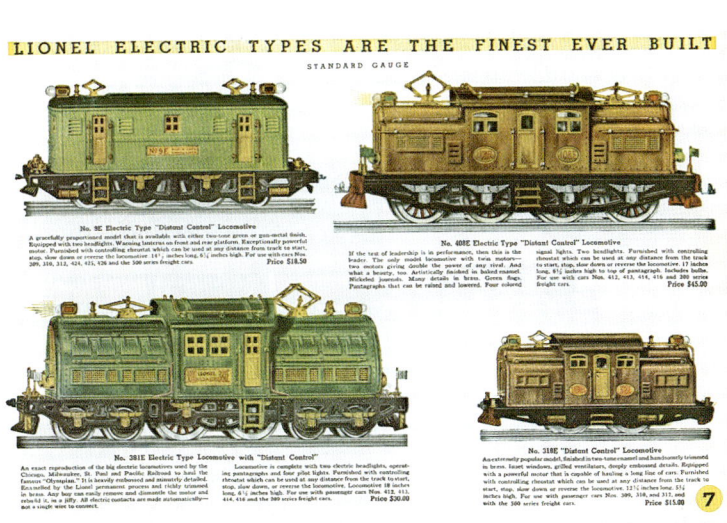

1934 LIONEL CATALOG

O-GAUGE

254 0-B-0, ELECTRIC, 1924-34

256 0-B+B-0, ELECTRIC, 1924-30

263E 2-4-2, STEAM, 1936-39

264E 2-4-2 STEAM, 1935-40

O-Gauge

	VG	EX	LN	RARITY
254/254E ELECTRIC: 1924-34, 0-B-0.				
Dark green.	$200	$250	$325	6
Mojave.	200	250	300	4
Olive green.	150	200	250	3
Orange.	150	200	250	3
Pea green.	200	250	300	4
255E STEAM: 1935-36, 2-4-2 with 263W.	500	700	1,000	5
256 ELECTRIC: 1924-30, 0-B+B-0, orange.	500	800	1,200	6
257 STEAM: 1930-32, 2-4-0 with 257T or 259T tender.	125	200	300	3
Crackle finish paint.	225	300	400	5
258 STEAM: 1930, 2-4-0 or 2-4-2, with 257T or 1689T tender.				
Black.	70	125	200	4
Gunmetal.	75	110	150	3
259/259E STEAM: 1932-40, 2-4-2 black or gunmetal with 259T, 262T, 1588TX, 2689T or 1689W.	50	80	125	3
260E STEAM: 1930, with 260T, 263T or 263W.				
Black.	350	450	550	4
Gunmetal.	450	550	650	5
261/261E STEAM: 1931, 1935, 2-4-2, black, with 257T or 261T.	125	175	225	3
262 STEAM: 1931-32, 2-4-2, black, with 262T.	200	250	325	3
262E STEAM: 1931-36, 2-4-2, black, with 262T, 265T or 265W tender.	100	140	200	3
263E STEAM: 1936-39, 2-4-2, gunmetal with 263W or 2263W tender.	300	450	625	5
Two-tone blue.	400	650	1,000	6
264E STEAM: 1935-40, 2-4-2, black with 261T or 265T tender.	200	275	375	5
Red.	125	200	300	4

265E 2-4-2 STEAM, 1935-40

289E 2-4-2 STEAM

529 PULLMAN, 1926-32

601 PULLMAN

601 OBSERVATION

O-Gauge

	VG	EX	LN	RARITY
265E STEAM: 1935-40, black, or gunmetal with 261TX, 2225T, 2225W, 265TX or 265WX tender.	$150	$225	$350	4
Blue.	425	625	850	6
289E STEAM: about 1936-37, black or gunmetal with 1588, 1688T, 1688W, 1689T or 1689W.	100	200	325	5
450 ELECTRIC: 1928-31, 0-B-0 red or apple green.	400	750	1,125	
529 PULLMAN: 1926-32, olive or terracotta.	20	30	40	2
530 OBSERVATION: 1926-32, olive or terracotta.	20	30	40	2
600 PULLMAN: 1915-1925, four wheels; 1933-42, eight wheels.				
Brown.	40	55	75	4
Maroon.	30	40	50	3
Dark green.	90	115	150	6
Gray.	40	60	90	3
Two-tone red, light blue and aluminum.	50	75	110	5
601 PULLMAN or OBSERVATION: 1915-1925, four wheels; 1933-42, eight wheels.				
Brown.	40	55	75	4
Maroon.	30	40	50	3
Dark green.	90	115	150	6
Gray.	40	60	90	3
Two-tone red, light blue and aluminum.	50	75	110	5
602 BAGGAGE CAR: 1915-1925, four wheels; 1933-42, eight wheels.				
Brown.	40	55	75	4
Maroon.	30	40	50	3
Dark green.	90	115	150	6
Gray.	40	60	90	3
Two-tone red, light blue and aluminum.	50	75	110	5

1936 LIONEL CATALOG

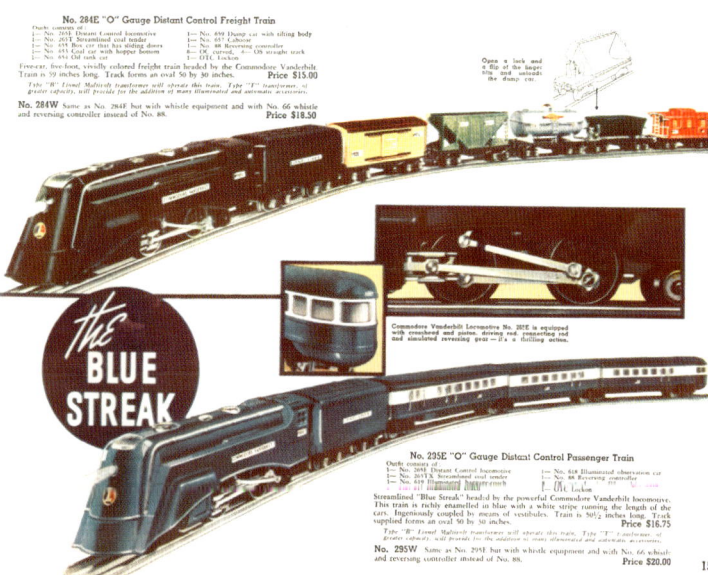

1936 LIONEL CATALOG

O-Gauge

1936 LIONEL CATALOG

1936 LIONEL CATALOG

O-Gauge

603 PULLMAN, 1920-1925

603 PULLMAN, 1932

606 OBSERVATION, 1925-32

607 PULLMAN, 1926-37

O-Gauge

	VG	EX	LN	RARITY
603 PULLMAN: 1920-36, 6-1/2", 7" or 7-1/2" long.				
Yellow-orange.	$25	$35	$50	3
Red with black roof.	30	45	60	4
Maroon with black roof.	75	100	140	6
Green.	30	45	60	4
Light red.	30	45	60	4
604 OBSERVATION: 1920-36, 6-1/2", 7" or 7-1/2" long.				
Yellow-orange.	25	35	50	3
Red with black roof.	30	45	60	4
Maroon with black roof.	75	100	140	6
Green.	30	45	60	4
Light red.	30	45	60	4
605 PULLMAN: 1925-32.				
Gray.	75	110	175	4
Red, "Illinois Central."	250	300	350	6
Orange, "Illinois Central."	300	350	400	7
Red, "The Lionel Lines."	150	200	250	6
Orange, "The Lionel Lines."	150	200	250	6
"Macy Special."	250	300	350	7
606 OBSERVATION: 1925-32.				
Gray.	75	110	175	4
Red, "Illinois Central."	250	300	350	6
Orange, "Illinois Central."	300	350	400	7
Red, "The Lionel Lines."	150	200	250	6
Orange, "The Lionel Lines."	150	200	250	6
"Macy Special."	250	300	350	7
607 PULLMAN: 1926-37, peacock.	40	50	65	3
Red or Stephen Girard green.	75	85	100	5
608 OBSERVATION: 1926-37, peacock.	40	50	65	3
Red or Stephen Girard green.	75	85	100	5
609 PULLMAN: 1937-42, blue and silver.	60	75	100	5

1941 LIONEL AD

O-GAUGE

1936 LIONEL CATALOG

1936 LIONEL CATALOG

610 PULLMAN, 1926

610 PULLMAN, circa 1935

611 OBSERVATION, 1937-42

614 OBSERVATION, 1931-40

O-Gauge

	VG	EX	LN	RARITY
610 PULLMAN: 1915-42, dark green; olive green.	$50	$60	$75	3
Pea green.	75	95	125	5
Mojave or maroon.	55	75	100	5
Decal lettering.	75	95	125	5
Terracotta.	100	125	150	4
"ILLINOIS CENTRAL."	100	125	150	6
Light red with aluminum-color roof.	100	125	150	4
Blue with aluminum-color roof.	125	175	225	7
Red-lettered Macy Special.	200	300	400	8
611 OBSERVATION: 1937-42, blue and silver.	60	75	100	5
612 OBSERVATION: 1915-42, dark green, olive green.	50	60	75	3
Pea green.	75	95	125	5
Mojave or maroon.	55	75	100	5
Decal lettering.	75	95	125	5
Terracotta.	100	125	150	4
"ILLINOIS CENTRAL."	100	125	150	6
Light red with aluminum-color roof.	100	125	150	4
Blue with aluminum-color roof.	125	175	225	7
Red-lettered Macy Special.	200	300	400	8
613 PULLMAN: 1931-40.				
Terracotta.	100	140	200	6
Two-tone blue.	175	250	350	6
Light red and aluminum.	200	300	400	7
614 OBSERVATION: 1931-40.				
Terracotta.	100	140	200	6
Two-tone blue.	175	250	350	6
Light red and aluminum.	200	300	400	7
615 BAGGAGE: 1931-40.				
Terracotta.	100	140	200	6
Two-tone blue.	175	250	350	6

1938 LIONEL CATALOG

1938 LIONEL CATALOG

O-GAUGE

1938 LIONEL CATALOG

1938 LIONEL CATALOG

O-Gauge

616 FLYING YANKEE, 1935-41

652 GONDOLA, 1935-42

653 HOPPER, 1933-42

656 STOCK CAR, 1935-42

O-Gauge

	VG	EX	LN	RARITY
Light red and aluminum.	$200	$300	$400	7
616 FLYING YANKEE: 1935-41. The 616E or the similar whistle-equipped 616W headed replicas of the streamlined, articulated Boston and Maine "Flying Yankee." Chrome or painted aluminum, with gunmetal, black, red or olive green trim. Complete train.	300	400	550	4
617 COACH: Matches 616, or blue.	50	60	75	4
618 OBSERVATION: Matches 617.	50	60	75	4
619 COMBINATION: Matches 617.	100	140	200	5
620 SEARCHLIGHT CAR: 1937-38, red.	50	65	85	3
629 PULLMAN: 1924-32, dark green, peacock, orange or red.	25	32	40	3
630 OBSERVATION: 1924-32, dark green, peacock, orange or red.	25	32	40	3
636W UP CITY OF DENVER POWER UNIT: 1936-39, streamlined diesel painted yellow with a brown roof. Came with two 637 coaches, and one 638 observation car from 1936 through 1939. Price for set.	500	650	1,100	6
651 FLATCAR: 1935-38, green.	20	30	45	2
652 GONDOLA: 1935-42, yellow or orange.	25	35	50	2
653 HOPPER: 1933-42, Stephen Girard green.	30	50	75	3
654 TANK CAR: 1933-42, aluminum, orange, gray, Sunoco or Shell.	25	35	50	3
655 BOXCAR: 1933-41, cream body, maroon roof.	30	40	55	4
Cream body, Tuscan roof.	45	60	80	4

O-Gauge

700 0-B-0 ELECTRIC, 1915-16

700E 4-6-4 STEAM, 1937-42

701 0-B-0 ELECTRIC, 1915-1916

710 PULLMAN, 1924-34

O-Gauge

	VG	EX	LN	RARITY
656 STOCK CAR: 1935-42, light gray.	$60	$75	$100	5
Orange.	75	100	140	5
657 CABOOSE: 1933-42, red.	15	25	35	1
659 ORE DUMP: 1935-42, dark green.	50	60	75	5
700 ELECTRIC: 1915-16, 0-B-0.	500	625	775	8
700E STEAM: 1937-42, 4-6-4 Hudson, scale-detailed.	1,300	2,000	2,800	5
700EWX STEAM: 4-6-4 Hudson. A number of customers liked the scale detailed appearance of Lionel's Hudson, but had extensive model railroad systems made of conventional tubular track. The 700EWX, available by special order, had blind (lacking flanges) center drivers, while the profile of the flanges of the other drivers was also slightly different.	1,500	2,250	3,000	6
700K STEAM: 1938-42, 4-6-4 Scale-detailed Hudson in kit form.				
Assembled:	2,500	1,000	4,000	6
Unassembled:	5,000	8,000	12,000	8
701 ELECTRIC: 1915-1916, 0-B-0.	400	500	625	7
701 STEAM: 1939-42, 0-6-0 switcher with 701T tender, cab lettered "8976."	350	500	700	6
702 BAGGAGE CAR: 1917-21, unlettered gray, for armored train.	125	200	300	7
703 ELECTRIC: 1915-16, 2-B-2, dark green.	1,100	1,700	2,500	8
706 ELECTRIC: 1915-1916, 0-B-0, dark green.	325	475	650	7
710 PULLMAN: 1924-34, "NEW YORK CENTRAL LINES."	125	175	225	4
Orange, "THE LIONEL LINES," four-wheel trucks.	125	175	225	4

O-Gauge

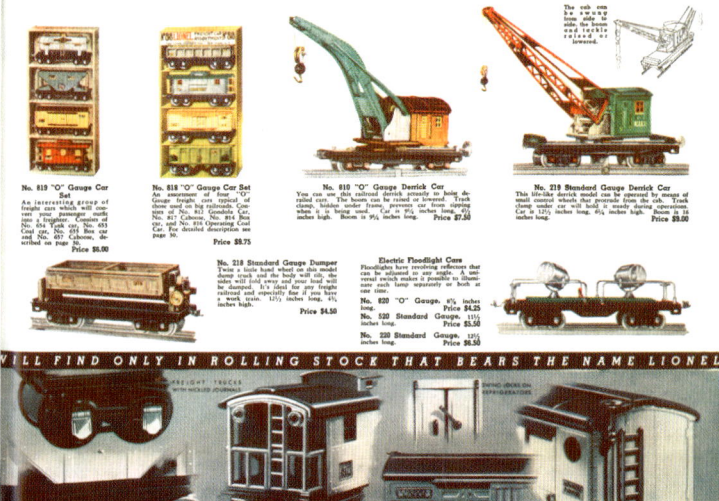

1936 LIONEL CATALOG

1936 LIONEL CATALOG

O-GAUGE

1938 LIONEL CATALOG

1936 LIONEL CATALOG

O-Gauge

714 BOXCAR, 1940-42

715 TANK CAR, 1940

715 TANK CAR, 1941-42

716 HOPPER, 1940-42

717 CABOOSE, 1940-42

O-Gauge

	VG	EX	LN	RARITY
"ILLINOIS CENTRAL LINES."	$225	$275	$325	6
Orange, "THE LIONEL LINES," six-wheel trucks.	225	275	325	6
Red or blue, "THE LIONEL LINES," six-wheel trucks.	300	375	475	7
Red, "THE LIONEL LINES," four-wheel trucks.	225	275	325	6
712 OBSERVATION: 1924-34, "NEW YORK CENTRAL LINES."	125	175	225	4
Orange, "THE LIONEL LINES," four-wheel trucks.	125	175	225	4
"ILLINOIS CENTRAL LINES."	225	275	325	6
Orange, "THE LIONEL LINES," six-wheel trucks.	225	275	325	6
Red or blue, "THE LIONEL LINES," six-wheel trucks.	300	375	475	7
Red, "THE LIONEL LINES," four-wheel trucks.	225	275	325	6
714 BOXCAR: 1940-42, scale replica Pennsylvania boxcar.	425	575	750	5
714K BOXCAR: 1940-42, unpainted and unassembled scale boxcar.	600	1,000	1,500	8
Assembled.	300	400	550	7
715 TANK CAR: scale model tank car, 1940 Shell.	300	500	725	6
1941-42 Sunoco.	400	600	850	7
715K TANK CAR: 1940-42, unpainted and unassembled scale tank car.	500	850	1,300	8
Assembled.	350	550	800	6
716 HOPPER: 1940-42, black die-cast scale hopper.	300	450	625	6
716K HOPPER: 1940-42, primered only, unassembled scale hopper car.	600	900	1,500	8
Assembled.	275	425	575	7

O-Gauge

752 Union Pacific M10000, 1935-41, four-car, yellow and brown.

752 Union Pacific M10000, 1935-41, four-car, painted aluminum.

763 4-6-4, STEAM, 1937-40

792/793/794 RAIL CHIEF CARS

O-Gauge

	VG	EX	LN	RARITY
717 CABOOSE: 1940-42, scale caboose.	$350	$475	$650	6
717K CABOOSE: 1940-42, unpainted and unassembled scale tank car.	600	1,000	1,500	8
Assembled.	300	400	550	7
728 ELECTRIC: 1916, 0-B-0, "Quaker."		Too infrequently traded to establish accurate values.		
732 ELECTRIC: 1916, 0-B-0, "Quaker."		Too infrequently traded to establish accurate values.		
752 UNION PACIFIC M10000: 1935-41, yellow and brown or painted aluminum finish; three- or four-car sets. Price listed for three-car sets, additional cars add $100-$200, yellow and brown adds a similar premium.	600	1,000	1,400	6
763 STEAM: 1937-40, semi-scale Hudson. Black or gunmetal, with 263W, 2263W, 2226W, or 2226WX tender.	1,100	1,800	2,750	4
782/783/784 HIAWATHA CARS: Orange sides, gray roof, maroon frame. Part of streamlined articulated Hiawatha passenger set pulled by 250E locomotive. Value per car.	600	900	1,200	6
792/793/794 RAIL CHIEF CARS: Red sides, maroon roof, maroon frame. Part of streamlined articulated Rail Chief passenger set pulled by 700E locomotive. Value per car.	750	1,125	1,575	6
800 BOXCAR: 1915-27, orange.				
Wabash or Pennsylvania, 6399 stamped on side, 5-1/2" long.	60	75	100	7
Pennsylvania, 4862 stamped on side, 5-1/2" long.	25	40	50	4
801 CABOOSE: 1915-26.	30	40	65	3
802 STOCK CAR: 1915-27, green.	25	40	55	4

"O" GAUGE FREIGHT CARS

EVERY CAR ON THIS PAGE NOW WITH ELECTRIC COUPLERS!

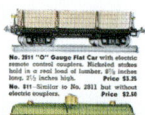

1938 LIONEL CATALOG

EVERY LIONEL "027" OUTFIT INCLUDES A SPEED-CONTROL TRANSFORMER

1939 LIONEL CATALOG

O-GAUGE

EVERY LIONEL "O" GAUGE TRAIN HAS ELECTRIC COUPLERS
— and Any Outfit Can Be Obtained with a Built-in Locomotive Whistle

LIONEL is the one and only builder of trains able to give you all the thrilling, exciting, action features that have been invented for remote control operation of the model railroad.

Every one of these developments is included in this year's great, new fleet of Lionel "O" gauge outfits:

*built-in electric couplers;
built-in locomotive whistles;
freight cars that unload electrically,
electric, remote control train reversing.*

But, railroading with Lionel "O" gauge trains has even more than these new, amazing remote control features. It is the enthusiastic first choice of men and boys everywhere because it includes:

*scale-proportioned, fully detailed engines;
all-steel, enameled cars, illuminated Pullmans;
faultless, time-tested, heavy duty motors;
patented, non-derailing, electric switches.*

Even more important — in "O" gauge there are Lionel signals, semaphores, crossing gates, stations, bridges, tunnels and everything else that is needed to assemble a modern, completely equipped railroad system.

This is the reason why boys throughout America are now using more Lionel Electric Trains than all other makes combined. It is also the reason why "O" gauge is more popular than any other size or style.

Millions of Lionel locomotives have, in nearly forty years, been operated many millions of miles. Out of this vast experience has come a Lionel motor design of incomparable excellence — sturdy, rugged, powerful — built with as much engineering forethought as if it were to drive a real engine and be responsible for the safety of real passengers. A cut-away illustration and description of the motor appears on the following page.

"O" gauge locomotives are accurate, authentic copies of real railroad equipment, made from real railroad blueprints. There is no skimping of detail and no crude, unfinished abbreviations. Every pipe or handrail is in its place and every pump, seam or rivet head as clean, sharp and clearly defined as if it were cut with a jeweler's tool.

Lionel "O" gauge cars are all-steel and finished in rich, lustrous enamel that is baked in by a secret, intense-heat process. Colors will not chip, check or fade.

The word "gauge" is used to indicate the distance between the running rails of track. The word "scale" describes the proportion of the model to the original. "O" gauge is 1¼ inches. The gauge of real track in America is 56½ inches. "O" gauge is therefore approximately one forty-eighth actual size — a quarter-inch in the model being equal to a foot in the original. It is commonly called "quarter-inch scale". Eight sections of Lionel "O" gauge track form a circle occupying a space 30½ inches square.

If you have sufficient room for building an "O" gauge railroad with all the loops and switches and sidings you want it to have, then by all means choose "O" gauge. In this catalog are "O" gauge outfits of every type, style and price. There is one to fit your needs — exactly.

1939 LIONEL CATALOG

No. 267   No. 267W   No. 299W
$12.50   **$16.50**   **$16.50**

it as well as electric switches and a few added accessories. Half the fun of model railroading, however, is in building a complete system. It is therefore always advisable to purchase a transformer of larger capacity in order to provide for this future expansion.

No. 267W FLYING YANKEE STREAMLINE PASSENGER TRAIN OUTFIT
Chromium-plated replica of the Boston and Maine's fast Flying Yankee. Built of steel and richly embellished by a wealth of accurate detail. Equipped with built-in whistle. Outfit consists of: No. 616W Power car, two No. 617 Coaches, No. 618 Observation car, whistling controller, eight sections of OC curved track, four sections of OS straight track and UTC Lockon. Train is 42 inches long. Track supplied forms an oval measuring 51⅞ by 30⅞ inches. **Price $16.50**

No. 267. Similar to No. 267W outfit, as described above, but without built-in whistle and whistle-controller. **Price $12.50**
No. 616W—Power car complete with whistle and whistle-controller. Price $10.00
No. 617—"Flying Yankee" Coach complete with one vestibule. Price $ 3.75

No. 299W UNION PACIFIC STREAMLINE PASSENGER TRAIN OUTFIT
Authentic reproduction of the yellow and golden-brown Pride of the West, the Union Pacific's "City of Denver". Equipped with built-in remote control whistle. Outfit consists of: No. 636W Power car, two No. 637 Illuminated coaches, No. 638 Illuminated observation car, whistling controller, eight sections of OC curved track, four sections of OS straight track and UTC Lockon. Train measures 42½ inches. Track oval, 51⅞ by 30⅞ inches. **Price $16.50**
No. 636W—Power car complete with whistle and whistle-controller. Price $10.00
No. 637—Union Pacific Coach with one vestibule. Price $ 3.75

Type "Q" Trainmaster Transformer will operate either train illustrated above. Type "R", of greater capacity, will provide for numerous accessories.

1939 LIONEL CATALOG

O-GAUGE

806 CATTLE CAR, 1927-34

810 DERRICK, 1930-42

813 STOCK CAR, 1926-42

814 BOXCAR, 1926-42

O-Gauge

	VG	EX	LN	RARITY
803 HOPPER: 1923-34, dark green or peacock.	$25	$35	$50	3
804 TANKER: 1923-41, gray, terracotta, aluminum-painted.	15	25	35	2
Yellow-orange.	35	45	60	5
805 BOXCAR: 1927-34, pea green, cream or orange.	20	35	50	4
806 CATTLE CAR: 1927-34, overall pea green.	60	90	125	6
Orange with maroon roof, no journal boxes.	40	55	75	5
Orange with maroon roof, copper journal boxes.	25	40	55	4
Orange with pea green roof.	30	45	65	4
Orange with orange roof.	50	65	85	6
807 CABOOSE: 1927-42, peacock.	40	50	65	4
Red.	35	45	55	3
809 DUMP CAR: 1930-32, orange or green dump bin.	60	70	85	5
810 DERRICK: 1930-42, terracotta cab.	175	210	250	6
Cream cab.	125	150	175	4
Yellow cab.	175	210	250	6
811 FLATCAR: 1926-42, maroon body.	35	45	60	2
Aluminum-colored body.	60	75	100	4
812 GONDOLA: 1926-42.				
Mojave.	50	60	75	4
Dark green.	25	35	45	3
45N green.	35	45	60	4
Stephen Girard green.	60	75	100	6
Orange.	60	75	100	6
813 STOCK CAR: 1926-42, orange.	75	110	150	4
Cream.	150	225	300	7
Tuscan body, rubber-stamped lettering.	1,500	2,250	3,250	8

O-GAUGE

814R, REFRIGERATOR CAR, 1929-42.

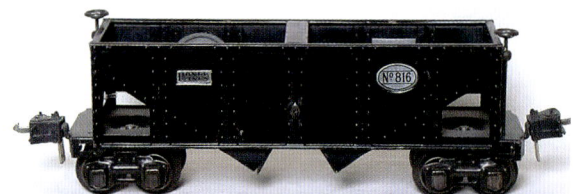

816 HOPPER, black with nickel plates, 1940.

816 HOPPER, black with rubber-stamped lettering, 1941-42.

820 SEARCHLIGHT CAR, 1931-42.

O-Gauge

	VG	EX	LN	RARITY
814 BOXCAR: 1926-42, cream, orange roof.	$60	$90	$125	3
Yellow, brown roof.	75	110	150	4
Cream, maroon roof.	100	150	225	6
Orange, brown roof.	100	150	225	6
814R: 1929-42, ivory, peacock roof.	100	150	225	4
Gloss white, blue roof.	200	275	400	6
Semi-gloss white, brown roof.	1,500	2,000	2,750	8
815 TANK CAR: 1926-42, pea green, maroon frame.	300	500	750	7
Pea green, black frame.	50	75	110	2
Silver, black frame.	75	110	150	4
Orange, with lettering plates.	200	300	550	7
Orange, with stamped lettering.	200	300	550	7
816 HOPPER: 1927-42, olive green.	80	125	175	4
Red, brass nameplates.	60	100	150	3
Red, nickel nameplates.	80	125	175	4
Black, nickel nameplates.	1,400	2,500	3,500	8
Black, rubber stamped.	400	600	1,000	7
817 CABOOSE: 1926-31, peacock.	35	55	75	2
Red, brass rails.	50	75	100	4
Red, silver rails.	20	30	45	1
Red, brown roof, nickel nameplates.	200	300	400	6
Red, brown roof, rubber-stamped lettering.	75	100	125	5
820 SEARCHLIGHT CAR: 1931-42, terracotta or green light base.	100	125	160	
820 BOXCAR: 1915-26.				
Dark olive A.T. & S.F	175	225	300	7
Yellow-orange "ILLINOIS CENTRAL RAILROAD."	40	55	80	4
Orange "UNION PACIFIC."	40	55	80	4
Dark orange, "UNION PACIFIC."	50	65	90	6

O-Gauge

902 GONDOLA, 1927-31

1011 PULLMAN, 1931-32

1015 0-4-0 STEAM, 1931-32

1020 BAGGAGE

O-Gauge

	VG	EX	LN	RARITY
821 STOCK CAR: 1925-26, green.	$50	$65	$90	6
831 FLATCAR: 1927-42, black or dark green, no journal boxes.	75	110	150	6
Dark, pale or 45N green with journal boxes.	20	30	40	2
900 AMMUNITION BOXCAR: 1917-21, unlettered gray, included with 203 armored motor car.	125	225	350	5
901 GONDOLA: 1917-27, brown, no journal boxes.	60	75	100	6
Brown, maroon, gray or green.	35	45	60	4
902 GONDOLA: 1927-31, dark green, peacock or Stephen Girard green.	20	30	40	3
1010 ELECTRIC: 1931-32, 0-B-0, orange.	75	110	150	3
1011 PULLMAN: 1931-32, light orange body with green or olive roof.	50	60	75	4
1015 STEAM: 1931-32, 0-4-0 with 1016 tender.	100	150	200	3
1019 OBSERVATION: Orange body, with green or olive roof.	50	60	75	4
1020 BAGGAGE: Light orange body, with green or olive roof.	60	75	100	5
1035 STEAM: 1931-32, 0-4-0 black with copper trim.	75	100	125	4
1506 STEAM: 1935, 0-4-0, clockwork, with Mickey Mouse riding in its 1509 tender.	225	325	450	6
1506L STEAM: 1933-34, 0-4-0, clockwork. No Mickey Mouse rode on this version.	80	100	125	4
1508 STEAM: 1935, 0-4-0, clockwork, streamlined, painted red, with Mickey Mouse riding in its 1509 tender.	325	450	600	6

1515 TANK CAR 1931-37

1517 CABOOSE, 1931-37

1518 through 1520 Mickey Mouse cars with locomotive and tender.

1631 OBSERVATION, 1938-41

O-Gauge

	VG	EX	LN	RARITY
1511 STEAM: 1936-37, 0-4-0, clockwork, black or red, with 1516T oil-style tender.	$100	$125	$150	2
1512 GONDOLA: 1931-37, blue or blue-green.	5	10	20	3
1514 BOXCAR: 1931-37, light yellow, with or without Baby Ruth logo.	15	20	30	3
1515 TANK CAR: 1931-37, aluminum-colored, lithographed Union Tank Lines.	25	45	70	7
Aluminum-colored tank, Sunoco.	15	25	35	4
Aluminum-colored tank, Lionel/Sunoco.	15	25	35	4
1517 CABOOSE: 1931-37, no Lionel markings whatsoever. Red, orange "NEW YORK – CENTRAL – LINES" legend.	20	30	40	2
1518 CIRCUS DINING CAR: 1935, part of an uncataloged Mickey Mouse-themed circus outfit.	100	150	225	7
1519 MICKEY MOUSE BAND: 1935, part of an uncataloged Mickey Mouse-themed circus outfit.	100	150	225	7
1520 MICKEY MOUSE CIRCUS: 1935, part of an uncataloged Mickey Mouse-themed circus outfit.	100	150	225	7
1588 STEAM: 1936-37, clockwork, black, with 1588T tender.	125	175	225	3
1630 PULLMAN: 1938-41, blue with gray or aluminum-colored windows, roof and underframe.	30	45	65	3
1631 OBSERVATION: 1938-41, blue with gray or aluminum-colored windows, roof and underframe.	30	45	65	3

O-GAUGE

1664 2-4-2 STEAM, 1938-42

1666E 2-6-2 STEAM LOCOMOTIVE, 1938-40

1668 2-6-2 STEAM, 1937-41

1679 BOXCAR, 1933-39

O-Gauge

	VG	EX	LN	RARITY
1651E ELECTRIC: 1933, 0-B-0, red.	$100	$140	$200	4
1661E STEAM: 1933, 2-4-0 with 1661T tender.	70	100	150	3
1662 STEAM: 1940-42, 0-4-0, with 2201T or 2203B tender.	225	300	400	4
1663 STEAM: 1940-42, 0-4-0, with 2201T.	200	300	400	5
1664/1664E STEAM: 1938-42, 2-4-2 black or gunmetal, with 1689T, 1689W or 2666W.	50	75	100	2
1666/1666E STEAM: 1938-42, 2-6-2 with 1689W, 2689T, 2689W, 2666T, or 2666W tender.				
Gunmetal.	100	130	175	4
Black.	75	100	125	3
1668/1668E STEAM: 1937-41, 2-4-2, Pennsylvania, streamlined, gunmetal or black, with 1689W tender.	75	100	125	2
1677 GONDOLA: 1933-38, peacock.	30	40	50	5
Blue or red.	20	30	40	3
1679 BOXCAR: 1933-39, yellow "Baby Ruth" or "CURTISS BABY RUTH" on sides.				
Maroon or light blue roof.	12	18	25	2
Brown roof.	25	30	40	5
1679X BOXCAR: 1936-42, the 1679X differed from the normal production by lacking journal boxes.	20	25	30	4
1680 TANK CAR: 1931-42, lithographed orange, or aluminum-colored lithographed tank, lettered "Motor Oil," Sunoco, Shell or "PETROLEUM – PRODUCTS."	15	22	30	3
Gray.	30	40	55	6
1680X TANK CAR: 1936-42, orange, or aluminum-colored with Sunoco, Shell or "Gas-Sunoco-Oils" markings.	15	22	30	3
Gray.	30	40	55	6

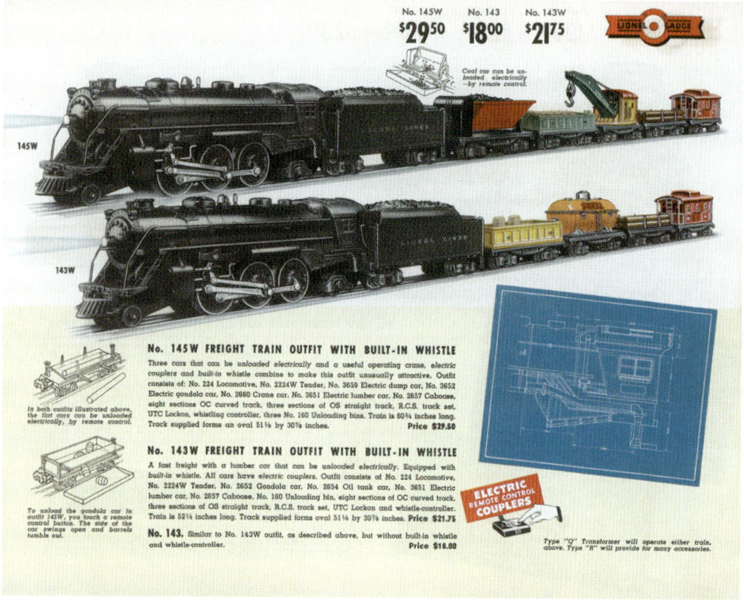
No. 145W
$29.50
No. 143
$18.00
No. 143W
$21.75
LIONEL O GAUGE
Coal car can be unloaded electrically —by remote control.
145W
143W
No. 145W FREIGHT TRAIN OUTFIT WITH BUILT-IN WHISTLE
Three cars that can be unloaded electrically and a useful operating crane, electric couplers and built-in whistle combine to make this outfit unusually attractive. Outfit consists of: No. 224 Locomotive, No. 2224W Tender, No. 3659 Electric dump car, No. 3652 Electric gondola car, No. 2660 Crane car, No. 3651 Electric lumber car, No. 2657 Caboose, eight sections OC curved track, three sections of OS straight track, R.C.S. track set, UTC Lockon, whistling controller, three No. 160 Unloading bins. Train is 60¾ inches long. Track supplied forms an oval 51⅛ by 30⅞ inches. Price $29.50
In both outfits illustrated above, the flat cars can be unloaded electrically, by remote control.
No. 143W FREIGHT TRAIN OUTFIT WITH BUILT-IN WHISTLE
A fast freight with a lumber car that can be unloaded electrically. Equipped with built-in whistle. All cars have electric couplers. Outfit consists of No. 224 Locomotive, No. 2224W Tender, No. 2652 Gondola car, No. 2654 Oil tank car, No. 3651 Electric lumber car, No. 2657 Caboose, No. 160 Unloading bin, eight sections of OC curved track, three sections of OS straight track, R.C.S. track set, UTC Lockon and whistle-controller. Train is 52¼ inches long. Track supplied forms oval 51⅛ by 30⅞ inches. Price $21.75
To unload the gondola car in outfit 145W, you touch a remote control button. The side of the car swings open and barrels tumble out.
No. 143. Similar to No. 143W outfit, as described above, but without built-in whistle and whistle-controller. Price $18.00
ELECTRIC REMOTE CONTROL COUPLERS
Type "Q" Transformer will operate either train, above. Type "R" will provide for many accessories.

1939 LIONEL CATALOG

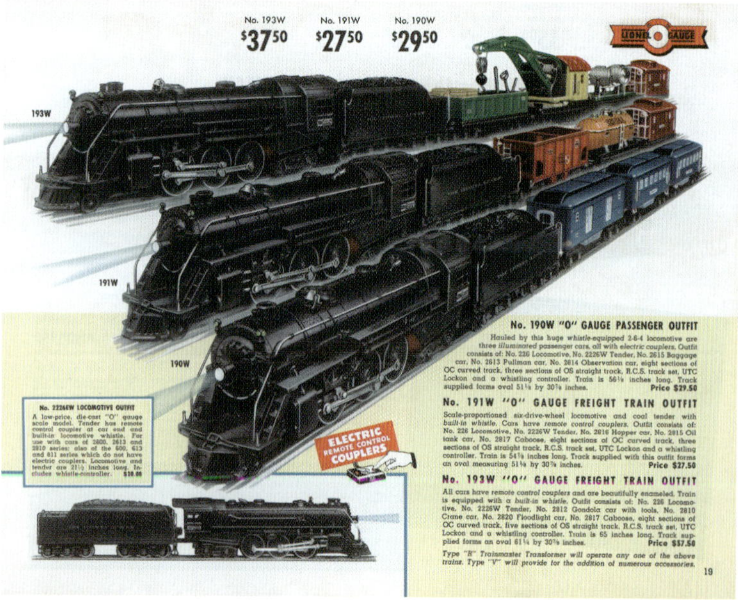
No. 193W
$37.50
No. 191W
$27.50
No. 190W
$29.50
LIONEL O GAUGE
193W
191W
190W
No. 190W "O" GAUGE PASSENGER OUTFIT
Hauled by this huge whistle-equipped 2-6-4 locomotive are three illuminated passenger cars, all with electric couplers. Outfit consists of: No. 226 Locomotive, No. 2226W Tender, No. 2615 Baggage car, No. 2613 Pullman car, No. 2614 Observation car, eight sections of OC curved track, three sections of OS straight track, R.C.S. track set, UTC Lockon and a whistling controller. Train is 56½ inches long. Track supplied forms oval 51⅛ by 30⅞ inches. Price $29.50
No. 191W "O" GAUGE FREIGHT TRAIN OUTFIT
Scale-proportioned six-drive-wheel locomotive and coal tender with built-in whistle. Cars have remote control couplers. Outfit consists of: No. 226 Locomotive, No. 2226W Tender, No. 2816 Hopper car, No. 2815 Oil tank car, No. 2817 Caboose, eight sections of OC curved track, three sections of OS straight track, R.C.S. track set, UTC Lockon and a whistling controller. Train is 54⅞ inches long. Track supplied with this outfit forms an oval measuring 51⅛ by 30⅞ inches. Price $27.50
No. 2226EW LOCOMOTIVE OUTFIT
A low-price, die-cast "O" gauge scale model. Tender has remote control coupler at car end and built-in locomotive whistle. For use with cars of 2600, 2613 and 2810 series; also of the 600, 613 and 811 series which do not have electric couplers. Locomotive and tender are 21½ inches long. Includes whistle-controller. $20.00
ELECTRIC REMOTE CONTROL COUPLERS
No. 193W "O" GAUGE FREIGHT TRAIN OUTFIT
All cars have remote control couplers and are beautifully enameled. Train is equipped with a built-in whistle. Outfit consists of: No. 226 Locomotive, No. 2226W Tender, No. 2812 Gondola car with tools, No. 2810 Crane car, No. 2820 Floodlight car, No. 2817 Caboose, eight sections of OC curved track, five sections of OS straight track, R.C.S. track set, UTC Lockon and a whistling controller. Train is 65 inches long. Track supplied forms an oval 61¼ by 30⅞ inches. Price $37.50
Type "R" Trainmaster Transformer will operate any one of the above trains. Type "V" will provide for the addition of numerous accessories.
19

1939 LIONEL CATALOG

O-GAUGE

1939 LIONEL CATALOG

1939 LIONEL CATALOG

O-GAUGE

1685 PASSENGER CAR, 1933-37

1689E STEAM, 1936-37

1691 OBSERVATION, 1933-1940

1700E DIESEL, 1935-37

O-Gauge

	VG	EX	LN	RARITY
1681/1681E: 1934, 2-4-0, with 1661T tender.				
Black with red frame.	$50	$80	$110	3
Overall red.	75	100	150	5
1682 CABOOSE: 1933-41, vermilion, red or brown body.	20	30	40	4
1684 STEAM: 1941-42, 2-4-2 die-cast, black or gunmetal.	40	55	75	3
1685 PASSENGER CAR: 1933-37.				
Gray with six-wheel trucks.	250	350	500	7
Red, four-wheel trucks.	175	275	350	5
Blue, four-wheel trucks.	175	275	350	5
1686 BAGGAGE CAR: 1933-37.				
Gray with six-wheel trucks.	250	350	500	7
Red, four-wheel trucks.	175	275	350	5
Blue, four-wheel trucks.	175	275	350	5
1687 OBSERVATION CAR: 1933-37.				
Gray with six-wheel trucks.	250	350	500	7
Red, four-wheel trucks.	175	275	350	5
Blue, four-wheel trucks.	175	275	350	5
1688/1688E STEAM: 1936-40, 2-4-2, Pennsylvania streamlined boiler and cab, gunmetal or black, with 1689T or 1689W tender.	40	55	75	3
1689E STEAM: 1936-37, 2-4-2, black or gunmetal Commodore Vanderbilt-style streamlined locomotive with 1689T, 1689W, 1688T or 1688W tender.	75	100	125	2
1690 PULLMAN: 1933-1940, dark red with yellow windows, medium red and cream windows or orange-red.	30	40	55	4
1691 OBSERVATION: 1933-1940, dark red with yellow windows, medium red and cream windows or orange-red.	30	40	55	4

O-GAUGE

1717 GONDOLA, 1933-40

1722 CABOOSE, 1933-42

1812 OBSERVATION, 1934-37

1813 BAGGAGE, 1934-37

O-Gauge

	VG	EX	LN	RARITY
1692 PULLMAN: 1939, lithographed blue.	$40	$50	$65	5
1693 OBSERVATION: 1939, lithographed blue.	40	50	65	5
1700E DIESEL: 1935-37, chrome finished, or painted yellow, orange or aluminum. Yellow too scarce to value.	150	200	250	4
1701 COACH: 1935-37, chrome finished, or painted red, yellow, orange or aluminum. Yellow too scarce to value.	25	35	50	4
1702 OBSERVATION: 1935-37, chrome finished, or painted red, yellow, orange or aluminum. Yellow too scarce to value.	25	35	50	4
1703 FRONT END CAR: 1935-37, chrome finished, or painted red, yellow, orange or aluminum. Yellow too scarce to value.	50	75	100	5
1717 GONDOLA: 1933-40, yellow.	15	25	35	4
1717X GONDOLA: 1940, yellow, equipped with latch couplers.	30	45	60	4
1719 BOXCAR: 1933-42, lithographed Stephen Girard or light green.	20	30	40	4
1719X BOXCAR: 1942, lithographed light Stephen Girard green.	25	35	45	5
1722 CABOOSE: 1933-42, orange, light red or orange red.	20	30	40	2
1722X CABOOSE: 1939-1940, orange-red.	20	30	40	2
1811 PULLMAN: 1934-37, peacock, gray or red.	30	45	65	3
1812 OBSERVATION: 1934-37, peacock, gray or red.	30	45	65	3
1813 BAGGAGE: 1934-37, peacock, gray or red.	30	45	65	3

O-Gauge

2600 PULLMAN, 1938-40

2601 OBSERVATION, 1938-40

2602 BAGGAGE, 1938-40

O-Gauge

	VG	EX	LN	RARITY
1816 DIESEL: 1935, clockwork-powered, chrome finished, came with a matching 1817 coach and 1818 observation with orange vestibules and frames.	$100	$150	$200	5
1816W DIESEL: 1936-37, clockwork-powered, chrome finished, came with a matching 1817 coach and 1818 observation with orange vestibules and frames.	110	160	225	6
1817 COACH: 1935-37, chrome-finished, fluted body. Sold in sets with matching 1816 or 1816W locomotive and 1818 observation.	20	35	50	5
1818 OBSERVATION: 1935-37, chrome-finished, fluted body. Sold in sets with matching 1816 or 1816W locomotive and 1818 observation.	20	35	50	5
2600 PULLMAN: 1938-40.	80	125	175	5
2601 OBSERVATION: 1938-40.	80	125	175	5
2602 BAGGAGE: 1938-40.	80	125	175	5
2613 PULLMAN: 1938-42.				
Blue body with two-tone blue roofs.	90	165	250	4
State green with a two-tone State green and dark green roof.	200	300	400	6
2614 OBSERVATION: 1938-42.				
Blue body with two-tone blue roofs.	90	165	250	4
State green with a two-tone State green and dark green roof.	200	300	400	6
2615 BAGGAGE: 1938-42.				
Blue body with two-tone blue roofs.	90	165	250	4

2623 PULLMAN, 1941-42

2630 PULLMAN, 1938-42

2641 OBSERVATION, 1938-42

2653 HOPPER, 1938-42

O-Gauge

	VG	EX	LN	RARITY
State green with a two-tone State green and dark green roof.	$200	$300	$400	6
2620 SEARCHLIGHT CAR: 1938-40.				
Red, aluminum-colored light housing.	50	80	120	3
Red, gray light housing.	80	110	150	5
2623 PULLMAN: 1941-42, "2623 IRVINGTON 2623."	200	300	425	6
2623 PULLMAN: 1941-42, "2623 MANHATTAN 2623."	125	200	300	6
2624 PULLMAN: "2624 MANHATTAN 2624."	800	1,500	3,000	8
2630 PULLMAN: 1938-42, blue with aluminum roof.	25	50	75	2
Blue with gray roof.	35	60	90	4
2631 OBSERVATION: 1938-42, blue with aluminum roof.	25	50	75	2
Blue with gray roof.	35	60	90	4
2640 PULLMAN: 1938-42, illuminated, blue or State green.	25	50	75	2
2641 OBSERVATION: 1938-42, illuminated, blue or State green.	25	50	75	2
2642 PULLMAN: 1941-42, Tuscan with gray windows.	40	60	85	4
2643 OBSERVATION: 1941-42, Tuscan with gray windows.	40	60	85	4
2651 FLATCAR: 1938-40, green.	25	35	50	2
Black.	50	75	115	5
2652 GONDOLA: 1939-42, yellow.	25	35	50	2
Orange.	40	50	65	4
2653 HOPPER: 1938-39, Stephen Girard Green.	30	50	75	3
Black.	75	200	350	7
2654 TANK CAR: 1938-42, aluminum-colored, orange or gray, Sunoco or Shell.	30	40	55	3

O-GAUGE

1938 LIONEL CATALOG

1938 LIONEL CATALOG

O-GAUGE

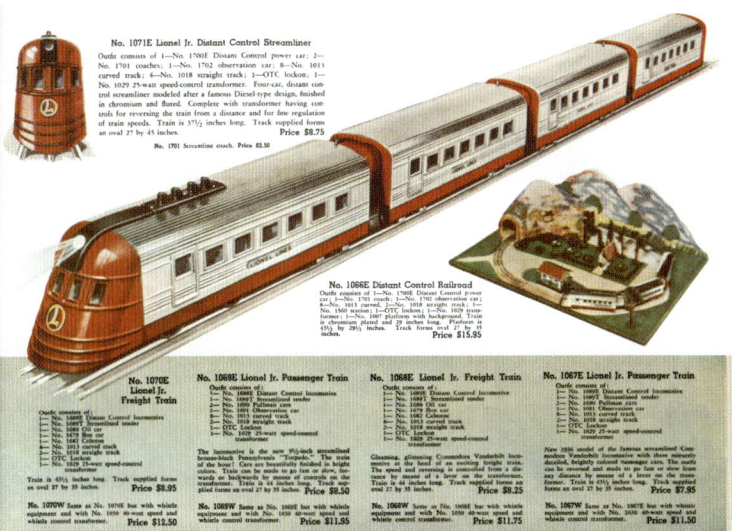

1936 LIONEL CATALOG

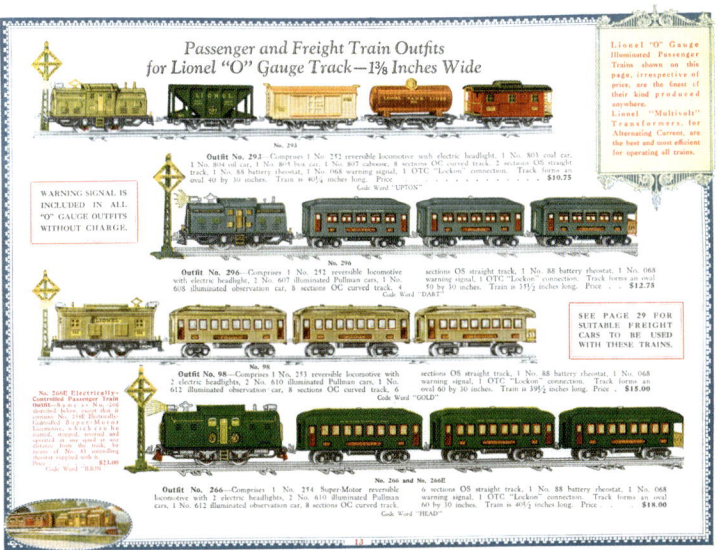

1927 LIONEL CATALOG

2660 CRANE, 1938-42

2677 GONDOLA, 1940-42

2755 TANK CAR, 1941-42

2757 CABOOSE, 1941-1942

O-Gauge

	VG	EX	LN	RARITY
2655 BOXCAR: 1938-41, yellow with maroon or Tuscan roof.	$40	$55	$75	4
2656 STOCK CAR: 1938-40, light gray.	60	75	100	4
Burnt orange.	100	125	165	7
2657 CABOOSE: 1938-42, light red.	15	22	30	1
2657X CABOOSE: 1938-42, light red, equipped with electrocouplers for use with switcher sets.	20	30	40	2
2659 DUMP CAR: 1938-42, with dark green dump bin.	75	100	125	6
2660 CRANE: 1938-42.	60	75	100	4
2672 CABOOSE: 1942, Pennsylvania, painted Tuscan. No window frames, smokejack or steps.	20	30	40	2
2677 GONDOLA: 1940-42, dark red lithographed gondola.	35	50	70	5
2679 BOXCAR: 1938-42, yellow lithographed, "Baby Ruth" or a "Curtiss Baby Ruth Candy."	15	25	40	3
2680 TANK CAR: 1938-42, aluminum-painted, Sunoco.	15	25	35	4
Orange with Shell markings.	15	25	35	4
Gray, Gas-Sunoco-Oils.	15	25	35	4
2682 CABOOSE: 1938-41, red "Lionel Lines"or Tuscan "New York Central."	15	22	30	1
2682X CABOOSE: 1940-41, caboose with two automatic couplers.	20	30	40	2
2717 GONDOLA: 1938-42, lithographed, yellow.	20	30	40	4
2719 BOXCAR: 1938-42, lithographed light peacock.	15	25	40	4
2722 CABOOSE: 1938-42, orange-red body.	20	30	45	2

2811 FLATCAR, 1938-42

2813 STOCK CAR, 1938-39

2814 BOXCAR, 1938-42

2814R REFRIGERATOR CAR, 1938-40

O-GAUGE

	VG	EX	LN	RARITY
2755 TANK CAR: 1941-42, Aluminum color.	$50	$80	$125	4
Gray.	100	150	225	6
2757 CABOOSE: 1941-1942, Tuscan with Pennsylvania markings, separately installed steps, smokejack and red window frames.	20	30	45	2
2757X CABOOSE: 1941-42, same as 2757, but with automatic box couplers on both ends. Requires box for full value.	30	45	60	4
2758 AUTOMOBILE BOXCAR: 1941-42, Tuscan double door.	40	50	65	4
2810 CRANE: 1938-42, cream cab.	175	210	250	5
Yellow cab.	185	225	275	6
2811 FLATCAR: 1938-42, aluminum-colored.	65	95	135	6
2812 GONDOLA: 1938-42, 45N green.	30	40	50	3
Orange, nickel nameplates.	40	50	70	5
Orange, rubber stamped.	40	50	60	4
2812X GONDOLA: 1940-42, dark orange car.	40	50	70	5
2813 STOCK CAR: 1938-39, cream or Tuscan.	150	225	350	6
2814 BOXCAR: 1938-42, cream body.	75	150	250	5
Orange body.	750	1,500	2,500	8
2814R REFRIGERATOR CAR: 1938-40, white with blue roof.	250	325	450	7
White with brown roof.	750	1,500	2,500	8
2815 TANK CAR: 1938-42, aluminum-colored Sunoco or orange Shell.	100	150	225	3
2816 HOPPER: 1938-42, red.	125	175	250	5
Black.	125	250	425	7

O-Gauge

2954 BOXCAR, 1940-42

2955 TANK CAR, 1941-42

2956 HOPPER, 1940-42

2957 CABOOSE, 1940-42

3814 MERCHANDISE CAR, 1939-40

O-Gauge

	VG	EX	LN	RARITY
2817 CABOOSE: 1938-42.				
Red body, red roof.	$75	$100	$125	4
Red body, brown roof, nickel plates.	300	450	600	7
Red body, brown roof, heat-stamped.	100	200	300	6
2820 SEARCHLIGHT CAR: 1938-42, nickel lights.	125	175	225	4
Gray die-cast lights.	200	275	350	6
2954 BOXCAR: 1940-42, semi-scale Tuscan Pennsylvania boxcar.	150	250	400	6
2955 TANK CAR: 1940, black with Shell markings.	200	350	525	5
1941-42 Sunoco markings.	350	525	725	7
2956 HOPPER: 1940-42, semi-scale hopper.	200	400	625	7
2957 CABOOSE: 1940-42, semi scale.	125	250	400	4
3651 LOG DUMP: 1939-40, black.	20	35	60	2
3652 OPERATING GONDOLA: 1939-41, yellow, nickel plates.	30	50	75	3
Yellow, red rubber-stamped lettering.	50	70	100	6
Yellow, black rubber-stamped lettering.	50	70	100	5
3659 OPERATING DUMP CAR: 1938-42, red dump bin.	30	50	75	3
3811 LOG DUMP CAR: 1939-42, black.	35	50	80	3
3814 MERCHANDISE CAR: 1939-40, Tuscan boxcar with operating mechanism, includes cube-like plastic "boxes."				
Decal lettering.	125	175	225	4
Stamped lettering.	175	225	275	4
3859 OPERATING DUMP CAR: 1938-42, light red.	60	85	115	5

1937 ADVERTISEMENT

O-GAUGE

1937 LIONEL CATALOG

1937 LIONEL CATALOG

OO-Gauge

Most likely two forces within the toy train hobby came together in the early 1930s, resulting in Lionel's introduction of OO-Gauge trains. First was the increasing demand for more realistic trains. Whereas during the first three decades of the company, the trains were unmistakably toys aimed at children, there was a growing demand for realistic model trains for use by hobbyists, who were primarily adult males. In O-Gauge, this manifested itself in the fabulous 700E locomotive and related cars, as well as the Pennsylvania B-6 switcher.

The second force was closely related to the first. Whereas many children were perfectly content to play with their trains on the floor, as so often depicted in the catalogs of the period, this wouldn't do for

OO-Gauge

the adult hobbyist. They envisioned their trains traversing complete miniature worlds, with realistic scenery and landscaping, an environment that required a permanent, tabletop display. Lionel's Standard and O-Gauge trains required vast amounts of space to accomplish this. But OO, and the slightly smaller HO, trains required only about 1/8 the volume of space for a given display (the wider radius of Lionel's two-rail OO track violates this principle).

Unfortunately, the Depression, World War II and Lionel's somewhat timid entry into this market combined to undermine this effort. Despite its popularity in Europe, OO never took hold in the U.S., and consequently OO did not return to Lionel's catalogs in the postwar era.

OO-Gauge

001 4-6-4 STEAM LOCOMOTIVE, 1938-42, three-rail.

002 4-6-4 STEAM LOCOMOTIVE, 1939-42, three-rail, with 0027 caboose.

003 4-6-4 STEAM LOCOMOTIVE, 1938-42, two-rail.

0014 BOXCAR, 1938 version shown.

OO-Gauge

	VG	EX	LN	RARITY

001 STEAM LOCOMOTIVE: 1938-42, replica of a New York Central J-3a 4-6-4 Hudson. The locomotive and tender were 15-1/2" long and the number "5342" was rubber stamped beneath the cab window. "New York Central" was rubber stamped in silver on the sides of the 12-wheel tender. It came with or without a whistle mechanism; locomotives with non-whistling tenders are today estimated at $70 less than the values listed. In 1938, the locomotive and tender were joined by a miniature drawbar pin with its own retaining chain. — $250 / $450 / $700 / 5

In 1939-42, a spring-loaded pin was used to connect the tender drawbar to the locomotive. — 200 / 400 / 600 / 4

002 STEAM LOCOMOTIVE: 1939-42, less-detailed than 001. — 175 / 350 / 550 / 4

003 STEAM LOCOMOTIVE: 1939-42, designed to operate on two-rail track. — 250 / 450 / 700 / 5

004 STEAM LOCOMOTIVE: 1939-42, less-detailed two-rail locomotive. — 150 / 300 / 500 / 6

0014 BOXCAR: 1938-1942, 6-7/8" long super-detailed boxcar.

	VG	EX	LN	RARITY
1938, yellow and maroon.	75	125	200	6
1939-42, Tuscan.	50	65	80	4

A note on Lionel OO freight cars: "Super-detailed" freight cars have a simulated air brake reservoir, whereas semi-scale cars do not. Interestingly, no semi-scale hopper cars were produced. All kit cars came with insulated wheels, permitting them to be operated on two-rail track. These cars, as well two-rail cars, could also be run on three-rail track. However, cars designed for three-rail operation cause a short circuit if placed on two-rail track.

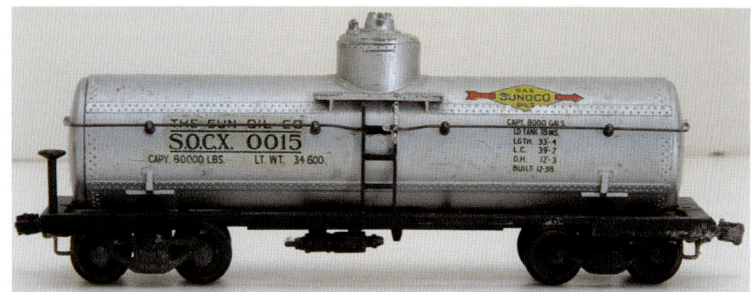

0015 TANK CAR, 1941 version shown.

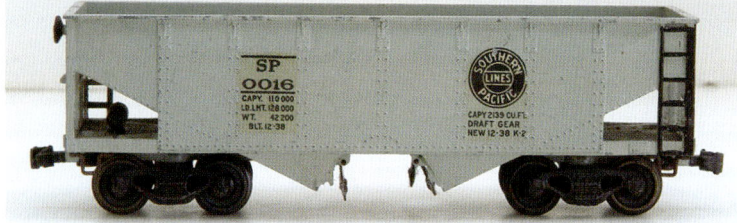

0016 HOPPER CAR, 1938 version.

0017 CABOOSE, 1938 version.

0031 TWO-RAIL CURVED TRACK, 1939-42

OO-Gauge

	VG	EX	LN	RARITY

0015 TANK CAR: 1938-42, 5-3/4" long, super-detailed, die-cast tanker.

	VG	EX	LN	RARITY
1938, silver with black frame, lettered "THE SUN OIL CO." and "S.O.C.X. 0015."	$50	$75	$100	6
1939-40, black, lettered "SHELL," "S.E.P.X. 8126."	40	60	80	5
1941, silver with black frame, lettered "THE SUN OIL CO." and "S.U.N.X. 2599."	40	60	80	5

0016 HOPPER CAR: 1938-42, 5-1/2" long die-cast hopper car.

	VG	EX	LN	RARITY
1938, painted gray and black lettered "SP 0016" with round "SOUTHERN PACIFIC LINES" herald.	75	125	175	6
1939-42, painted black and white lettered "SP 0016" with round "SOUTHERN PACIFIC LINES" herald.	60	100	150	4

0017 CABOOSE: 1938-42, 4-5/8" long caboose

	VG	EX	LN	RARITY
1938, red lettered "PENNSYLVANIA 0017."	75	115	150	5
1939-42, darker red, lettered "N.Y.C. 0017."	50	75	100	3

0024 BOXCAR: 1939-42, semi-scale 6-7/8" long boxcar lettered "PENNSYLVANIA 0024."

	VG	EX	LN	RARITY
	45	60	75	4

0025 TANK CAR: 1939-42, 5-3/4" long tanker.

	VG	EX	LN	RARITY
1939-40, black, lettered "SHELL," "S.E.P.X. 8126."	40	60	80	3
1941, silver with black frame, lettered "THE SUN OIL CO." and "S.U.N.X. 2599."	40	60	80	3

0027 CABOOSE: 1939-1942, 4-5/8" long semi-scale three-rail red caboose lettered "N.Y.C. 0027."

	VG	EX	LN	RARITY
	40	60	80	3

0031 CURVED TRACK: 1939-42, standard two-rail 24" radius OO curved track. Twelve sections were required to form a circle.

	VG	EX	LN	RARITY
	8	14	20	4

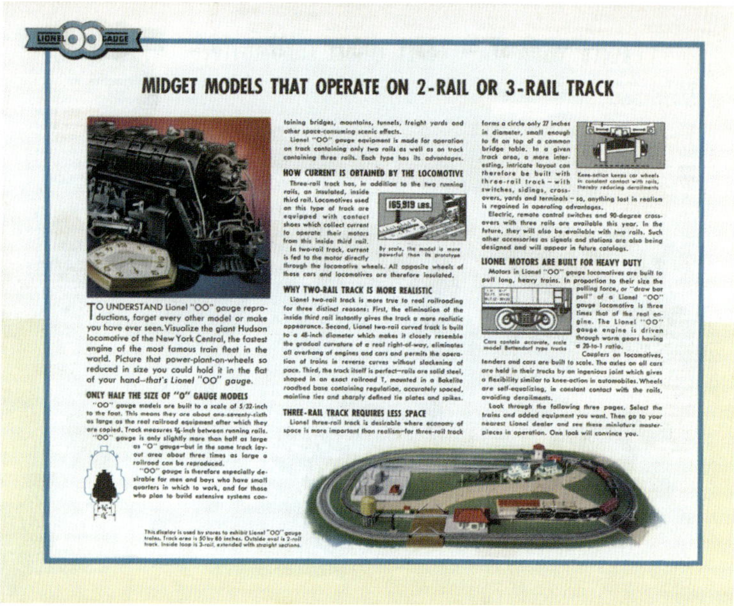

MIDGET MODELS THAT OPERATE ON 2-RAIL OR 3-RAIL TRACK

TO UNDERSTAND Lionel "OO" gauge reproductions, forget every other model or make you have ever seen. Visualize the giant Hudson locomotive of the New York Central, the fastest engine of the most famous train fleet in the world. Picture that power-plant-on-wheels so reduced in size you could hold it in the flat of your hand—*that's Lionel "OO" gauge.*

ONLY HALF THE SIZE OF "O" GAUGE MODELS

"OO" gauge models are built to a scale of 5/32-inch to the foot. This means they are about one-seventy-sixth as large as the real railroad equipment after which they are copied. Track measures ¾-inch between running rails.

"OO" gauge is only slightly more than half as large as "O" gauge—but in the same track layout area about three times as large a railroad can be reproduced.

"OO" gauge is therefore especially desirable for men and boys who have small quarters in which to work, and for those who plan to build extensive systems containing bridges, mountains, tunnels, freight yards and other space-consuming scenic effects.

Lionel "OO" gauge equipment is made for operation on track containing only two rails as well as on track containing three rails. Each type has its advantages.

HOW CURRENT IS OBTAINED BY THE LOCOMOTIVE

Three-rail track has, in addition to the two running rails, an insulated, inside third rail. Locomotives used on this type of track are equipped with contact shoes which collect current to operate their motors from this inside third rail.

In two-rail track, current is fed to the motor directly through the locomotive wheels. All opposite wheels of these cars and locomotives are therefore insulated.

165,919 LBS.

By scale, the model is more powerful than its prototype

WHY TWO-RAIL TRACK IS MORE REALISTIC

Lionel two-rail track is more true to real railroading for three distinct reasons: First, the elimination of the inside third rail instantly gives the track a more realistic appearance. Second, Lionel two-rail curved track is built to a 48-inch diameter which makes it closely resemble the gradual curvature of a real right-of-way, eliminates all overhang of engines and cars and permits the operation of trains in reverse curves without slackening of pace. Third, the track itself is perfect—rails are solid steel, shaped in an exact railroad T, mounted in a Bakelite roadbed base containing regulation, accurately spaced, mainline ties and sharply defined tie plates and spikes.

THREE-RAIL TRACK REQUIRES LESS SPACE

Lionel three-rail track is desirable where economy of space is more important than realism—for three-rail track forms a circle only 27 inches in diameter, small enough to fit on top of a common bridge table. In a given track area, a more interesting, intricate layout can therefore be built with three-rail track—with switches, sidings, crossovers, yards and terminals—so, anything lost in realism is regained in operating advantages.

Knee-action keeps car wheels in constant contact with rails, thereby reducing derailments

Electric, remote control switches and 90-degree crossovers with three rails are available this year. In the future, they will also be available with two rails. Such other accessories as signals and stations are also being designed and will appear in future catalogs.

LIONEL MOTORS ARE BUILT FOR HEAVY DUTY

Motors in Lionel "OO" gauge locomotives are built to pull long, heavy trains. In proportion to their size the pulling force, or "draw bar pull" of a Lionel "OO" gauge locomotive is three times that of the real engine. The Lionel "OO" gauge engine is driven through worm gears having a 20-to-1 ratio.

Cars contain accurate, scale model Bettendorf type trucks

Couplers on locomotives, tenders and cars are built to scale. The axles on all cars are held in their trucks by an ingenious joint which gives a flexibility similar to knee-action in automobiles. Wheels are self-equalizing, in constant contact with the rails, avoiding derailments.

Look through the following three pages. Select the trains and added equipment you want. Then go to your nearest Lionel dealer and see these miniature masterpieces in operation. One look will convince you.

This display is used by stores to exhibit Lionel "OO" gauge trains. Track area is 50 by 86 inches. Outside oval is 2-rail track. Inside loop is 3-rail, extended with straight sections.

1939 CATALOG

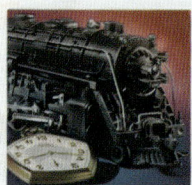

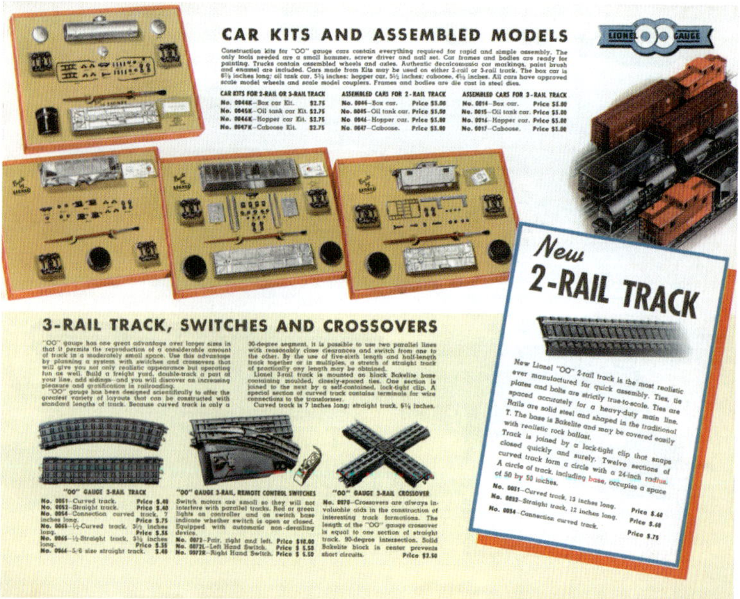

CAR KITS AND ASSEMBLED MODELS

Construction kits for "OO" gauge cars contain everything required for rapid and simple assembly. The only tools needed are a small hammer, screw driver and nail set. Car frames and bodies are ready for painting. Trucks contain assembled wheels and axles. Authentic decalcomania car markings, paint brush and enamel are included. Cars made from Kits may be used on either 2-rail or 3-rail track. The box car is 6⅔ inches long; oil tank car, 5¾ inches; hopper car, 5½ inches; caboose, 4⅔ inches. All cars have approved scale model wheels and scale model couplers. Frames and bodies are die cast in steel dies.

CAR KITS FOR 2-RAIL OR 3-RAIL TRACK

- No. 0044K—Box car Kit. $2.75
- No. 0045K—Oil tank car Kit. $2.75
- No. 0046K—Hopper car Kit. $2.75
- No. 0047K—Caboose Kit. $2.75

ASSEMBLED CARS FOR 2-RAIL TRACK

- No. 0044—Box car. Price $5.00
- No. 0045—Oil tank car. Price $5.00
- No. 0046—Hopper car. Price $5.00
- No. 0047—Caboose. Price $5.00

ASSEMBLED CARS FOR 3-RAIL TRACK

- No. 0014—Box car. Price $5.00
- No. 0015—Oil tank car. Price $5.00
- No. 0016—Hopper car. Price $5.00
- No. 0017—Caboose. Price $5.00

3-RAIL TRACK, SWITCHES AND CROSSOVERS

"OO" gauge has one great advantage over larger sizes in that it permits the reproduction of a considerable amount of track in a moderately small space. Use this advantage by planning a system with switches and crossovers that will give you not only realistic appearance but operating fun as well. Build a freight yard, double-track a part of your line, add sidings—and you will discover an increasing pleasure and gratification in railroading.

"OO" gauge has been designed scientifically to offer the greatest variety of layouts that can be constructed with standard lengths of track. Because curved track is only a 30-degree segment, it is possible to use two parallel lines with reasonably close clearances and switch from one to the other. By the use of five-sixth length and half-length track together or in multiples, a stretch of straight track of practically any length may be obtained.

Lionel 3-rail track is mounted on black Bakelite base containing moulded, closely-spaced ties. One section is joined to the next by a self-contained, lock-tight clip. A special section of curved track contains terminals for wire connections to the transformer.

Curved track is 7 inches long; straight track, 6¼ inches.

"OO" GAUGE 3-RAIL TRACK

- No. 0051—Curved track. Price $.40
- No. 0052—Straight track. Price $.40
- No. 0054—Connection curved track, 7 inches long. Price $.75
- No. 0063—½-Curved track, 3½ inches long. Price $.55
- No. 0065—½-Straight track, 3⅛ inches long. Price $.55
- No. 0066—5/6 size straight track. $.40

"OO" GAUGE 3-RAIL, REMOTE CONTROL SWITCHES

Switch motors are small so they will not interfere with parallel tracks. Red or green lights on controller and on switch base indicate whether switch is open or closed. Equipped with automatic non-derailing device.

- No. 0072—Pair, right and left. Price $10.00
- No. 0072L—Left Hand Switch. Price $ 5.50
- No. 0072R—Right Hand Switch. Price $ 5.50

"OO" GAUGE 3-RAIL CROSSOVER

No. 0070—Crossovers are always invaluable aids in the construction of interesting track formations. The length of the "OO" gauge crossover is equal to one section of straight track. 90-degree intersection. Solid Bakelite block in center prevents short circuits. Price $2.50

New 2-RAIL TRACK

New Lionel "OO" 2-rail track is the most realistic ever manufactured for quick assembly. Ties, tie plates and bolts are strictly true-to-scale. Ties are spaced accurately for a heavy-duty main line. Rails are solid steel and shaped in the traditional T. The base is Bakelite and may be covered easily with realistic rock ballast.

Track is joined by a lock-tight clip that snaps closed quickly and surely. Twelve sections of curved track form a circle with a 24-inch radius. A circle of track, including base, occupies a space of 50 by 50 inches.

- No. 0031—Curved track, 13 inches long. Price $.40
- No. 0032—Straight track, 12 inches long. Price $.40
- No. 0034—Connection curved track. Price $.75

1939 CATALOG

OO-Gauge

1938 CATALOG

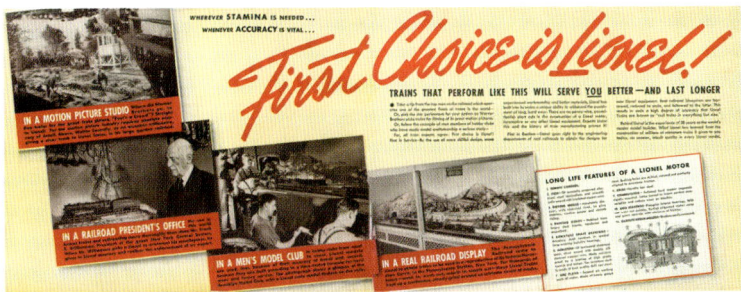

1938 CATALOG

1939 CATALOG

OO-Gauge

0045 TANK CAR, 1939-40

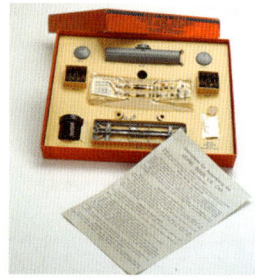

0045K TANK CAR KIT, 1939-42

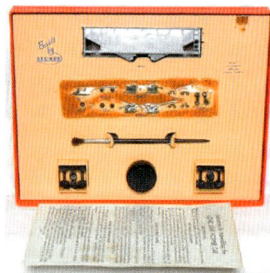

0046K HOPPER CAR KIT, 1939-42

0046 HOPPER CAR, 1939-42

0047 CABOOSE, 1939-42

OO-Gauge

	VG	EX	LN	RARITY
0034 CURVED TRACK:	$12	$18	$25	5
0044 BOXCAR: 1939-42, 6-7/8" long super-detailed die-cast two-rail Pennsylvania boxcar.	45	70	100	5
0044K BOXCAR: 1939-42, unassembled version of the 6-7/8" long super-detailed die-cast boxcar in primer.	70	125	350	6
0045 TANK CAR: 1939-42, super-detailed 5-3/4" long tank car for two-rail operation.				
1939-40, black, lettered "SHELL," "S.E.P.X. 8126."	40	60	80	5
1941-42, silver with black frame, lettered "THE SUN OIL CO." and "S.U.N.X. 2599."	40	60	80	3
0045K TANK CAR: 1939-42, unassembled version of the 5-3/4" long super-detailed die-cast tank car, in primer.	70	125	350	6
0046 HOPPER CAR: 1939-42, black 5-1/2" long super-detailed Southern Pacific hopper.	40	70	100	4
0046K HOPPER CAR: 1939-42, unassembled version of the 5-1/2" long super-detailed die-cast hopper car, in primer.	70	125	350	6
0047 CABOOSE: 1939-42, 4-5/8" long super-detailed caboose for two-rail operation.	30	60	90	4
0047K CABOOSE: 1939-42, unassembled version of the 4-5/8" long super-detailed die-cast caboose, in primer.	70	125	350	6
0051 CURVED TRACK: 1939-42, standard three-rail 27" radius OO curved track.	6	12	18	4
0052 STRAIGHT TRACK: 1939-42, standard three-rail 7" long OO straight track.	12	18	30	5

OO-GAUGE

0063 CURVED TRACK, 1939-42, box of six sections.

0070 90-DEGREE CROSSING, 1939-42

0072 PAIR OF REMOTE CONTROL SWITCHES, 1949-42

0072R REMOTE CONTROL SWITCH, 1939-42

OO-Gauge

	VG	EX	LN	RARITY
0054 CURVED TERMINAL TRACK: 1939-42, standard three-rail 27" radius with two side-mounted electrical connections.	$12	$18	$25	5
0061 CURVED TRACK: 1938.	5	10	15	4
0062 STRAIGHT TRACK: 1938.	6	12	18	6
0063 CURVED TRACK: 1939-42, 3" long "half section" of three-rail tubular OO curved track.	12	18	24	6
0064 CURVED TERMINAL TRACK: 1938, terminal track.	12	18	25	5
0065 STRAIGHT TRACK: 1939-42, 3-3/8" long "half section" of three-rail tubular OO straight track.	12	18	24	6
0066 STRAIGHT TRACK: 1939-42, 5-5/8" long section of three-rail tubular OO track.	12	18	24	6
0070 90-DEGREE CROSSING: 1939-42, 00 Gauge 90-degree crossing.	4	8	12	5
0072 PAIR OF REMOTE CONTROL SWITCHES: 1949-42.	125	200	300	6
0072L REMOTE CONTROL SWITCH: 1939-42.	60	90	140	6
0072R REMOTE CONTROL SWITCH: 1939-42.	60	90	140	6
0074 BOXCAR: 1939-42, 6-7/8" long semi-scale die-cast two-rail boxcar.	45	70	100	5
0075 TANK CAR: semi-scale 5-3/4" long tank car for two-rail operation.				
1939-40, black, lettered "SHELL," "S.E.P.X. 8126."	20	40	60	3
1941-42, silver with black frame, lettered "THE SUN OIL CO." and "S.U.N.X. 2599."	20	40	60	3
0077 CABOOSE: 1939-1942, red 4-5/8" long two-rail semi-scale caboose.	20	40	60	3

Accessories, Toys and Novelties

Accessories, Toys

One of the key elements in Lionel's success, both pre and postwar was their numerous operating accessories. Joshua Cowen felt it was important to provide a means for children and adults to interact with the trains, as well as provide a semi-realistic setting to operate them in.

Today Lionel's accessories retain their appeal to operators and collectors alike. Children, young or old, still delight in watching day to day tasks being performed in miniature by these accessories.

Accessories, Toys and Novelties

and Novelties

Despite their appeal compared to trains and starter sets in particular all accessories are relatively scarce. The rarity ratings given in this chapter are relative to other accessories, not the Lionel product line as a whole. Even the most common of accessories like the 145 Gateman is more difficult to locate than a common train car, such as the 6462 Gondola.

ACCESSORIES, TOYS AND NOVELTIES

1 BILD-A-MOTOR, 1928-31

2 BILD-A-MOTOR, 1928-31

26-020-2

023 BUMPER, 1915-33

ACCESSORIES, TOYS AND NOVELTIES

	VG	EX	LN	RARITY
1 BILD-A-MOTOR: 1928-31, mounted on a red or black base.	$60	$90	$150	7
2 BILD-A-MOTOR: 1928-31.	100	125	225	7
011 PAIR OF REMOTE CONTROL SWITCHES: 1933-37.	20	30	40	3
011L LEFT-HAND REMOTE CONTROL SWITCH: 1933-37.	10	15	20	3
011R RIGHT-HAND REMOTE CONTROL SWITCH: 1933-37.	10	15	20	3
012 PAIR OF REMOTE CONTROL SWITCHES: 1927-33.	25	30	40	3
012L LEFT-HAND REMOTE CONTROL SWITCH: 1927-33.	12	15	20	3
012R RIGHT-HAND REMOTE CONTROL SWITCH: 1927-33.	12	15	20	3
013 REMOTE CONTROL SWITCH SET: 1929-31.	100	140	200	6
020 90-DEGREE CROSSING: 1915-42.	4	6	8	1
020X 45-DEGREE CROSSING: 1915-42.	4	7	10	2
021 PAIR OF MANUAL SWITCHES: 1915-27.	15	25	40	2
021L LEFT-HAND MANUAL SWITCH: 1915-37.	7	12	20	2
021R RIGHT-HAND MANUAL SWITCH: 1915-37.	7	12	20	2
022 PAIR OF MANUAL SWITCHES: 1915-26. Priced per pair.	25	40	65	6
022 REMOTE CONTROL SWITCHES: 1938-42.	60	75	90	4
022L LEFT-HAND REMOTE CONTROL SWITCH: 1938-42.	35	45	55	4
022R RIGHT-HAND REMOTE CONTROL SWITCH: 1938-42.	35	45	55	4

ACCESSORIES, TOYS AND NOVELTIES

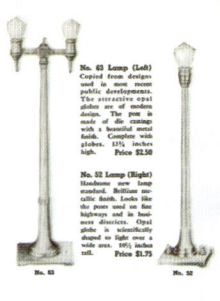

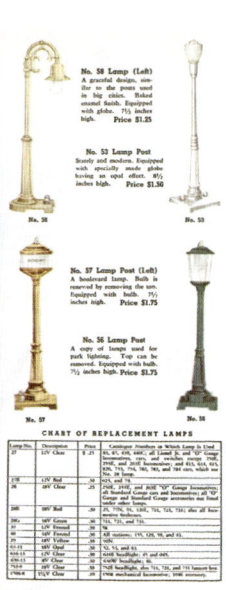

1936 LIONEL CATALOG

1936 LIONEL CATALOG

Accessories, Toys and Novelties

1943 DEALER BROCHURE (left photo cover & right photo back cover)

1943 DEALER BROCHURE (interior pages)

ACCESSORIES, TOYS AND NOVELTIES

43 LIONEL CRAFT PLEASURE BOAT, 1933-36

44 LIONEL CRAFT RACING BOAT, 1935-36

47 DOUBLE CROSSING GATE, 1933-42

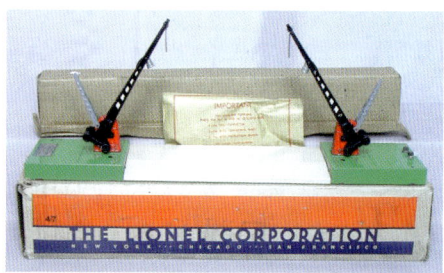

50 WARTIME FREIGHT TRAIN, 1943

Accessories, Toys and Novelties

	VG	EX	LN	RARITY
023 BUMPER: 1915-33, red or black.	$15	$25	$35	5
025 ILLUMINATED BUMPER: 1928-42, cream or black.	15	20	25	3
27 LIGHTING SET: 1911-23.	15	30	45	3
32 MINIATURE FIGURES: 1909-18.	70	100	150	5
35 BOULEVARD LAMP: 1940-42, 1945-49. Painted aluminum color or gray.	20	35	55	
41 CONTACTOR: 1936-42.	1	5	8	1
042 PAIR OF MANUAL SWITCHES: 1938-42, 1946-59.	40	50	60	4
042L LEFT-HAND MANUAL SWITCH: 1938-42, 1946-59.	20	25	30	4
042R RIGHT-HAND MANUAL SWITCH: 1938-42, 1946-59.	20	25	30	4
43/043 BILD-A-MOTOR GEAR SET: 1929.	40	60	90	5
43 LIONEL CRAFT PLEASURE BOAT: 1933-36.	325	550	750	5
44 LIONEL CRAFT RACING BOAT: 1935-36.	500	800	1,250	7
45 AUTOMATIC GATEMAN, 045 AUTOMATIC GATEMAN, 45N AUTOMATIC GATEMAN: 1935-42, 1945.	30	45	60	2
46 SINGLE CROSSING GATE: 1939-42. Roadway area painted ivory; the remainder of the accessory base was painted 45N green.	75	100	125	3
47 DOUBLE CROSSING GATE: 1933-42. Roadway area painted ivory; the remainder of the accessory base was painted 45N green.	60	100	150	3
48W WHISTLE STATION: 1937-42.	30	45	60	4
49 AIRPORT: 1937-39.	400	700	1,100	5
50 REMOTE CONTROL AIRPLANE: 1936.	425	650	850	6

ACCESSORIES, TOYS AND NOVELTIES

1936 LIONEL CATALOG

1936 LIONEL CATALOG

ACCESSORIES, TOYS AND NOVELTIES

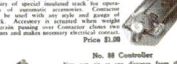

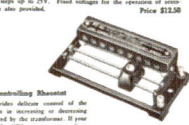
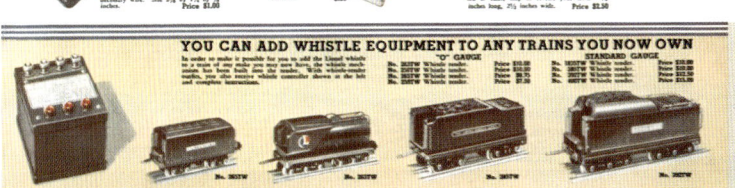

1936 LIONEL CATALOG

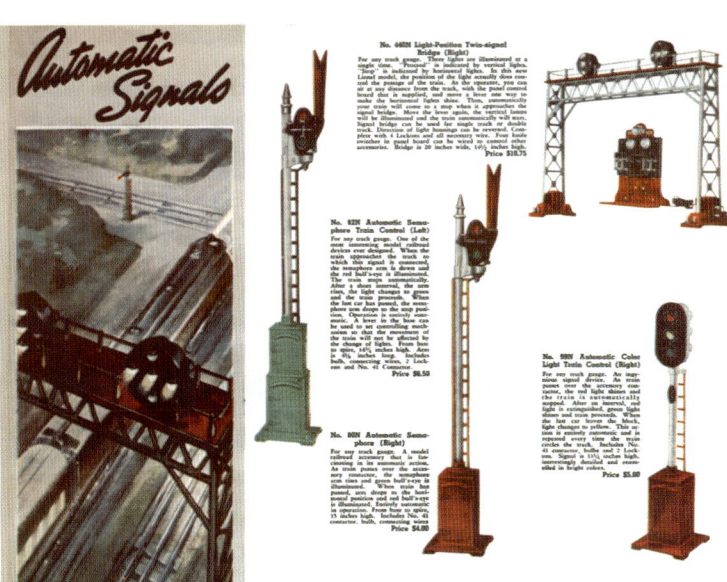

1936 LIONEL CATALOG

ACCESSORIES, TOYS AND NOVELTIES

54 LAMPPOST, 1929-35

57 LAMPPOST, 1922-42

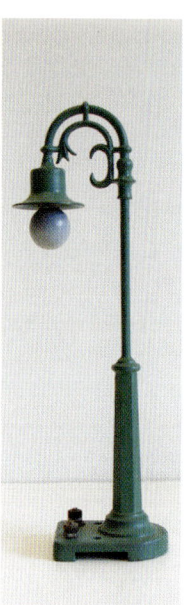

58 LAMPPOST, 1922-42

59 LAMPPOST, 1920-36

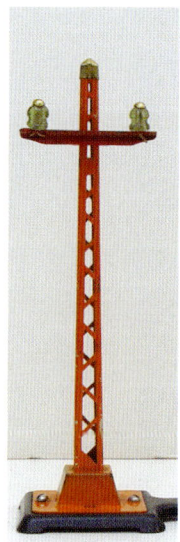

060 TELEGRAPH POST, 1929-42

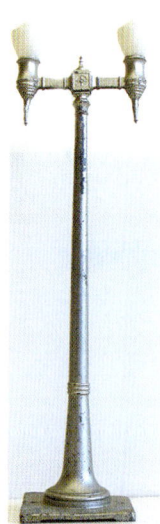

63 LAMPPOST, 1933-42

ACCESSORIES, TOYS AND NOVELTIES

	VG	EX	LN	RARITY
50 WARTIME FREIGHT TRAIN: 1943.	$200	$300	$500	6
51 AIRPORT: 1936, 1938.	200	300	500	6
52 LAMPPOST: 1933-41.	35	55	75	5
53 LAMPPOST: 1931-42, ivory, aluminum, light Mojave, gray or white.	25	35	45	3
54 LAMPPOST: 1929-35, maroon, pea green or State brown.	40	60	80	5
55 REMOTE CONTROL AIRPLANE: 1937-39.	325	550	750	5
56 LAMPPOST: 1924-42, 1946-49, copper.	40	55	90	6
Green, pea green, dark green, gray, dark gray or aluminum.	30	45	60	4
57 LAMPPOST: 1922-42, orange.	30	45	60	2
"BROADWAY," "42nd STREET," "FIFTH AVENUE," "21st STREET."	60	85	115	6
58 LAMPPOST: 1922-42, dark green, pea green, orange, cream, peacock or maroon.	30	40	60	3
59 LAMPPOST: 1920-36, dark green, olive green, light green, maroon, State brown or red.	35	55	75	3
060 TELEGRAPH POST: 1929-42, orange, gray, green, aluminum or gray.	20	25	30	3
61 LAMPPOST: 1914-32, 1934-36, olive green, mojave, dark green, pea green, maroon, State brown and black.	40	50	60	4
62 SEMAPHORE: 1920-32, bases painted dark green, olive green, apple green, pea green.	30	40	50	4
Yellow.	40	50	60	6
63 SEMAPHORE: 1915-21, red and black.	25	40	55	6
63 LAMPPOST: 1933-42.	150	200	250	6

Lionel All-Steel Illuminated Stations

No. 124 Illuminated Station—De Luxe Model. There is elegance, grace and architectural dignity to this all-steel station, difficult to show in an illustration. It is an exact reproduction of stations seen in most suburban towns. It is equipped with two corner platform lights and reflectors, all finished in polished nickel. These corner lighting brackets have beautifully designed supporting arms. This station is also fitted with inside light supported on a nickeled fixture. Roof is removable so that interior lamp can be easily reached. A most essential accessory to complete your model railroad. 13½ inches long, 9 inches wide and 13 inches high.
Price, complete with electric lamps and connecting wires **$9.00**
Code Word "READE"

No. 122 Illuminated Station—This is in every way similar to No. 124 Station described above, but has one inside electric light supported on a nickeled fixture.
Price, complete with electric lamp and connecting wires **$6.25**
Code Word "CENT"

No. 126 Illuminated Station—This station has been specially designed for use with our smaller train outfits and has many of the architectural and structural features of our larger models. The interior light is supported on a fixture placed beneath the removable roof. A beautifully proportioned model that retails at a low price. 10¼ inches long, 7¼ inches wide and 7 inches high.
Price, complete with electric lamp and connecting wires **$4.50**
Code Word "ALITE"

No. 127 Illuminated Station—This is particularly adaptable for use with any of our "O" Gauge Trains. Interior light is rigidly fastened to a supporting fixture. Roof is removable so that interior lamp can be easily reached. A better built or lower priced miniature station has never before been offered. 8½ inches long, 4¼ inches wide and 5 inches high.
Price, complete with electric lamp and connecting wires **$2.95**
Code Word "TONLY"

THE NEW LIONEL ILLUMINATED SWITCH-SIGNAL TOWER—(Illustrated on Next Page)

No. 437 Illuminated Switch-Signal Tower—In keeping with our policy to introduce everything new in model railroading, we are proud to present our new Switch-Signal Tower, which every boy will want to add to his model railroad layout.

It is built absolutely to scale and has a panel board on the rear (see illustration on next page) with six knife-switches which may be used for operating illuminated accessories, such as Stations, Lamp Posts, Bungalows and Villas. The lights in these accessories can be turned on and off by means of these switches, so that it is not necessary to have them illuminated all the time the train is in operation.

One or more controlling levers for "Lionel Standard" or "O" Gauge Electrically-Controlled Switches (illustrated on Page 40) can be attached to the upper part.

The interior of the switch-signal tower is fitted with an electric lamp. The illumination adds realism to this very desirable accessory. The Signal Tower is made of very heavy steel, beautifully enameled in various colors. The windows, doors, sashes and other parts are separable pieces inserted in the main body. The roof is removable so that the interior can easily be reached.

In every way this Switch-Signal Tower is typical of Lionel quality and perfection in model railroad accessories. No railroad layout is complete without one. 10¼ inches long, 9½ inches high, 7¼ inches wide. Price, complete with electric lamp and connecting wires . **$8.50**
Code Word "ZEV"

38

1927 LIONEL CATALOG

Lionel Power Stations. Illuminated Switch-Signal Towers

No. 437 Illuminated Switch Signal-Tower—Front view, showing wonderful detail in the windows, doors and panels, which are separable inserted pieces, beautifully enameled to harmonize with the walls of the structure.

No. 437 Illuminated Switch Signal-Tower—Rear view, showing panel board equipped with six knife-switches. In the upper part of the panel board provision is made for attaching from one to four controlling levers of "Lionel Standard" or "O" Gauge Electrically-Controlled Switches, described on Page 40.

The new Lionel Power Stations—Boys, you see them in every town and on all electrified railroads. Lionel, as usual, is first to reproduce them.

The illustration below shows how simple it is to house a Lionel "Multivolt" Transformer (illustrated and described on Pages 32 and 33) within the Power Station. Transformer is operated by raising the grid in the roof. Lionel Power Stations are made in two sizes to accommodate all types of Lionel "Multivolt" Transformers. In appearance they suggest the massive concrete buildings in which electric current is generated. Notice the beautiful embossing and die work, inserted windows and doors—see how the great chimney stack is reproduced in true proportion.

No. 435 Power Station—For use with Type A or B Transformers. 5¾ inches long, 4½ inches wide, 5⅝ inches high to the roof. Chimney stack rises 4¾ inches above the roof. Base, which measures [illegible], is hollow, so that Power Station can be easily placed over transformer. Grid in roof is removable.
Price **$2.50**
Code Word "JENA"

Illustration above shows transformer housed within the new Lionel Power Station.

No. 436 Power Station—For use with Type T, C or K Transformers. Similar in construction to No. 435 Power Station. Dimensions 7½ inches long, 6 inches wide, 6½ inches high. Chimney stack [illegible] above the roof. Grid in roof is removable. Base measures 9¼ inches by 7¼ inches.
Price **$3.35**
Code Word "WATTS"

No. 092 Illuminated Signal-Tower—A desirable accessory for "O" Gauge Railroads. Dimensions 5 inches long, 4 inches wide, 5½ inches high. Roof is removable. A handsomely nickeled light fixture is rigidly attached to the base. Price includes electric lamp and connecting wires.
Price . . **$2.10**
Code Word "CYRIL"

No. 438 Illuminated Signal Tower—The proportions of the Signal-Tower are the same as No. 092 illustrated to the left. We have mounted it on a beautiful structural-steel elevation, embossed with rivets, etc. The base represents reinforced concrete. A brass ladder runs up the entire length of the steel work and the Signal-Tower is surrounded by a brass railing. The illustration clearly shows the wonderful detail and architectural beauty of this desirable new accessory which can be used with all Lionel equipment. Complete height is 10½ inches. Base measures 6x4¾ inches. Price includes electric lamp and connecting wires. Price . . **$4.25**
Code Word "CARP"

39

1927 LIONEL CATALOG

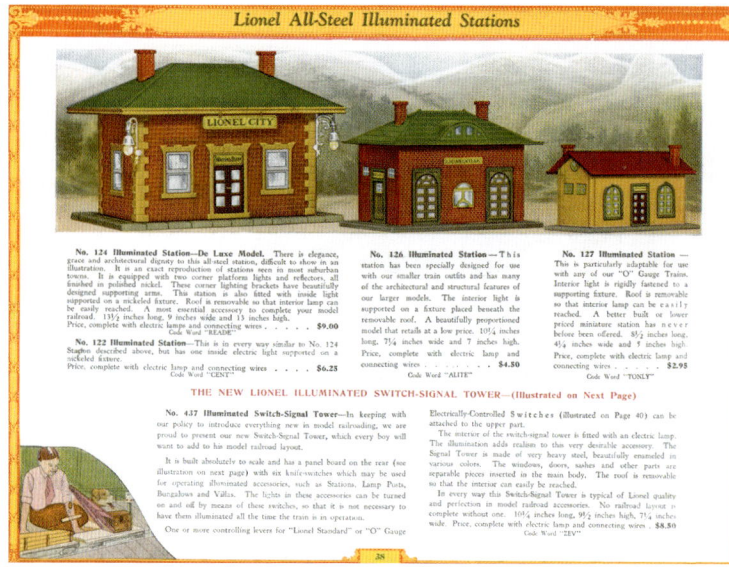

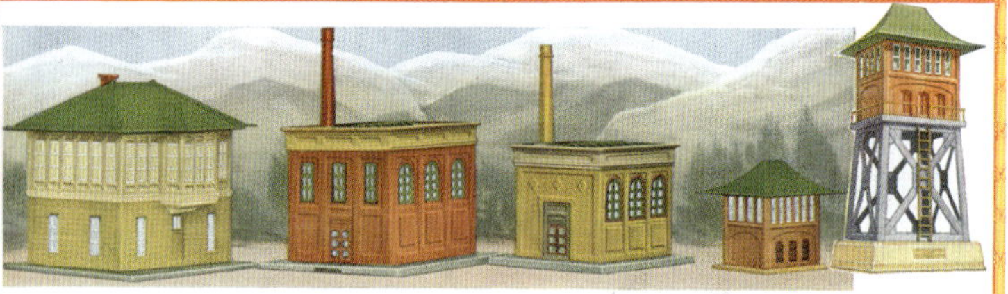

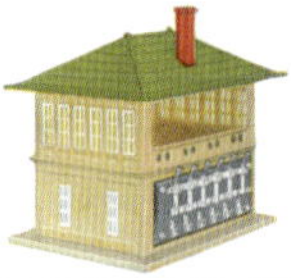

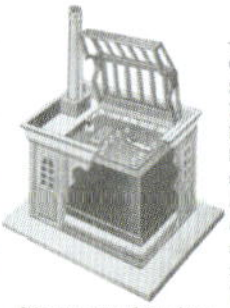

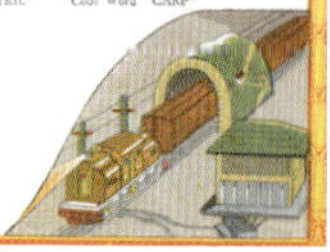

ACCESSORIES, TOYS AND NOVELTIES

No. 155 Illuminated Freight Shed
A beautifully designed all-steel railroad accessory. Just the thing for completing a railroad freight siding and to lend the right atmosphere to your freight train. The platform has ample space for accommodating hand trucks, baggage trucks and dump trucks, described below. It is illuminated by 2 lamps under the eaves. 18 inches long, 11 inches high, 9 inches wide. Price $7.50

No. 163 Freight Set
Consists of 2 hand trucks, a dump truck and a baggage truck. Each has strong, wide, die-cast wheels. The dump truck operates as the real ones do. The outfit is ideally suitable for use with freight platform, illustrated above. Price $2.75

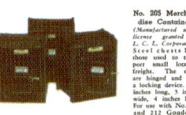

No. 205 Merchandise Containers
(Manufactured under license granted by L. C. L. Corporation) Steel chests like those used to transport small lots of freight. The doors are hinged and have a locking device. 3½ inches long, 5 inches wide, 4 inches high. For use with No. 512 and 212 Gondolas. Price: Set of 3, $2.50

Freight

No. 441 Standard Gauge Weighing Scale
Beam scale is accurately calibrated so that you can weigh your rolling stock by running it on the specially constructed track platform. An assortment of various weights is included. The weighing house is illuminated. The doors swing open. 29½ inches long, 4⅝ inches high, 9½ inches wide. Price $5.00

No. 209 Four Barrels
Made of wood. Open in center. 2¼ inches high. Price $.50
No. 0209 Six Barrels
1½ inches high. Price $.35

No. 208 Tools and Chest
Miniature pick and shovel, axe, rake, hoe, sledge—all important tools on real railroads, packed in neat nickeled chest with nickeled handle. Price $.75

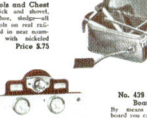

No. 439 Panel Board
By means of this board you can operate your accessories at any distance from the track. Six knife switches are mounted on a composition panel. Provision is made for mounting a pair of switch controls. The electric bulb at the top illuminates small dummy meters. 8¼ inches high, 7½ inches wide. Price $3.75

1936 LIONEL CATALOG

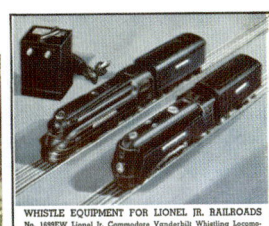

WHISTLE EQUIPMENT FOR LIONEL JR. RAILROADS
No. 1692EW Lionel Jr. Commodore Vanderbilt Whistling Locomotive Outfit—You get not only whistle equipment, but a brand new, elaborately detailed Commodore Vanderbilt Distant Control locomotive and tender and a 40-watt whistle and speed control transformer in this new outfit. Price $9.00

No. 1690EW Lionel Jr. "Torpedo" Whistling Locomotive Outfit—Pennsylvania "Torpedo," a beauty in design. Equipped with whistling streamlined tender and No. 1050 40-watt whistle and speed control transformer. Overall length, 16½ inches. Price $9.50

LIONEL JR. TRANSFORMERS
No. 1029 Lionel Jr. 25-watt transformer, 110 volts, A.C. Price $2.25
No. 1030 Lionel Jr. 40-watt transformer with speed and whistle control, 110 volts, A.C. Price $4.00

LIONEL JR. TRACK EQUIPMENT

No. 1061 Freight Car Set
If you have a Lionel Jr. passenger outfit, add these cars to make up a freight train. Price $2.25

No. 1021 Lionel Jr. 90 Degree Crossing
Bakelite center insulation prevents short circuits. The crossing is a great help in making interesting track layouts. Price $.85

No. 1013 Lionel Jr. Curved Track
Eight pieces form circle measuring 27 inches in diameter. Price $.15

No. 1018 Lionel Jr. Straight Track
9 inches long. Price $.15

No. 1024 Lionel Jr. Switches
Solidly constructed and perfectly insulated. Operated by hand lever. Price per pair $2.75
No. 1024R Right hand switch. Price $1.75
No. 1024L Left hand switch. Price $1.75

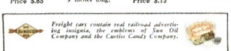

No. 1060 Passenger Car Set
Low and long, like real railroad rolling stock. Four-wheel trucks, automatic couplers. Price $2.00

1936 LIONEL CATALOG

ACCESSORIES, TOYS AND NOVELTIES

69 ELECTRIC WARNING BELL SIGNAL, 1921-35

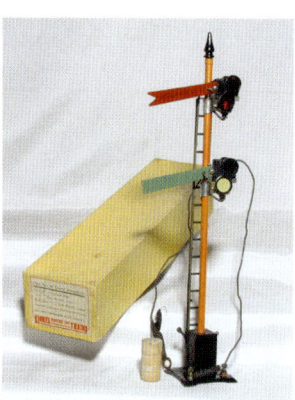

66 SEMAPHORE, 1915-26

68 WARNING SIGNAL, 1920-39

71 TELEGRAPH POST SET, 1929-42

76 WARNING BELL AND SHACK, 1939-42

ACCESSORIES, TOYS AND NOVELTIES

	VG	EX	LN	RARITY
64 HIGHWAY LAMPPOST: 1940-49, green.	$45	$60	$75	6
64 SEMAPHORE: 1915-21.	30	45	65	5
65 SEMAPHORE: 1915-26.	30	45	65	6
65 WHISTLE CONTROLLER: 1935.	3	5	7	2
66 SEMAPHORE: 1915-26, upper arm red and black, lower arm green and black.	30	45	65	5
66 WHISTLE CONTROLLER: 1936-38.	3	5	7	2
67 LAMPPOST: 1915-32, dark or State green, rarely in peacock.	75	115	150	5
67 WHISTLE CONTROLLER: 1936-38.	3	5	7	2
68 WARNING SIGNAL: 1920-39, dark olive, orange, maroon, pea green, peacock or white.	5	10	15	1
068 WARNING SIGNAL: 1925-42, orange or pea green.	5	10	15	1
69 ELECTRIC WARNING BELL SIGNAL, 069 ELECTRIC WARNING BELL SIGNAL, 69N ELECTRIC WARNING BELL SIGNAL: 1921-35, olive, maroon, dark green, white, red, aluminum or 9E orange paint and black lettering.	30	45	60	4
70 ACCESSORY OUTFIT: 1921-32.	75	125	175	7
71/071 TELEGRAPH POST SET: 1929-42, gray with light red crossarms, green with red crossarms or orange with maroon crossarms.	75	125	175	7
76 BLOCK SIGNAL, 076 BLOCK SIGNAL: 1923-28.	30	50	80	4
76 WARNING BELL AND SHACK: 1939-42, brass or die-cast sign.	85	150	250	5

ACCESSORIES, TOYS AND NOVELTIES

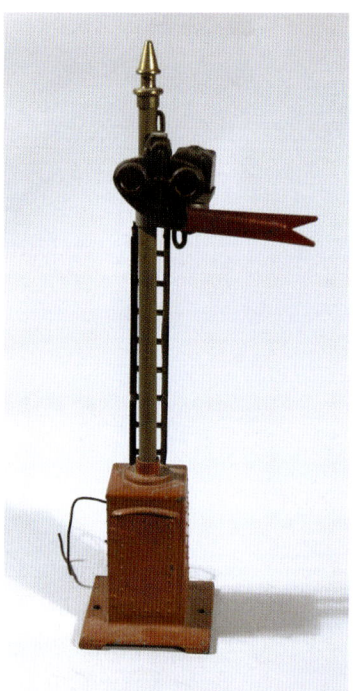

80 SEMAPHORE, 080 SEMAPHORE,
1926-35

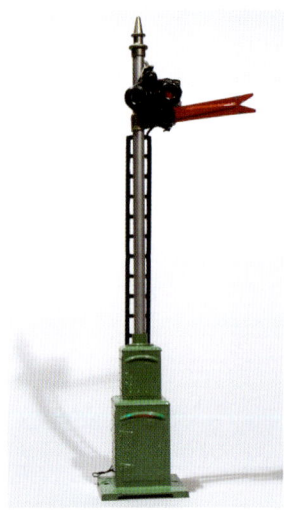

82N SEMAPHORE,
1936-42

83 TRAFFIC AND
CROSSING SIGNAL,
1927-42

ACCESSORIES, TOYS AND NOVELTIES

	VG	EX	LN	RARITY
77 AUTOMATIC CROSSING GATE, 077 AUTOMATIC CROSSING GATE, 77N AUTOMATIC CROSSING GATE: 1923-39.	$30	$40	$50	4
78 TRAIN CONTROL BLOCK SIGNAL, 078 TRAIN CONTROL BLOCK SIGNAL: 1924-32. Various colors.	40	70	100	6
79 FLASHING HIGHWAY SIGNAL: 1928-40, cream base, and a pole painted either cream or Mojave.	100	125	150	5
80 SEMAPHORE, 080 SEMAPHORE: 1926-35, various colors.	50	75	110	5
80N SEMAPHORE: 1936-42, light red base, aluminum-painted pole and black ladder.	50	75	110	5
80 RACING AUTOMOBILE SET: 1912-16, 8-1/2" long sheet metal car, painted either orange or red, 36" diameter sheet metal track.	1,500	2,200	3,500	8
81 RACING AUTOMOBILE SET: 1912-16, 8-1/2" long sheet metal car, painted either orange or red, 30" diameter track and was designed so it could be combined with the 80 to form a two-lane race track.	1,500	2,200	3,500	8
81 RHEOSTAT: 1927-33	5	10	15	3
82 TRAIN CONTROL SEMAPHORE, 082 TRAIN CONTROL SEMAPHORE: 1927-35, peacock or 45N-green base.	50	80	110	5
82N SEMAPHORE: 1936-42, green base, aluminum-painted pole, black ladder and nickel finial.	50	80	110	5
83 TRAFFIC AND CROSSING SIGNAL: 1927-42 1927-34, Mojave base, cream relay box and white signal head.	75	150	250	6

ACCESSORIES, TOYS AND NOVELTIES

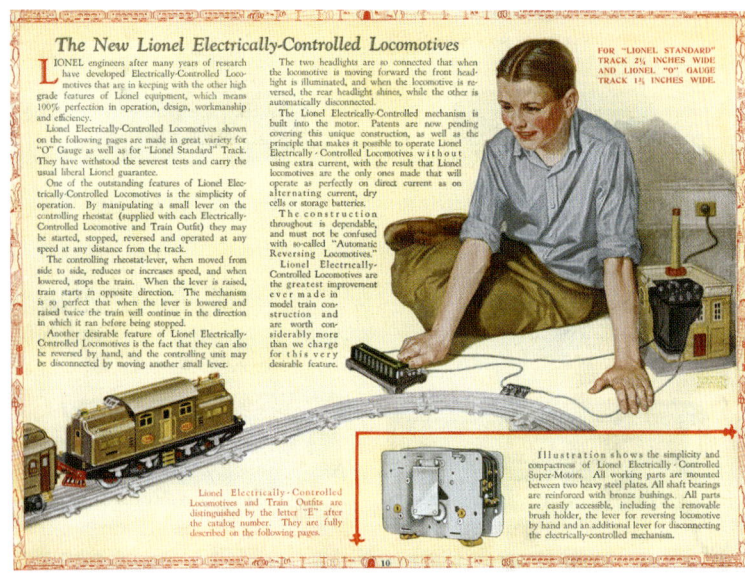

1927 LIONEL CATALOG

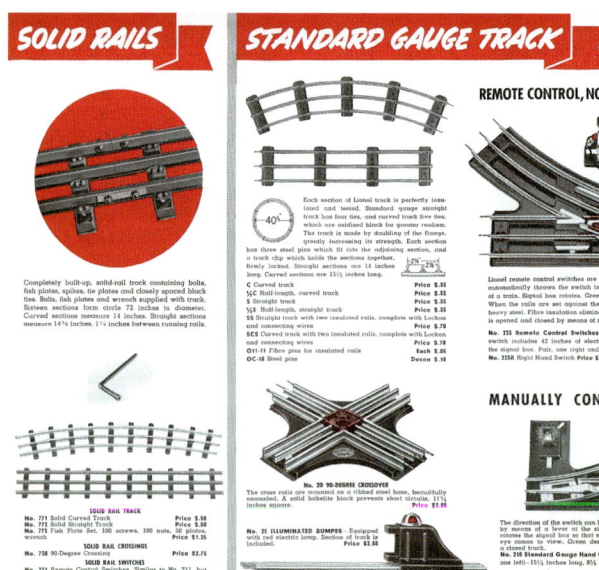

1938 LIONEL CATALOG

ACCESSORIES, TOYS AND NOVELTIES

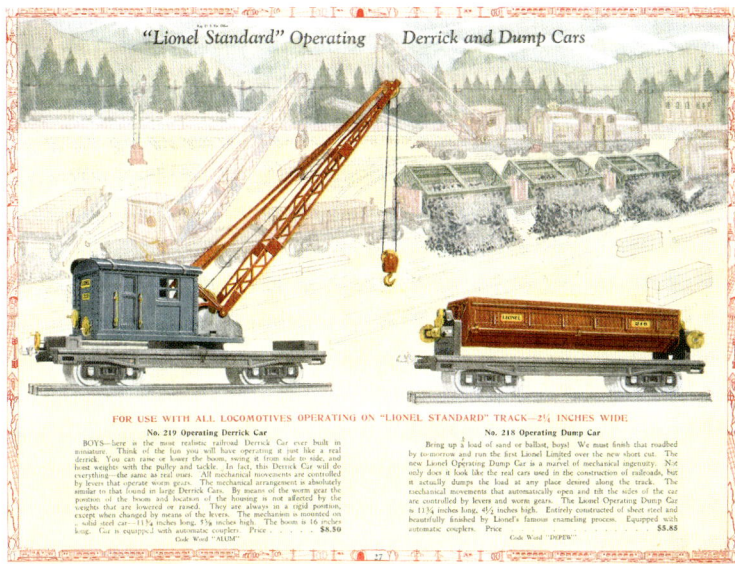

1927 LIONEL CATALOG

1938 LIONEL CATALOG

Accessories, Toys and Novelties

86 TELEGRAPH POST SET, 1929-42

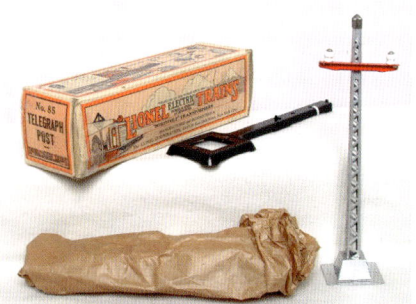

85 TELEGRAPH POST, 1929-42

91 CIRCUIT BREAKER, 1930-42

092 ILLUMINATED SIGNAL TOWER, 1923-27

Accessories, Toys and Novelties

	VG	EX	LN	RARITY
1935-42, light red base, cream relay box and white signal head.	$50	$110	$190	4
84 SEMAPHORE, 084 SEMAPHORE: 1927-32. Dark green or maroon base, orange or cream pole.	40	80	130	5
84 DOUBLE RACING AUTOMOBILE SET: 1912-16, combination of the 80 and 81 sets.	2,500	3,300	4,500	8
85 DOUBLE RACING AUTOMOBILE SET: 1912-16, combination of the 80 and 81 sets plus eight pieces of straight track.	3,000	4,000	5,700	8
85 TELEGRAPH POST: 1929-42, orange post.	12	25	45	2
Aluminum-colored post.	20	40	65	5
86 TELEGRAPH POST SET: 1929-42, six posts, original box critical to value Orange-colored posts.	100	200	400	5
Aluminum-colored posts.	125	250	500	6
87 RAILROAD CROSSING SIGNAL: 1927-42, orange, tan, or Mojave base.	75	125	200	5
Dark green base.	125	225	350	6
88 BATTERY RHEOSTAT: 1915-27.	5	10	15	5
88 DIRECTION CONTROLLER: 1933-42.	5	10	15	2
89 FLAG POLE: 1923-34.	50	75	110	2
90 FLAG POLE: 1927-42. Brass, nickel or black pedestal.	75	110	150	3
91 CIRCUIT BREAKER: 1930-42. Mojave or State brown, two or three terminals.	25	35	45	3
092 ILLUMINATED SIGNAL TOWER: 1923-27, Mojave base, terracotta walls, pea green roof, maroon doors and cream windows.	50	90	150	4

Accessories, Toys and Novelties

93 WATER TOWER, 1931-42

97 MOTORIZED COAL ELEVATOR, 1938-42

98 COAL BUNKER, 1938-40

96 COAL ELEVATOR, 1938-40

Accessories, Toys and Novelties

	VG	EX	LN	RARITY
Brown base, terracotta walls, pea green roof, cream windows and red or brown doors with black lines.	$50	$90	$150	4
A Mojave base supported a tower with white walls, red roof, red doors and pea green windows.	90	150	225	6
92 FLOODLIGHT TOWER: 1931-42 1931-34, terracotta base and pea green tower structure.	75	125	175	4
1935-41, red base and an aluminum-painted tower.	100	150	200	4
1941-42, light red base and gray tower.	125	175	225	6
93 WATER TOWER: 1931-42, 1946-49, pea green, aluminum or gray tank.	25	35	60	3
94 HIGH TENSION TOWER: 1932-42, terracotta base and gunmetal tower.	150	300	500	6
Terracotta base and Mojave tower.	150	300	500	6
Red base, aluminum-painted tower.	100	175	275	3
Gray base, aluminum-painted tower.	150	300	500	6
95 RHEOSTAT: 1934-42, brass or nickel instruction plate.	10	15	20	2
096 TELEGRAPH POST: 1934-35.	15	20	25	4
96 COAL ELEVATOR: 1938-40.	100	175	275	6
097 TELEGRAPH POST AND SIGNAL SET: 1934-35.	200	275	375	5
97 MOTORIZED COAL ELEVATOR: 1938-42, 1938-41, aluminum-painted supporting structure.	100	175	225	5
1942, gray-painted supporting structure.	125	200	275	7
98 COAL BUNKER: 1938-40, cream-colored house on aluminum structure.	200	325	500	6

Accessories, Toys and Novelties

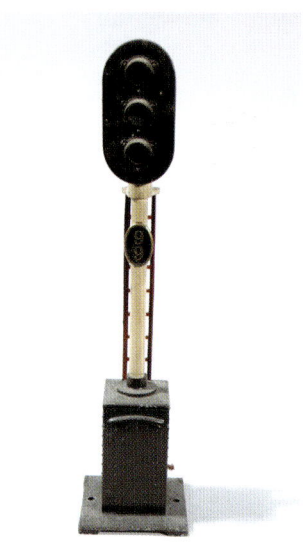

99/099 TRAIN CONTROL BLOCK
SIGNAL, 1932-35

99N TRAIN CONTROL BLOCK
SIGNAL, 1936-42

104 BRIDGE CENTER SPAN, 1920-31

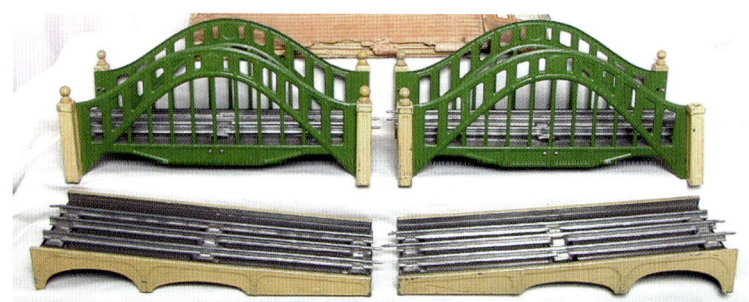

102 BRIDGE, 1920-31

Accessories, Toys and Novelties

	VG	EX	LN	RARITY
99/099 TRAIN CONTROL BLOCK SIGNAL: 1932-35, black or red base with cream or Mojave poles.	$40	$75	$125	3
99N TRAIN CONTROL BLOCK SIGNAL: 1936-42, red base and ladder with aluminum-painted pole.	40	75	125	3
100 BRIDGE APPROACHES: 1920-31, pair of Standard Gauge sheet-metal ramps.	10	20	40	2
101 BRIDGE: 1920-31, Standard Gauge 104 Bridge Center Span and one pair of 100 approaches when sold as a combination. The original box is a significant portion of the value listed.	100	150	225	4
102 BRIDGE: 1920-31, two 104 Bridge Center Spans and one pair of 100 approaches. The original box is a significant portion of the value listed.	125	175	250	4
103 BRIDGE: 1920-31, Standard Gauge bridge consisted of three 104 Bridge Center Spans and one pair of 100 approaches. The original box is a significant portion of the value listed.	150	200	275	5
104 BRIDGE CENTER SPAN: 1920-31, pea green miniature version of Lionel's 300 Hellgate bridge, holding a single section of S Standard Gauge.	20	30	40	2
105 BRIDGE APPROACHES: 1920-31, O-Gauge.	10	20	30	4
106 BRIDGE: 1920-31, O-Gauge, cream, light mustard, or pea green sides.	50	75	110	4
107 DC REDUCER: 1911-38.	Too infrequently traded to establish accurate value.
108 BRIDGE: 1920-31, O-Gauge, cream or light mustard sides.	75	100	150	5

ACCESSORIES, TOYS AND NOVELTIES

112 STATION, 1931-34

114 STATION, 1931-34

115 STATION, 1935-42

116 STATION, 1935-42

ACCESSORIES, TOYS AND NOVELTIES

	VG	EX	LN	RARITY
109 BRIDGE: 1920-31, O-Gauge, cream or light mustard sides.	$100	$150	$200	5
110 BRIDGE CENTER SPAN: 1920-31, pea green.	20	30	40	2
111 BULB ASSORTMENT: 1920-31, set of wooden individual bulb containers with bulbs.	500	1,000	2,000	8
Cardboard individual bulb containers with bulbs.	250	500	1,000	7
112 STATION: 1931-34, cream, beige or ivory walls.	150	250	375	5
113 STATION: 1931-34.	200	400	600	6
114 STATION: 1931-34, cream, beige or ivory walls.	500	1,000	1,600	6
115 STATION: 1935-42, 1946-49. Includes train-stop circuit.	250	350	500	5
116 STATION: 1935-42, Mojave or red base.	700	1,200	1,800	6
117 STATION: 1935-42.	100	200	300	4
118 TUNNEL: 1915-32.	20	35	50	2
118L TUNNEL: 1927, illuminated version of the 118.	40	75	150	6
119 TUNNEL: 1915-42.	20	35	50	2
119L TUNNEL: 1927-33, illuminated version of the 119.	40	75	150	6
120 TUNNEL: 1915-27, papier-mâché or steel.	35	75	125	4
120L TUNNEL: 1927-42, illuminated version of 120.	50	100	200	4
121 STATION: 1908-26, wooden or steel construction.	150	200	250	4
122 STATION: 1920-31, gray or gray-speckled base.	75	150	225	4
123 STATION: 1920-23.	150	225	350	6
123 TUNNEL: 1933-42.	75	150	225	4

Accessories, Toys and Novelties

The 124 Station produced, 1920-30 and 1933-36, came in variety of color combinations.

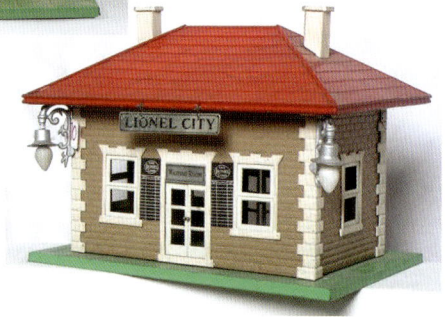

The 127 Station, also produced 1923-36, similarly came in variety of color combinations.

Accessories, Toys and Novelties

	VG	EX	LN	RARITY
124 STATION: 1920-30, 1933-36, terracotta walls, tan, dark gray base.	$100	$200	$300	4
Pea green base	200	300	400	5
125 STATION: 1923-25, red brick and a dark Mojave base with a pea green roof and white windows.	100	150	225	4
125 TRACK TEMPLATE: 1938.	2	5	10	7
126 STATION: 1923-36, lithographed or red-painted walls.	75	125	200	4
Mustard-painted walls.	200	275	375	6
127 STATION: 1923-36, white, cream, or ivory-colored walls.	75	110	150	3
Mustard-painted walls.	100	150	225	6

The 126 Station, produced 1923-36, came in variety of color combinations.

The 127 Station, also produced 1923-36, similarly came in variety of color combinations.

ACCESSORIES, TOYS AND NOVELTIES

The 128 STATION AND TERRACE came with a variety of stations from 1928 through 1942.

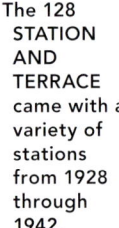

129 TERRACE, 1928-42

134 STATION, 1937-42

136 STATION, 1937-42

ACCESSORIES, TOYS AND NOVELTIES

	VG	EX	LN	RARITY
128 STATION AND TERRACE: 1928-42, 129 terrace in combination with various station.				
1928-30, with 124 Station.	$1,000	$1,500	$2,100	6
1931-34, with 113 Station.	1,050	1,600	2,200	6
1935-42, with 115 stop Station.	1,200	1,800	2,500	6
128 TUNNEL: 1920.	Too rarely, if ever, traded to establish market pricing.			
129 TERRACE: 1928-42, light Mojave and pea green.	600	900	1,200	6
Cream with red trim.	800	1,200	1,700	7
129 TUNNEL: 1920.	Too rarely, if ever, traded to establish market pricing.			
130 TUNNEL: 1920.	Too rarely, if ever, traded to establish market pricing.			
130 TUNNEL: 1926.	200	400	1,000	8
130L TUNNEL: 1927-33.				
1927.	200	400	1,000	8
1928-33 (18-1/2" x 14-1/2" base).	100	200	500	6
131 CORNER ELEVATION: 1924-28.	125	250	500	6
132 CORNER GRASS PLOT: 1924-28.	125	250	500	6
133 HEARTSHAPE GRASS PLOT: 1924-28.	125	250	500	6
134 OVAL GRASS PLOT: 1924-28.	125	250	500	6
134 STATION: 1937-42.	175	275	450	5
135 SMALL CIRCULAR GRASS PLOT: 1924-28.	100	200	400	6
136 LARGE ELEVATION: 1924-28.	125	250	500	6
136 STATION: 1937-42, cream walls.	75	125	175	4
Mustard walls.	125	250	400	6

ACCESSORIES, TOYS AND NOVELTIES

No. 300 Bridge for "O" Gauge or Standard Gauge
In New York City there is a famous bridge that spans the East River. It has imposing archways, majestic super-structure and is called Hell Gate. Lionel No. 300 is an accurate reproduction. The great archways at each end are embossed and enamelled to represent limestone. There are four doorways for pedestrians and two sidewalk elevations. The train passes through the bridge at regular track level, thus avoiding the necessity of grade approaches. 28½ inches long, 11 inches high, 10½ inches wide. Price $16.50

No. 270 Single-Span Bridge for "O" Gauge
Bridges of this type are used by nearly all real railroads. The Lionel model is made of heavy steel with plates and rivets deeply embossed. Finished in bright enamel. Complete with section of track. 10½ inches long. Price $1.75

No. 271 Two-Span Bridge for "O" Gauge
Consists of 2 spans of No. 270 bridge complete with 2 sections of track. 20½ inches long. Price $3.50

No. 272 Three-Span Bridge for "O" Gauge
Consists of 3 spans of No. 270 bridge, complete with 3 sections of track. 30½ inches long. Price $5.25

Bridges

No. 280 Single-Span Bridge for Standard Gauge
Built of steel to represent modern heavy girder construction. On each side of the right of way are portals and walks for pedestrians. Handsomely enamelled by Lionel's exclusive process. Complete with track. 14 inches long. Price $2.50

No. 281 Two-Span Bridge for Standard Gauge
Consists of 2 spans of No. 280 bridge. Complete with 2 sections of track. 28 inches long. Price $5.00

No. 282 Three-Span Bridge for Standard Gauge
Consists of 3 spans of No. 280 bridge, as shown in the illustration below. An extremely long and impressive construction. Complete with track. 42 inches long. Price $7.50

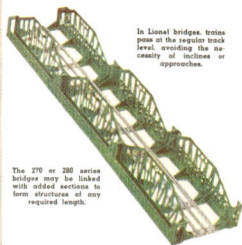

In Lionel bridges, trains pass at the regular track level, avoiding the necessity of inclines or approaches.

The 270 or 280 series bridges may be linked with added sections to form structures of any required length.

1936 LIONEL CATALOG

No. 437 Illuminated Switch Signal Tower
Realistically detailed with embossings and inset doors and windows. Six knife switches, to control the illumination of accessories, are attached to the panel board in the rear. 10½ inches long, 6½ inches high, 6½ inches wide. Price $7.50

No. 840 Industrial Power Station
Masterpiece of miniature buildings. These are few accessories more desirable or fitting for the miniature railroad. Original and extremely ornamental in design. Equipped with inner doors and windows and with a pressure water tank. The power station can be filled off the platform and transformers can be fitted into the hollows planned for them on the inside. Transformer switches can be operated from the grid roofs. A panel board on one side contains six knife switches, from which all of your illuminated and signal accessories can be operated. 26 inches long, 23½ inches wide, 18 inches to top of smokestack. Price $17.50

Signal Towers

No. 436 Power Station
You can house your transformer in this neat power station. The skylight is removable. Constructed of heavy steel and enamelled in bright colors. 9½ inches long, 7½ inches wide, 10½ inches to top of chimney. Price $3.00

No. 435 Power Station
Same as No. 436, but smaller in size. Will house only A, B, L or F transformers. 7⅝ inches long, 6 inches wide, 9½ inches to top of chimney. Price $2.00

No. 438 Illuminated Signal Tower
A true copy of switching towers seen on all big railroads. Girder steel elevation is embossed with rivets. Brass ladder. Removable roof. Equipped with 2 knife switches for operation of accessories. 12 inches high, base measures 6 inches by 5½ inches. Price $4.75

1936 LIONEL CATALOG

ACCESSORIES, TOYS AND NOVELTIES

1936 LIONEL CATALOG

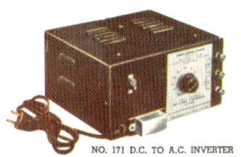

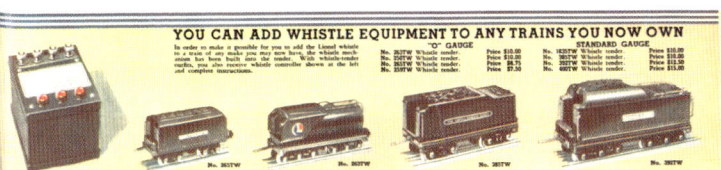

1936 LIONEL CATALOG

Accessories, Toys and Novelties

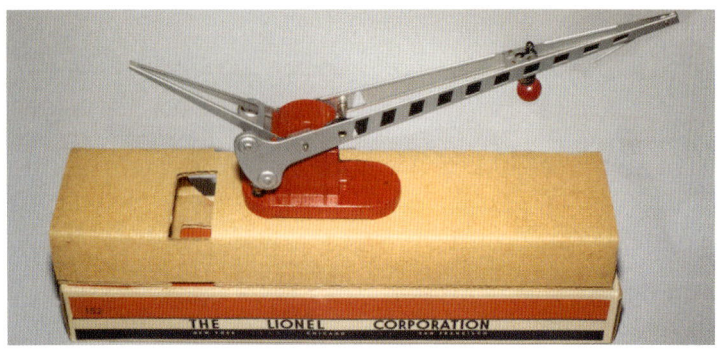

152 AUTOMATIC CROSSING GATE, 1940-42

153 AUTOMATIC BLOCK SIGNAL AND CONTROL, 1940-42

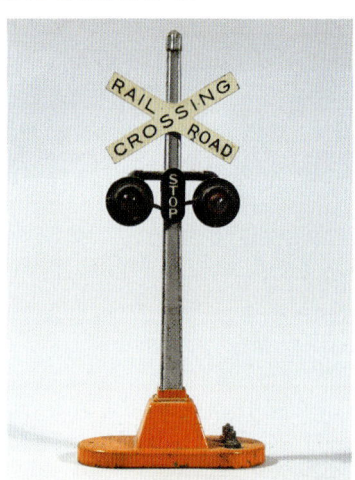

154 AUTOMATIC HIGHWAY SIGNAL, 1940-69

155 FREIGHT SHED, 1930-42

ACCESSORIES, TOYS AND NOVELTIES

	VG	EX	LN	RARITY
137 STATION: 1937-42, ivory walls, vermilion roof, green or yellow door and window frames.	$100	$150	$225	4
140L TUNNEL: 1927-32.	600	1,200	2,000	7
152 AUTOMATIC CROSSING GATE: 1940-42, aluminum or gray gate.	20	40	55	5
153 AUTOMATIC BLOCK SIGNAL AND CONTROL: 1940-42, silver-colored post on a green die-cast base.	30	40	50	3
Gray post on a green die-cast base.	40	55	70	6
153C CONTACTOR: 1940-42.	1	2	10	1
154 AUTOMATIC HIGHWAY SIGNAL: 1940-69, black base with silver-colored pole.	30	40	50	3
Gray post on a black die-cast base.	40	55	70	6
Hiawatha orange base silver-colored pole.	50	75	100	7
155 FREIGHT SHED: 1930-42, yellow base with maroon roof.	175	250	350	5
White base and gray roof.	225	325	450	6
White base and gray roof and posts.	325	425	550	6
156 ILLUMINATED STATION PLATFORM: 1939-42, 1946-51, green base and red roof, silver posts.	60	100	150	4
Gray posts.	90	150	225	6
157 HAND TRUCK: 1930-32, 1942, red.	20	30	40	2
158 STATION SET: 1940-42.	400	700	1,000	7
159C BLOCK CONTROL CONTACTOR SET: 1940-42.	10	15	25	4
160 UNLOADING BIN: 1938-42.	1	1	2	1
161 BAGGAGE TRUCK: 1930-32, 1942.	30	40	55	3

ACCESSORIES, TOYS AND NOVELTIES

163 FREIGHT ACCESSORY SET, 1930-42

184 BUNGALOW, 1923-42

165 MAGNETIC CRANE, 1940-42

164 LOG LOADER, 1940-42

Accessories, Toys and Novelties

	VG	EX	LN	RARITY
162 DUMP TRUCK: 1930-32, 1942, orange, terracotta or yellow hand truck with dump bin, rare in red.	$30	$50	$75	4
163 FREIGHT ACCESSORY SET: 1930-42.	175	250	350	5
164 LOG LOADER: 1940-42, 1946-50.				
Aluminum-painted supporting structures.	150	225	350	4
Gray-painted supporting structures.	200	275	400	5
Orange roof.	225	325	450	7
165 MAGNETIC CRANE: 1940-42.				
Aluminum-painted supporting structure.	200	275	375	4
Gray-painted supporting structure.	300	375	475	6
166 WHISTLE CONTROLLER: 1938-39.	5	7	10	1
167 WHISTLE AND DIRECTION CONTROLLER: 1939-42.	4	8	15	1
167X WHISTLE AND DIRECTION CONTROLLER: 1940-42.	10	20	30	6
168 MAGIC ELECTROL CONTROLLER: 1940-42, styled like 167 whistle control or 1019 controller.	10	20	30	6
169 DIRECTION CONTROLLER: 1940-42.	10	20	30	6
170 DC REDUCER: 1914-38.	10	20	30	6
171 DC TO AC INVERTER: 1936-42.	4	8	15	5
172 DC TO AC INVERTER: 1936-42.	4	8	15	5
184 BUNGALOW: 1923-42.	40	90	150	5
185 BUNGALOW: 1923-24.	50	100	175	6
186 ILLUMINATED BUNGALOW SET: 1923-32.	400	1,000	1,800	6

ACCESSORIES, TOYS AND NOVELTIES

186 LOG LOADER OUTFIT, 1940-41

188 COAL ELEVATOR OUTFIT, 1938-41

200 TURNTABLE, 1928-33

205 MERCHANDISE CONTAINERS, 1930-38

Accessories, Toys and Novelties

	VG	EX	LN	RARITY
186 LOG LOADER OUTFIT: 1940-41.	$500	$800	$1,200	6
187 BUNGALOW SET: 1931-32.	400	1,000	1,800	7
188 COAL ELEVATOR OUTFIT: 1938-41.	500	800	1,200	6
189 VILLA: 1923-32.	150	250	375	4
191 VILLA: 1923-32.	150	275	400	4
192 ILLUMINATED VILLA SET: 1923-32.	1,500	2,500	4,000	8
193 AUTOMATIC ACCESSORY SET: 1927-29.	250	500	800	6
194 AUTOMATIC ACCESSORY SET: 1927-29.	200	400	700	5
195 ILLUMINATED TERRACE: 1927-30.	400	800	1,600	8
196 ACCESSORY SET: 1927.	250	500	800	6
200 TURNTABLE: 1928-33, red rotating platform, pea green base.	75	125	200	4
Mojave rotating platform, pea green base.	75	125	200	4
Red platform, black base.	200	350	550	6
205 MERCHANDISE CONTAINERS: 1930-38.	125	225	350	6
206 ARTIFICIAL COAL: 1938-42.	5	10	15	3
207 SACK OF COAL: 1938-42.	5	10	15	3
208 TOOL SET: 1928-42, miniature section gang tools in metal toolbox.	50	150	275	5
209 BARRELS: 1930-34, with sides of the barrels arced.	150	225	300	6
0209 BARRELS: 1934-42, O-Gauge turned wooden representations of wooden or steel drums.	100	175	250	5
1935-42, barrels resembling steel drums.	150	225	300	6
210 PAIR OF MANUAL TURNOUTS: 1926-42, pair of illuminated manual Standard Gauge turnouts.	20	30	40	3

ACCESSORIES, TOYS AND NOVELTIES

210 PAIR OF MANUAL TURNOUTS, 1926-42

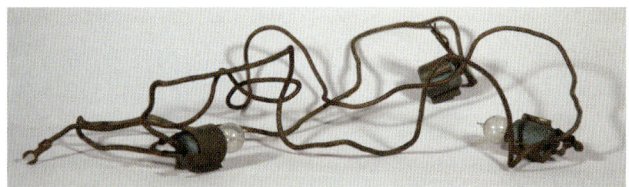

217 LIGHTING SET, 1914-23

The 280 BRIDGE, offered 1931-42, came in a variety of colors.

Accessories, Toys and Novelties

	VG	EX	LN	RARITY
210L LEFT-HAND MANUAL TURNOUT: 1926-42.	$10	$15	$20	3
210R RIGHT-HAND MANUAL TURNOUT: 1926-42.	10	15	20	3
217 LIGHTING SET: 1914-23.	20	35	50	4
220 PAIR OF MANUAL TURNOUTS: 1926.	20	40	70	5
222 PAIR OF REMOTE CONTROL TURNOUTS: 1926-31.	40	60	100	3
222L LEFT-HAND REMOTE CONTROL TURNOUT: 1926-31.	20	30	50	3
222R RIGHT-HAND REMOTE CONTROL TURNOUT: 1926-31.	20	30	50	3
223 PAIR OF REMOTE CONTROL TURNOUTS: 1932-42, pea green or black bases.	60	90	125	3
223L LEFT-HAND REMOTE CONTROL TURNOUT: 1932-42, pea green or black base.	30	45	60	3
223R RIGHT-HAND REMOTE CONTROL TURNOUT: 1932-42, pea green or black base.	30	45	60	3
225 REMOTE CONTROL TURNOUT SET: 1929-32.	125	250	400	7
270 BRIDGE: 1931-42, light red, maroon, vermilion.	25	35	50	4
270 LIGHTING SET: 1915-23, for DC current.	20	35	50	4
271 LIGHTING SET: 1915-23, for AC current.	20	35	50	4
271 BRIDGES: 1931-40, except 1934.	150	250	400	6
272 BRIDGES: 1931-40, except 1934.	250	450	750	8
280 BRIDGE: 1931-42, gray, red, pea or 45N green.	50	80	125	4
281 BRIDGES: 1931-40, except 1934.	150	250	400	6

ACCESSORIES, TOYS AND NOVELTIES

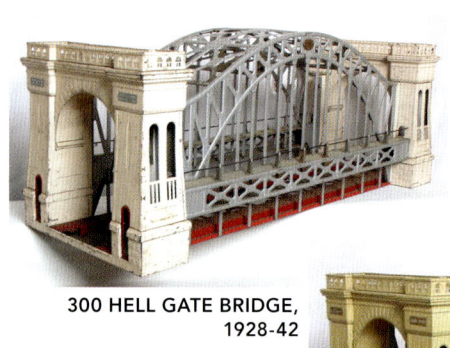

300 HELL GATE BRIDGE, 1928-42

313 BASCULE BRIDGE, 1940-42

340 SUSPENSION BRIDGE, 1902-05

ACCESSORIES, TOYS AND NOVELTIES

	VG	EX	LN	RARITY
282 BRIDGES: 1931-40, except 1934.	$250	$450	$750	8
300 HELL GATE BRIDGE: 1928-42.				
1928-34, green and cream.	800	1,100	1,400	6
1935-42, silver and cream.	1,000	1,500	2,100	7
1941-42, with black railings.	1,200	1,800	2,500	8
308 RAILROAD SIGN SET: 1940-42, 1945-49, green base with artificial grass, rectangular base painted white or round white bases.	35	50	75	5
310 TRACK: 1901-05.	75	125	200	8
313 BASCULE BRIDGE: 1940-42, 1946-49, silver superstructure.	300	525	675	5
Gray superstructure.	400	625	775	7
314 PLATE GIRDER BRIDGE: 1940-1941 silver, 1942 gray.	25	35	50	3
315 ILLUMINATED TRESTLE BRIDGE: 1940-42.				
1940-41, silver.	75	100	125	5
1942, gray.	100	125	150	6
316 TRESTLE BRIDGE: 1941, 1942 and 1949.				
Silver.	25	40	55	4
Gray.	30	50	70	6
320 SWITCH AND SIGNAL: 1902-05. Too rarely, if ever, traded to establish market pricing.				
330 CROSSING: 1902-05. Too rarely, if ever, traded to establish market pricing.				
340 SUSPENSION BRIDGE: 1902-05.	Too rarely, if ever, traded to establish market pricing.			
350 BUMPER: 1902-05.	Too rarely, if ever, traded to establish market pricing.			
380 ELEVATED PILLARS: 1904-05, set of 12 8-1/2" tall cast iron posts.	450	850	1,200	8
435 POWER STATION: 1926-38.				
"EDISON SERVICE" sign.	300	600	1,000	7

ACCESSORIES, TOYS AND NOVELTIES

"O" GAUGE

No. 615 "O" Gauge Illuminated Baggage Car—Four-wheel trucks and sliding doors. 10½ inches high. Price $3.25
No. 613 "O" Gauge Illuminated Pullman Car—Companion to No. 615. Price $3.25
No. 614 "O" Gauge Illuminated Observation Car—Companion to Nos. 613 and 615. Price $3.50

No. 607 "O" Gauge Illuminated Pullman Car—7½ inches long, 5½ inches high. Price $1.65
No. 608 "O" Gauge Illuminated Observation Car—Companion to No. 607. Price $1.75
Nos. 603 and 604—Same as Nos. 607 and 608, but without interior lights. Price, each $1.10

No. 601 "O" Gauge Illuminated Pullman Car—Removable roofs and four-wheel trucks. 9 inches long, 5½ inches high. Price $2.75
No. 600 "O" Gauge Illuminated Pullman Car—Companion to No. 601. Price $2.50
No. 602 "O" Gauge Illuminated Baggage Car—Companion to Nos. 600 and 601. Price $3.00

STANDARD GAUGE

No. 420 Standard Gauge Illuminated Pullman Car—Long, low and accurately proportioned. Has removable roof. Interior is fitted with two rows of swivel chairs that actually revolve. Doors swing open on pivot hinges. 18 inches long, 5 inches high. Price $11.00
No. 422 Standard Gauge Illuminated Observation Car—Companion to No. 420. Named "Tempel." Price $11.00
No. 421 Standard Gauge Illuminated Pullman Car—Same as 420 but named "Westphal." Price $11.00

No. 428 Standard Gauge Illuminated Observation Car—One of the finest model cars ever produced. Finished in two-tone green baked enamel with ivory trim. Inner windows and ventilators, swinging doors, six-wheel trucks, wide observation platform with colored warning discs. Roof is removable. 16 inches long. Price $9.50
No. 424 Standard Gauge Illuminated Pullman Car—Similar to No. 426 but without observation platform. Named "Liberty Bell." Price $9.50
No. 425 Standard Gauge Illuminated Passenger Car—Same as No. 424 but named "Stephan Gerard." Price $9.50

Cars 600, 601, and 602 are for use with Locomotives Nos. 258E, 249E, 255E, 265E, 262E, 261E. Cars 603, 604, 607, and 608 are for use with Locomotives Nos. 258E, 249E, 255E, 265E, 262E, 261E. Cars 613, 614, and 615 are for use with Locomotives Nos. 258E, 249E, 255E, 265E, 262E, 261E.

Standard Gauge cars Nos. 509, 510, 512 may be used with Locomotives Nos. 9E, 318E, 385E, 1835E. Nos. 332, 339, and 341 may be used with Locomotives Nos. 9E, 385E, 1835E. Nos. 424, 425, 426 may be used with Locomotives Nos. 9E, 385E, 392E, 1835E. Nos. 420, 421, 422 may be used with Locomotives Nos. 9E, 385E, 392E, 400E, 408E. Nos. 1766, 1767, 1768 may be used with Locomotives Nos. 9E, 385E, 1835E.

STANDARD GAUGE

No. 1766 Standard Gauge Illuminated Car—One of the most accurately proportioned Gauge passenger cars made. Inner windows, embossed details and swinging doors. Roof removable. 15 inches long, 6½ inches high.
No. 1767 Standard Gauge Illuminated Car—To be used with No. 1766. It has doors.

No. 1768 Standard Gauge Illuminated Car—Similar to No. 1766 but with decoform.

No. 310 Standard Gauge Illuminated Passenger Car—Steel construction, baked enamel, inner windows, swinging doors. 13½ inches high.
No. 309 Standard Gauge Illuminated Pullman—Companion to No. 310.
No. 512 Standard Gauge Illuminated Car—Companion to Nos. 310 and 309.

New, automatic and realistically tioned couplers illustrated below couple cars automatically on eit or straight track. The new couple and equipment on Passenger Cars 615 and 614 and on the No. Freight Cars.

INTERESTING DETAILS AND ACCURATE, STURDY CONSTRUCTION

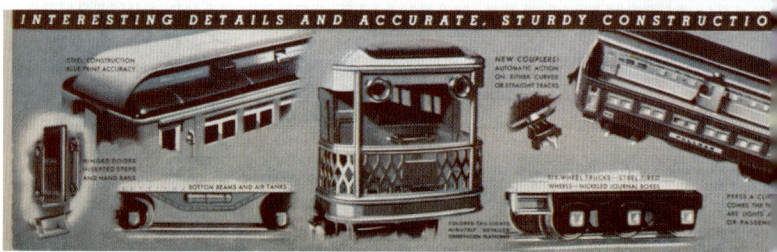

1936 LIONEL CATALOG

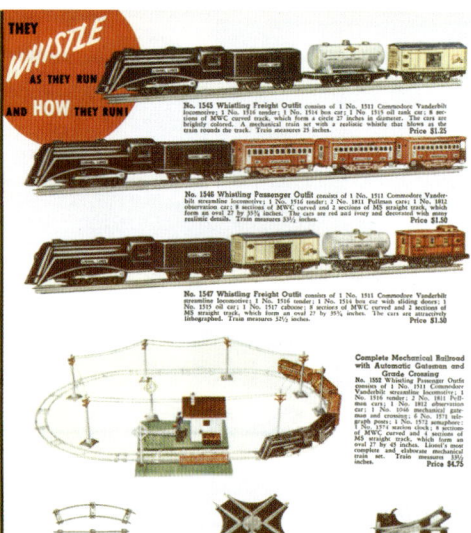

1936 LIONEL CATALOG

Accessories, Toys and Novelties

1936 LIONEL CATALOG

1927 LIONEL CATALOG

Accessories, Toys and Novelties

437 SWITCH SIGNAL TOWER, 1926-37

439 PANEL BOARD, 1928-42

438 SIGNAL TOWER, 1927-39

440 SIGNAL BRIDGE/
0440 SIGNAL BRIDGE, 1932-35

ACCESSORIES, TOYS AND NOVELTIES

	VG	EX	LN	RARITY
"POWER STATION" sign.	$125	$250	$400	3
With 45N green base.	200	400	700	6
436 POWER STATION: 1926-37.				
Yellow cornices, "POWER STATION" sign.	200	400	700	5
Cream cornices, "POWER STATION" sign.	150	275	425	4
Terracotta cornices, "POWER STATION" sign.	150	275	425	4
"EDISON SERVICE" sign.	500	900	1,700	8
437 SWITCH SIGNAL TOWER: 1926-37, terracotta lower walls, mustard upper walls, pea green roof.	200	350	550	4
Terracotta lower walls, cream upper walls, peacock roof.	300	475	700	5
Burnt orange lower walls, mustard upper walls, pea green roof.	200	350	550	4
Burnt orange lower walls, light mustard upper walls, pea green roof.	200	350	550	4
Yellow lower and upper walls, orange roof.	1,200	1,800	2,500	8
438 SIGNAL TOWER: 1927-39.				
1927, without knife switches.	300	475	700	6
Pea green supports.	200	325	500	4
Aluminum-painted supports.	300	475	700	6
439 PANEL BOARD: 1928-42, black simulated marble background.	75	125	175	4
White simulated marble background.	100	150	200	5
440 SIGNAL BRIDGE/0440 SIGNAL BRIDGE: 1932-35.				
Mojave bridge.	175	250	350	3
Aluminum-colored bridge.	200	325	450	6
440C PANEL BOARD: 1932-42, light, glossy or flat red, includes switches to control 440 signal bridge in addition to knife switches.	75	125	175	4

ACCESSORIES, TOYS AND NOVELTIES

442 LANDSCAPED DINER, 1938-42

444 ROUNDHOUSE, 1932-35

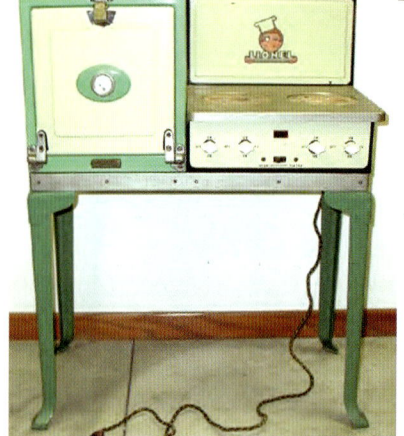

455 ELECTRIC RANGE, 1930, 1932-34

550 MINIATURE RAILROAD FIGURES, 1932-36

ACCESSORIES, TOYS AND NOVELTIES

	VG	EX	LN	RARITY
440N SIGNAL BRIDGE: 1936-42.				
With silver structure.	$175	$225	$275	3
Gray structure.	250	450	650	6
442 LANDSCAPED DINER: 1938-42, ivory or cream bodies with pink or red foundations and steps.	150	250	375	5
444 ROUNDHOUSE: 1932-35.	1,200	2,000	3,000	7
455 ELECTRIC RANGE: 1930, 1932-34, green and cream porcelain range.	400	800	1,500	6
500 PINE BUSHES: 1927-28.	Too rarely, if ever, traded to establish market pricing.			
501 SMALL PINE TREES: 1927-28.	Too rarely, if ever, traded to establish market pricing.			
502 MEDIUM PINE TREES: 1927-28.	Too rarely, if ever, traded to establish market pricing.			
503 LARGE PINE TREES: 1927-28.	Too rarely, if ever, traded to establish market pricing.			
504 ROSE BUSHES: 1927-28.	Too rarely, if ever, traded to establish market pricing.			
505 OAK TREES: 1927-28.	Too rarely, if ever, traded to establish market pricing.			
506 PLATFORM: 1924-28.	Too rarely, if ever, traded to establish market pricing.			
507 PLATFORM: 1924-28.	Too rarely, if ever, traded to establish market pricing.			
508 SKY: 1924-28.	Too rarely, if ever, traded to establish market pricing.			
509 COMPOSITION BOARD MOUNTAINS: 1924-28. **Too rarely traded to establish market pricing.**				
510 CANNA BUSHES: 1927-28.	Too rarely, if ever, traded to establish market pricing.			
550 MINIATURE RAILROAD FIGURES: 1932-36, original box significant portion of values listed.	225	375	550	6
551 ENGINEER: 1932-36, medium or dark blue clothing.	20	30	40	4
552 CONDUCTOR: 1932-36.	20	30	40	4

ACCESSORIES, TOYS AND NOVELTIES

760 072 TRACK, 1938-42

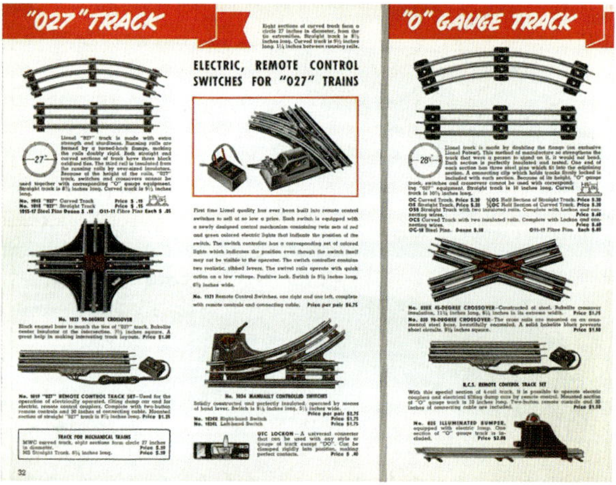

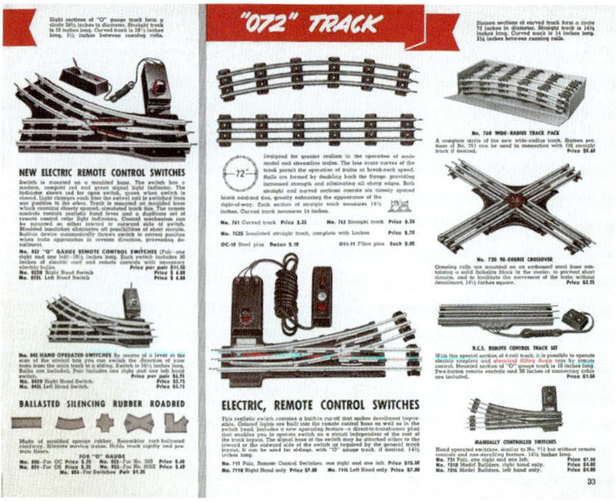

1938 LIONEL CATALOG

Accessories, Toys and Novelties

	VG	EX	LN	RARITY
553 PORTER: 1932-36, came with a removable yellow step box.	$20	$30	$40	4
554 MALE PASSENGER: 1932-36, brown or Mojave clothing.	20	30	40	4
555 FEMALE PASSENGER: 1932-36, variety of different colored clothing.	20	30	40	4
556 RED CAP: 1932-36, dark blue clothing and a red cap.	20	30	40	4
711 PAIR OF REMOTE CONTROL TURNOUTS: 1935-42.	75	125	200	4
711L LEFT-HAND REMOTE CONTROL TURNOUT: 1935-42.	40	60	100	4
711R RIGHT-HAND REMOTE CONTROL TURNOUT: 1935-42.	40	60	100	4
720 90-DEGREE CROSSING: 1935-42.	25	35	45	4
721 PAIR OF MANUAL TURNOUTS: 1935-42.	50	75	125	6
721L LEFT-HAND MANUAL TURNOUT: 1935-42.	25	40	60	6
721R RIGHT-HAND MANUAL TURNOUT: 1935-42.	25	40	60	6
730 90-DEGREE CROSSING: 1935-42.	30	45	60	6
731 PAIR OF REMOTE CONTROL TURNOUTS: 1935-42.	75	125	200	6
731L LEFT-HAND REMOTE CONTROL TURNOUT: 1935-42.	40	60	100	6
731R RIGHT-HAND REMOTE CONTROL TURNOUT: 1935-42.	40	60	100	6
760 072 TRACK: 1938-42, including box.	50	75	120	5
761 CURVED TRACK: 1934-42, 072.	1	2	3	4

ACCESSORIES, TOYS AND NOVELTIES

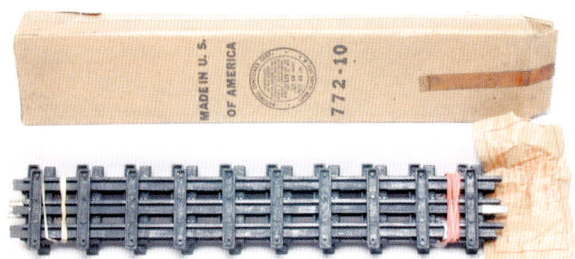

772 STRAIGHT TRACK, 1935-42 "T-RAIL"

840 INDUSTRIAL POWER STATION, 1928-40

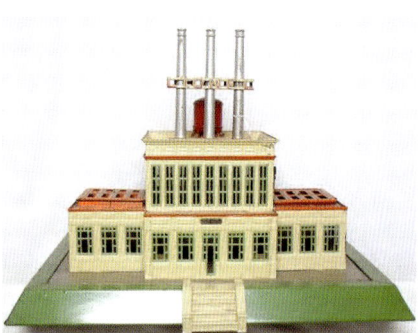

911 COUNTRY ESTATE, 1932-42

916 TUNNEL, 1932-42

Accessories, Toys and Novelties

	VG	EX	LN	RARITY
762 STRAIGHT TRACK: 1934-42, 072.	$1	$2	$3	5
762S STRAIGHT TRACK: 1934-42, 072 short straight.	1	2	3	6
771 CURVED TRACK: 1935-42, "T-rail."	5	10	15	6
772 STRAIGHT TRACK: 1935-42, "T-rail."	10	15	20	6
772S STRAIGHT TRACK: 1935-42, "T-rail."	20	30	40	7
773 FISH PLATE SET: 1935-42, "T-rail."	25	50	75	8
812T TOOL SET: 1930-41.	50	100	150	4
840 INDUSTRIAL POWER STATION: 1928-40, cream walls, orange roof.	1,000	1,700	2,500	7
White walls with red roof.	1,500	2,500	3,500	8
910 GROVE OF TREES: 1932-42.	100	250	500	5
911 COUNTRY ESTATE: 1932-42, variety of color combinations.	200	500	1,000	5
912 SUBURBAN HOME: 1932-42, variety of color combinations.	200	500	1,000	6
913 LANDSCAPED BUNGALOW: 1932-42.	150	300	550	5
914 PARK LANDSCAPE: 1932-36, cream-colored plywood base and urn.	150	350	650	5
915 TUNNEL: 1932-35, 60" long.	100	200	300	5
65" long.	150	300	650	8
916 TUNNEL: 1932-42, 29-1/4" long.	100	200	300	5
37" long.	150	300	550	7
917 SCENIC HILLSIDE: 1932-36.	150	200	250	5
918 SCENIC HILLSIDE: 1932-36.	150	200	250	5
919 ARTIFICIAL GRASS: 1932-42.	7	7	25	2

ACCESSORIES, TOYS AND NOVELTIES

920 SCENIC PARK, 1932-33

921 SCENIC PARK, 1932-33

921C PARK CENTER SECTION, 1932-33

ACCESSORIES, TOYS AND NOVELTIES

	VG	EX	LN	RARITY
920 SCENIC PARK: 1932-33.	$1,000	$2,000	$3,000	8
921 SCENIC PARK: 1932-33.	2,000	3,200	4,500	8
921C PARK CENTER SECTION: 1932-33.	750	1,500	2,250	8
922 LAMP TERRACE: 1932-36, with green, Mojave, pea green-colored lamppost.	100	150	200	6
With copper-colored lamppost.	200	350	550	8
923 TUNNEL: 1933-42.	100	200	400	6
924 TUNNEL: 1935-42. 1935, 29-1/4" x 20-1/2" x 13-1/2".	200	350	550	8
1936, 30-1/8" x 21-1/4" x 12-1/4".	100	200	400	6
925 LUBRICANT: 1935-42.	1	4	10	1
927 ORNAMENTAL FLAG PLOT: 1937-42, cream base.	100	200	400	6
1012 WINNER STATION: 1931-33, cream walls, orange roof two or three binding posts. Transformer mounted internally.	40	55	75	4
1012K WINNER STATION: 1932-33, same as 1012, but without transformer.	40	55	75	4
1013 CURVED TRACK: 1933-42.	.25	.50	1	1
1017 WINNER STATION: 1932-33.	40	55	75	4
1018 STRAIGHT TRACK: 1933-42.	.25	.50	1	1
1019 REMOTE CONTROL TRACK SET: 1938-42, 1946-50.	5	8	10	3
1021 90-DEGREE CROSSING: 1933-42, 1945-54.	2	4	8	3
1022 TUNNEL: 1935-42.	20	40	75	3
1023 TUNNEL: 1934-42.	20	40	75	3
1024 PAIR OF MANUAL TURNOUTS: 1935-42, 1946-52.	10	15	25	3
1024L LEFT HAND MANUAL TURNOUT: 1934-42.	5	8	10	3

Accessories, Toys and Novelties

Special Notice to Father

Nothing in the world can make you and your boy such close pals and such real friends as playing together and working together at the game of model railroading.

It's a thrill you owe to yourself—to watch the joy that will sparkle in his eyes when you tell your son that you have decided to enter into a railroad partnership with him.

Then enter into partnership—a real partnership of working things out together . . . a track layout . . . a signal system . . . a miniature village. You will be building far more than a model railroad that will delight his heart, and yours. You will be building a glorious father-son companionship. It will grow before you realize it and it will last as long as memory.

It's simple to build a model railroad—and far more thrilling than a round of golf or an hour or two of bridge. First you find the best space for it. Attic. Cellar. Gameroom. Sunporch. Even your son's bedroom might do—with a ledge around the room and terminals at either end.

Next you decide on the gauge you will use. The word gauge indicates the size of trains. Lionel makes trains of many sizes, from diminutive "OO" gauge (a whole train will operate on the top of a common bridge table) to the large and highly detailed Standard gauge.

Next, you think of switches, stations, tunnels, bridges and a signal system. These are the things that can be added from time to time. You start with the most essential accessories, such as switches, plenty of track, a crossover and maybe a station or two. Then you add the others, as often as possible, as gifts from the senior partner.

Now comes the real fun, the real interest, the place where your side of the partnership is most important. You must build a table or a wide ledge for the railroad to run over, because it's important for the trains to be up, off the floor, on a permanent right-of-way.

From this point on, there are a thousand and one things you and your boy can do together to enhance, improve and individualize your railroad. There are rolling country-sides that can be made by erecting an uneven framework out of sticks, covering it with chicken-wire, covering that with plain burlap, then painting the burlap roughly in brown and greens.

There is an engine house that can be made in an evening's time out of two-ply wood and a few pieces of hardware screening. A miniature gas station for miniature motorists. A real railroad grade crossing—with cattle guards and all—done with realistic effect in just two hours flat. All sorts of industrial buildings for your industrial sidings. Newsstands, baggage offices and all types of improvements for your passenger stations.

Lionel tells you how you can do all these things—and much, much more—with only a few pennies to spend here and there for ply-wood, tacks, paints and glue—and no special tools at all.

Pictures, diagrams, complete, concise instructions are printed in Lionel's magazine, The Model Builder. Trick wiring diagrams; signal systems; track layouts; photographs of other model railroads; everything you want to know about trains, big or little. All this, and more, in every bi-monthly issue.

Both you and your boy will enjoy reading The Model Builder and will make it your guide to many happy hours together. The coupon below will bring you the current issue promptly.

THE LIONEL CORPORATION, 15 East 26th Street, New York, N. Y.

☐ Enclosed is $1 (in stamps, check or well-wrapped currency). Send The Model Builder magazine bi-monthly for two years.

☐ Enclosed is 50c (in stamps or check). Send The Model Builder magazine bi-monthly for one year.

Name_____
PLEASE PRINT

Address_____

City_____ State____

OUTSIDE THE U. S. OR POSSESSIONS, 75c PER YEAR, IN U. S. FUNDS

1938 LIONEL CATALOG

ACCESSORIES, TOYS AND NOVELTIES

Fold back and forth on this line, then tear out neatly. Fill in the number of the outfit you want and your name, then hand this note to Dad. Tell him it's important.

Dear Dad;

One thing I want this Christmas more than anything else is a Lionel Electric Train No. ____ . Be sure it's a Lionel, Dad. That's the kind all the other fellows have and it's the one and only kind I want. You ought to see the way they run! Like a million dollars. And they whistle too. Real railroad whistle signals by remote control. You can couple and uncouple cars electrically, from a distance, just by touching a button; and reverse the train or speed it up or slow it down.

Please get me a Lionel, Dad. We'll have lots of fun together.

                Your son,

P.S. don't forget switches. We'll need them.

1938 LIONEL CATALOG

Accessories, Toys and Novelties

The 1100 HAND CAR, offered 1934-37, came in a variety of colors.

ACCESSORIES, TOYS AND NOVELTIES

	VG	EX	LN	RARITY
1024R RIGHT-HAND MANUAL TURNOUT: 1934-42.	$5	$8	$10	3
1025 ILLUMINATED BUMPER: 1940-42, 1946-47.	10	15	20	4
1027 LIONEL JUNIOR TRANSFORMER STATION: 1933-34, yellow.	40	60	85	4
1028 LIONEL JUNIOR TRANSFORMER STATION: 1935.	40	60	85	4
1029 LIONEL JUNIOR TRANSFORMER STATION: 1936.	40	60	85	4
1038 TRANSFORMER: 30-watt.	5	10	20	4
1039 TRANSFORMER: 1937-40, 35-watt.	5	10	20	2
1040 TRANSFORMER: 1937-39, 60-watt.	20	35	50	4
1041 TRANSFORMER: 1939-42, 60-watt.	20	35	50	4
1045 OPERATING WATCHMAN: 1938-42, 1946-50. With blue, dark blue, black or brown figure.	20	35	50	4
1100 HAND CAR: 1934-37, Mickey and Minnie Mouse.				
Red base.	350	600	1,100	6
Orange base.	500	900	1,600	7
Green base.	400	675	1,250	6
Maroon base	450	700	1,400	7

1937 LIONEL CATALOG

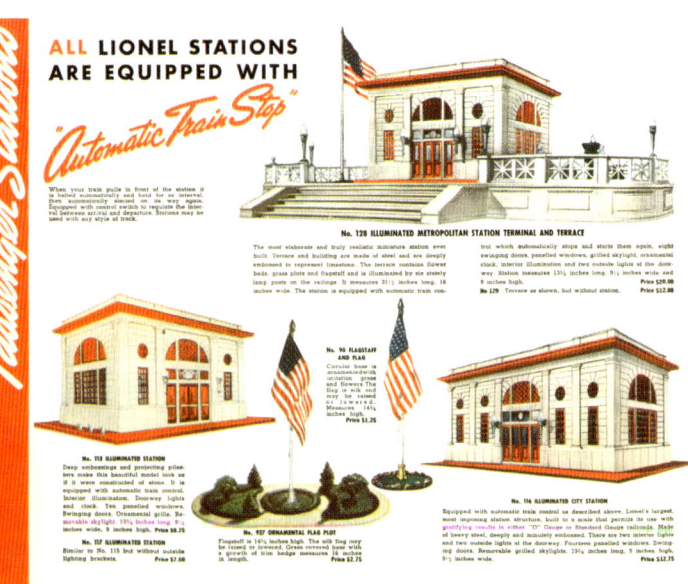

1937 LIONEL CATALOG

ACCESSORIES, TOYS AND NOVELTIES

LOOK WHAT STANDS BEHIND THE NAME THAT STANDS FOR *Leadership*

WORLD'S GREATEST MODEL RAILROAD WORKS. Back of Lionel stands a 36-year-old reputation for manufacturing excellence—and the greatest model railroad plant in all the world—covering acres of ground and producing trains that are the favorites in nearly every spot on the globe.

MILLIONS IN TOOLS AND DIES. Dominance and leadership is maintained year after year by continuous investments in new tools, new dies, new machinery to make new and better trains—and to keep progress on the miniature system in step with the fast-advancing strides of real roads.

PLUS, INVENTIVE GENIUS. Lionel genius invented the first and only true railroad whistle, created automatic signals, brought out model builders' solid rails, introduced remote control for trains and switches, developed each and every new, important improvement in miniature railroading including the power plant, the "Multivolt" transformer and including even a secret method of enameling cars.

PLUS, SCORES OF PATENTS. And now, no one but Lionel can make a Lionel Train or a model that even resembles its authentic operation—for Lionel is now, and has always been, the pioneer in model railroading and the law protects the pioneer with patents.

PLUS, A RARE INGREDIENT, CRAFTSMANSHIP. Lionel Trains *are the trains real railroad men buy for their boys*, because Lionel Trains are true-to-life. BUT, there is something more important than appearance. It's performance. Lionel Trains are not the product of mass production. Every engine, car or accessory is produced for hard service, as if it were the only one of its kind—at the hands of craftsmen, skilled and schooled in the work they do.

YET, ANY LIONEL IS A THRIFTY BUY. No premium is placed on Lionel perfection. You pay *no more* for a *genuine* Lionel that is true to life, inspiring in appearance, thrilling in operation, than you might pay for an ordinary *toy* train. Dollar for dollar, feature for feature, they have no equal. So, turn these pages and pick a favorite from the big parade.

THE LIONEL CORPORATION
15 East 26th Street, New York, N. Y.

1936 LIONEL CATALOG

1936 LIONEL CATALOG

Accessories, Toys and Novelties

The 1103 HAND CAR, known as the Peter Rabbit Chick Mobile, was sold 1935-37, in several variations.

ACCESSORIES, TOYS AND NOVELTIES

	VG	EX	LN	RARITY
1103 HAND CAR: 1935-37, Peter Rabbit Chick Mobile.				
Metal flanged wheels.	$300	$600	$900	6
Rubber wheels.	400	675	1,250	8
1105 HAND CAR: 1935-36, Santa with Mickey Mouse peering from sack.				
Red base.	500	1,000	2,000	7
Green base.	700	1,500	2,500	8

1106: Santa handcars were made without Mickey as well.

Too rarely, if ever, traded to establish market pricing.

1105 SANTA with MICKEY MOUSE

1106 Did Not Have MICKEY MOUSE & is shown with 1105 for comparison.

Accessories, Toys and Novelties

1107 WHITE AND GREEN

1107 ORANGE AND GREEN

Accessories, Toys and Novelties

	VG	EX	LN	RARITY
1107 RAIL CAR: 1936-37, Donald Duck and Pluto.				
White doghouse with green roof.	$400	$600	$900	6
White doghouse with red roof.	500	700	1,000	7
Orange doghouse with green roof.	700	1,000	1,500	8
1121 REMOTE CONTROL TURNOUTS: 1937-42, 1946-51.	20	35	45	3
1550 PAIR OF MANUAL TURNOUTS: 1933-37.	1	2	5	4
1555 90-DEGREE CROSSING: 1933-37.	1	2	5	4
1560 LIONEL JUNIOR STATION: 1933-37.	15	25	35	3
1569 LIONEL JUNIOR ACCESSORY SET: 1933-37, included four telegraph poles, one each semaphore, warning signal, clock and crossing gate, mounted on red or black bases. Box critical to value.	100	200	400	6
1571 TELEGRAPH POLE: 1933-37.	5	10	15	4
1572 SEMAPHORE: 1933-37, gray or pea green post mounted on black or red bases.	5	10	15	4
1575 CROSSING GATE: 1933-37, pea green or gray post.	5	10	15	4
A MINIATURE MOTOR: 1904.	50	75	100	7
A TRANSFORMER: 1921-37, 40 or 60 watts.	5	10	15	4
B NEW DEPARTURE MOTOR: 1906-16.	75	110	150	6
B TRANSFORMER: 1916-38, 50 or 75 watts.	5	10	25	5
C NEW DEPARTURE MOTOR: 1906-16.	100	130	175	6
C TRANSFORMER: 1922-31, 75 watts.	5	10	25	5

ACCESSORIES, TOYS AND NOVELTIES

1937 LIONEL CATALOG

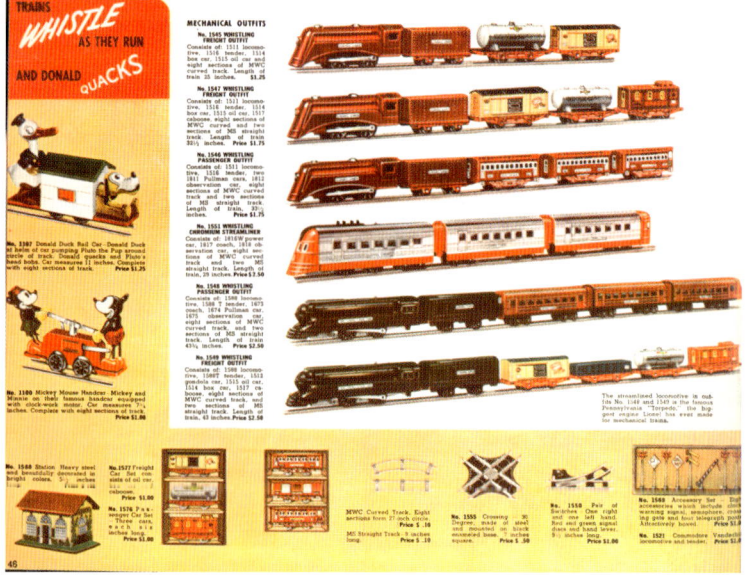

1937 LIONEL CATALOG

ACCESSORIES, TOYS AND NOVELTIES

No. 440R LIGHT-POSITION TWIN SIGNAL BRIDGE
For Every Style of Track

AUTOMATIC, ILLUMINATED DOUBLE ARM CROSSING GATES

No. 83 TRAFFIC SIGNAL — Price $3.25
No. 068 WARNING SIGNAL — Price $.40 / Price $.50
No. 87 SIGNAL — Price $3.75

No. 77N AUTOMATIC CROSSING GATE
For Every Style of Track — Price $4.00

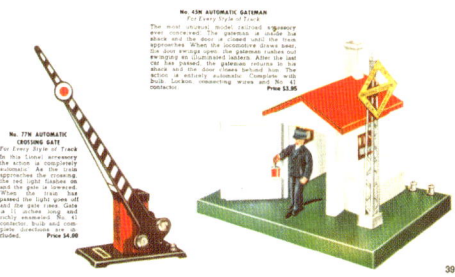

No. 45N AUTOMATIC GATEMAN
For Every Style of Track — Price $2.95

1937 LIONEL CATALOG

LIGHTS FLASH, BELLS RING, THE SEMAPHORE CALLS A HALT

Here's railroad color, action and atmosphere in abundance. Warning lights and bells that tell a miniature motorist when a train is approaching. Color light signals and semaphores that, by means of an ingenious thermal control, stop a train at a designated spot, hold it waiting for a moment, then start it again — automatically.

Automatic Signals

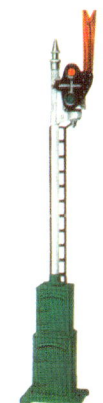

No. 79 FLASHING SIGNAL — Price $4.00
No. 69N AUTOMATIC ELECTRIC WARNING SIGNAL — Price $3.50
No. 79N AUTOMATIC COLOR LIGHT SIGNAL — Price $10.50
No. 80N AUTOMATIC SEMAPHORE — Price $4.25
No. 82N AUTOMATIC SEMAPHORE TRAIN CONTROL — Price $6.75

1937 LIONEL CATALOG

ACCESSORIES, TOYS AND NOVELTIES

Early Type K TRANSFORMER

Late Type K TRANSFORMER

Accessories, Toys and Novelties

	VG	EX	LN	RARITY
D NEW DEPARTURE MOTOR: 1906-16.	$100	$130	$175	6
E NEW DEPARTURE MOTOR: 1906-16.	100	130	175	6
F NEW DEPARTURE MOTOR: 1906-16.	100	130	175	6
F TRANSFORMER: 1931-37, 40 watts.	5	10	25	5
G FAN MOTOR: 1909-14.	100	130	175	6
H TRANSFORMER: 1938-39, 75 watts.	5	10	25	5
K SEWING MACHINE MOTOR: 1904-06.	100	130	175	6
K TRANSFORMER: 1913-38, 150 or 200 watts.	20	40	60	5
L SEWING MACHINE MOTOR: 1905.	75	100	125	5
L TRANSFORMER: 1913-38, 50 or 75 watts.	10	15	20	3
M PEERLESS MOTOR: 1915-20.	50	75	100	4
MS STRAIGHT TRACK: 1933-38, two-rail 027-type track.	.50	1	2	4
MWC CURVED TRACK: 1933-38, two-rail 027-type track.	.50	1	2	4
N TRANSFORMER: 1941-42, 50 watts.	5	10	15	3
OC CURVED TRACK: 1915-61, O-Gauge.	.25	.50	1	1
OCC CURVED TRACK: 1915-22, O-Gauge terminal track.	.25	.50	1	4
OCS CURVED TRACK: 1933-42, O-Gauge insulated.	.25	.50	1	4
OS STRAIGHT TRACK: 1915-61, O-Gauge.	.50	1	2	1
OSC STRAIGHT TRACK: 1915-22, O-Gauge terminal.	.50	1	2	4
OSS STRAIGHT TRACK: 1933-42, O-Gauge insulated.	.50	1	2	4
OTC LOCKON: 1923-36.	.25	.50	1	1
Q TRANSFORMER: 1914-42, 50 or 75 watts.	10	20	40	4

ACCESSORIES, TOYS AND NOVELTIES

Type V TRANSFORMER

UTC LOCKON

1939 LIONEL CATALOG

Accessories, Toys and Novelties

	VG	EX	LN	RARITY
R PEERLESS MOTOR: 1915-20.	$75	$100	$125	$5
R TRANSFORMER: 1939-42, 1946, 100 or 110 watts.	50	75	100	4
RCS REMOTE CONTROL TRACK: 1938-42, 1946-48, O-Gauge.	5	10	15	2
S TRANSFORMER: 1914-17, 1938-42, 1947, 50 or 80 watts.	20	35	60	5
SC STRAIGHT TRACK: 1915-22, Standard Gauge straight terminal track.	1	2	3	2
SCS CURVED TRACK: 1933-42, Standard Gauge curved track with one outside rail.	1	2	3	2
SMC CURVED TRACK: 1935-36, two-rail, 027-style track to activate the Mickey Mouse stoker.	1	2	3	5
SS STRAIGHT TRACK: 1933-42. Standard Gauge straight track with one outside rail insulated.	1	2	3	3
STC LOCKON: 1923-36, Standard Gauge lockon.	.25	.50	1	1
T TRANSFORMER (Type I): 1914-22, 75, 100, 110 or 150 watts.	10	15	25	6
U TRANSFORMER: 1932-33, 50 watts.	10	15	25	4
UTC LOCKON: 1936-42.	.25	.50	1	1
V TRANSFORMER: 1938-1942, 1946-47, 150 watts.	100	125	150	4
W CURVED TRACK: 1934-42, half section of Standard Gauge curved track, 8" long.	1	2	3	2
W TRANSFORMER: 1933-42, 75 watts.	10	15	25	4
WX TRANSFORMER: 1933-42, 75 watts, 25 cycle.	10	15	25	4
Y PEERLESS MOTOR: 1915-20.	50	75	100	4
Z TRANSFORMER: 1938-42, 1945-47, 250 watts.	100	125	150	4

ACCESSORIES, TOYS AND NOVELTIES

1927 LIONEL CATALOG

1927 LIONEL CATALOG

ACCESSORIES, TOYS AND NOVELTIES

1927 LIONEL CATALOG

1938 LIONEL CATALOG

Lionel Catalogs and

For many, the collecting of Lionel paper goods is a hobby unto itself. Indeed, so vast was Lionel's production of trains, it is difficult to comprehend that in fact there were more different paper products produced than trains themselves. A large display area indeed is required to display a "complete"—whatever that means—collection of both.

Beyond the celebrated color consumer catalog, during the later portion of the prewar era Lionel published a dealer advance catalog. Though often similar to the consumer catalog, dealer catalogs also illustrated store displays and promotional items that were not shown in the regular catalog. Also, these dealer catalogs often give us insight into how pieces evolved, for the illustrations in the dealer publication were often based on pre-production samples. Some items are shown that were never produced.

Far from the full-color 1942 catalog full of trains that closed the prewar era, the 1900 Lionel catalog was black and white, and illustrated no trains at all.

Lionel Catalogs and Paper Products

Paper Products

Virtually every operating piece Lionel produced at its own instructional document, often several editions as production continued on good selling items.

Booklets were printed for department store and hobby shop salespeople, teaching the "right" way to extol the virtues of Lionel's products.

Rather than trying to list and illustrate each paper product issued, which would require a massive volume, the listings will be confined to catalogs; consumer, dealer and accessory. A few other items of special interest are listed as well.

(Unlike the trains, only two values are listed for paper products, New and Excellent. Paper in less than Excellent condition is not generally considered collectible. Beware, however, that like the trains, rare and valuable catalogs have been reproduced, and those that are not marked as such are sometimes hard to distinguish.)

Lionel Catalogs and Paper Products

1900 CATALOG

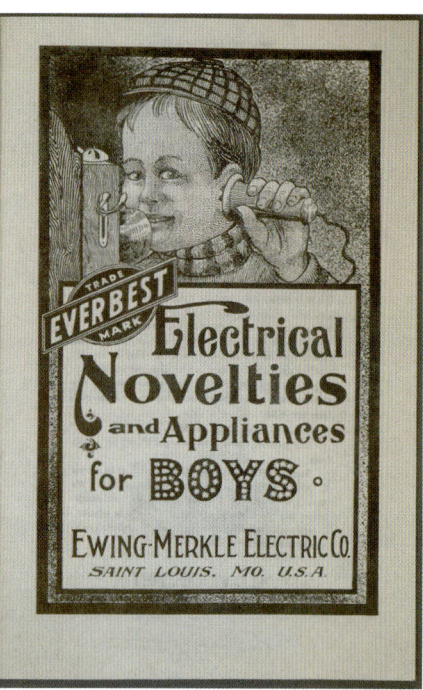

1903 CATALOG

1902 CATALOG

1904 CATALOG

Lionel Catalogs and Paper Products

	VG	EX	LN	RARITY

1900 CATALOG: The first catalog Lionel issued was a 12-page 3-1/2" x 5-7/8" flyer filled with medical devices and electric novelties—all kinds of materials, but no trains.

Too infrequently traded to establish accurate values.

1901 CATALOG: This four-page catalog was the first catalog to illustrate trains.

Too rarely traded to establish pricing.

1902 CATALOG: 16 pages, 3-1/2" x 6-1/4" vertical format catalog with cover made of light green paper printed with red ink.

Too rarely traded to establish pricing.

1903 CATALOG (Type I): 16 pages, 6" x 9" vertical format catalog bearing the name "Ewing-Merkle Electric Co., Saint Louis, Mo. U.S.A.," which was an early Lionel distributor.

Too rarely traded to establish pricing.

1903 CATALOG (Type II): 20 pages, 6-1/4" x 3-1/2" horizontal format catalog with 24-26 Murray Street address listed for Lionel.

Too rarely traded to establish pricing.

1904 CATALOG: 6" x 6-1/2", 12-page booklet promoting Lionel products with diagonal stripe on cover.

Too rarely traded to establish pricing.

1905 CATALOG: 6" x 6", 12-page catalog. The cover shows a 100 locomotive towing a 400 gondola over a 340 suspension bridge.

Too rarely traded to establish pricing.

1906 CATALOG: 4-1/2" x 6-1/2", 24-page black-and-white catalog.

Too rarely traded to establish pricing.

1907 CATALOG: 28 pages, 6" x 9" horizontal format catalog.

Too rarely traded to establish pricing.

1908 CATALOG: 28 pages, 6" x 9" horizontal format catalog.

Too rarely traded to establish pricing.

1909 CATALOG: 32 pages, 6" x 9" catalog.

Too rarely traded to establish pricing.

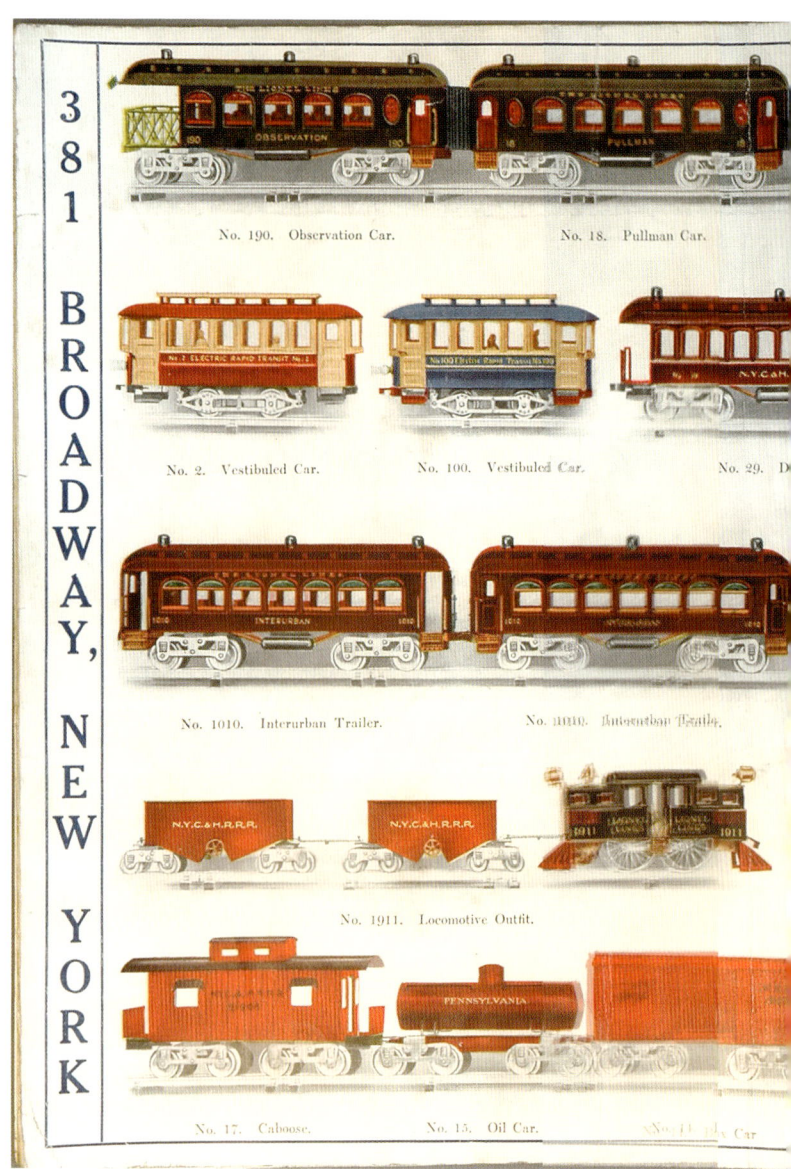

1910 LIONEL CATALOG

Lionel Catalogs and Paper Products

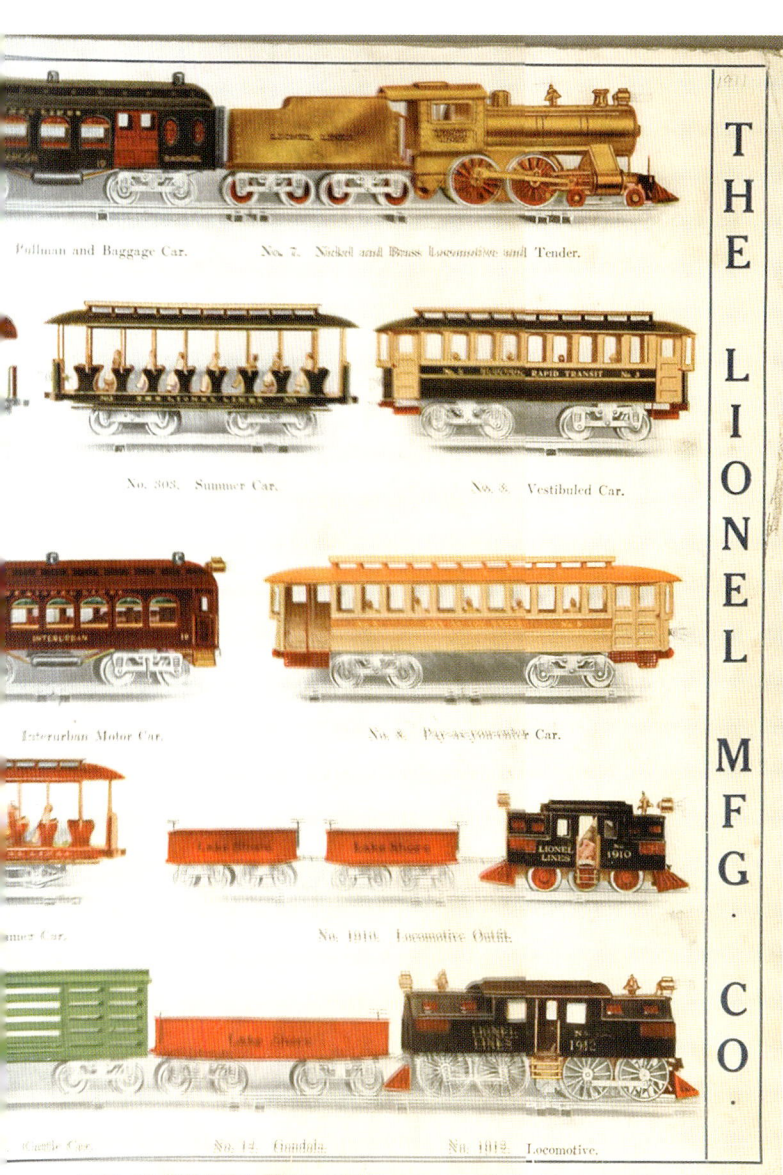

1910 CATALOG

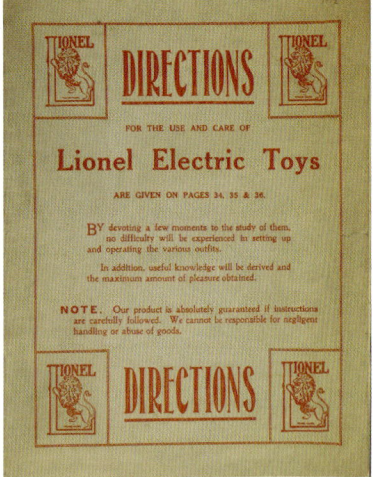

1912 CATALOG

Reproduction of 1913 Catalog.

1914 CATALOG

Lionel Catalogs and Paper Products

	VG	EX	LN	RARITY

1910 CATALOG (Type I): 28 pages, 8" x 10" vertical format catalog with illustration of Lionel factory centered at the bottom of the front cover.

Too rarely traded to establish pricing.

1910 CATALOG (Type II): Factory illustration omitted in favor of blank for dealers to print their addresses in.

Too rarely traded to establish pricing.

1910 CATALOG (Type III): Same catalog with full-color wraparound cover showing many trains.

Too rarely traded to establish pricing.

1911 CATALOG (Type I): 32 pages, 8" x 10" vertical format catalog.

Too rarely traded to establish pricing.

1911 CATALOG (Type II): Same catalog with full-color wraparound cover showing many trains.

Too rarely traded to establish pricing.

1912 CATALOG (Type I): 36 pages, 8" x 10" vertical format catalog.

Too rarely traded to establish pricing.

1912 CATALOG (Type II): Same catalog with full-color wraparound cover showing many trains.

Too rarely traded to establish pricing.

1913 CATALOG (Type I): 36 pages, 8" x 10" vertical format catalog.

Too rarely traded to establish pricing.

1913 CATALOG (Type II): 16 pages, 6" x 6-3/4". Note: Reproduction shown here.

Too rarely traded to establish pricing.

1914 CATALOG (Type I): 36 pages, 8" x 10" vertical format catalog.

Too rarely traded to establish pricing.

1914 CATALOG (Type II): 16 pages, 6" x 6-3/4" printed with green ink.

Too rarely traded to establish pricing.

1914 CATALOG (Type III): 16 pages, 6" x 6-3/4" printed with brown and orange ink.

Too rarely traded to establish pricing.

Lionel Catalogs and Paper Products

1917 CATALOG

1918 CATALOG

1920 FOLDER

Lionel Catalogs and Paper Products

	VG	EX	LN	RARITY

1915 CATALOG (Type I): 40 pages, 10" x 7" horizontal format catalog. Price of set 421 on left centerfold is $32.50.

Too rarely traded to establish pricing.

1915 CATALOG (Type II): 40 pages, 10" x 7" horizontal format catalog. Price of set 421 on left centerfold is $40.

Too rarely traded to establish pricing.

1916 CATALOG: 40 pages, 10" x 7" horizontal format catalog.

Too rarely traded to establish pricing.

1917 CATALOG (Type I): 40 pages, 10" x 7" horizontal format catalog.

Too rarely traded to establish pricing.

1917 CATALOG (Type II): 6" x 9" vertical format catalog. The cover on this version reads "1917 – CATALOGUE OF – LIONEL – ELECTRIC – TOYS."

Too rarely traded to establish pricing.

1917 CATALOG (Type III): 6" x 9" vertical format catalog. The cover on this version reads "1917 – CATALOGUE OF – LIONEL – ELECTRIC – TOY TRAINS." Note, reproduction shown here.

Too rarely traded to establish pricing.

1918 FOLDER: 6" x 9" vertical format catalog. The cover on this folder reads "LIONEL – ELECTRIC – TOY TRAINS – and Multivolt transformers – SOLD BY – MANUFACTURED AND GUARANTEED BY – The Lionel Manufacturing Company, 48-52 East 21st Street, New York."

Too rarely traded to establish pricing.

1919 FOLDER: 6" x 9" vertical format catalog. The cover on this folder reads "LIONEL – ELECTRIC – TOY TRAINS – and Multivolt transformers – SOLD BY – MANUFACTURED AND GUARANTEED BY – The Lionel Corporation, 48-52 East 21st Street, New York."

Too rarely traded to establish pricing.

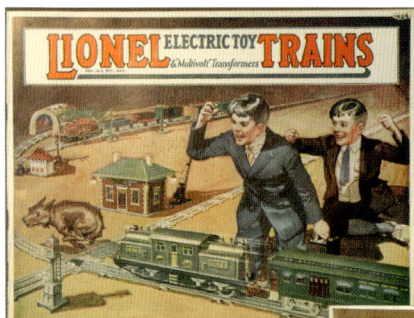

1924 CATALOG

1925 CATALOG

1926 CATALOG

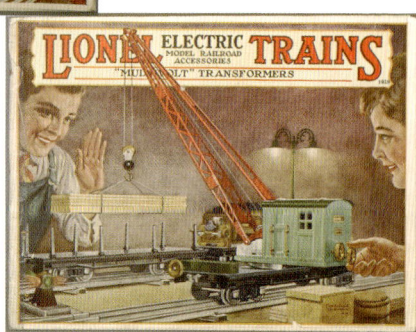

1928 CATALOG

Lionel Catalogs and Paper Products

	VG	EX	LN	RARITY
1920 CATALOG: 46 pages, 10" x 6-3/4" horizontal format catalog with gray cover.	Too rarely traded to establish pricing.			
1920 FOLDER: 7" x 5" double-sided full-color folder representing 32-page catalog. One "page" of the folder with the headline "STANDARD of the WORLD FOR TWENTY YEARS."	Too rarely traded to establish pricing.			
1921 FOLDER: 7" x 5" double-sided full-color folder representing 32-page catalog. One "page" of the folder with the headline "STANDARD of the WORLD FOR TWENTY-ONE YEARS."	Too rarely traded to establish pricing.			
1922 CATALOG: 40 pages, 10" x 6-3/4" horizontal format color catalog with gray cover.	$200	$300		6
1923 CATALOG: 48 pages, 10" x 7" horizontal format color catalog with color cover.	200	300		6
1924 CATALOG: 44 pages, 10-1/2" x 8" horizontal format color catalog with color cover.	175	250		5
1924 FOLDER: 3-5/16" x 6-1/4" folder printed in orange and black.	40	75		4
1925 CATALOG: 44 pages, 10-1/2" x 8" horizontal format color catalog with color cover.	125	200		5
1926 CATALOG: 48 pages, 10-1/2" x 8" horizontal format color catalog with color cover.	125	200		5
1927 CATALOG: 46 pages, 11-1/2" x 8-1/2" horizontal format color catalog with color cover.	125	200		5
1928 CATALOG: 46 pages, 11" x 8-1/2" horizontal format color catalog with color cover.	125	200		5

1929 CATALOG

1929 Pocket Edition catalog

1931 CATALOG

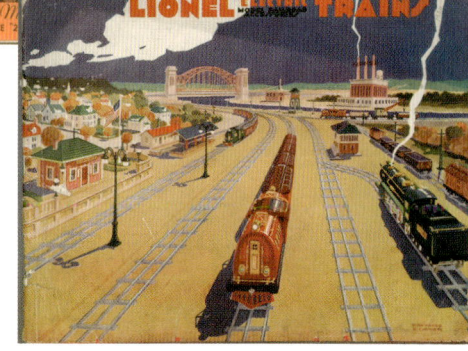
1930 CATALOG

Lionel Catalogs and Paper Products

	VG	EX	LN	RARITY
1929 CATALOG: 46 pages, 11-1/2" x 8-1/2" horizontal format color catalog with color cover.	$175	$250		5
1929 MINIATURE CATALOG: 32 pages, 7-5/8" x 5-3/4" horizontal format with color cover.	40	50		5
1930 ADVANCE CATALOG: Black and white.	Too rarely traded to establish accurate pricing.			
1930 TRADE PRICE LIST: 8-1/2" X 11-1/4", black and red ink on white paper, effective February 1930.	Too rarely traded to establish accurate pricing.			
1930 CONSUMER CATALOG: 48 pages, 11-1/2" x 8-1/2" horizontal format color catalog with color cover.	175	250		5
1930 MINIATURE FOLDER: Blue Comet on cover.	40	50		5
1930 WINNER BROCHURE: 11-1/2" x 17".	Too rarely traded to establish accurate pricing.			
1931 CONSUMER CATALOG: 52 pages, 11-1/2" x 8-1/2" horizontal format color catalog with color cover.	125	200		5
1932 CONSUMER CATALOG: 52 pages, 11-1/2" x 8-1/2" horizontal format color catalog with color cover.	100	175		4

1932 CATALOG

Lionel Catalogs and Paper Products

1933 CATALOG

1934 CATALOG

1935 CATALOG

1935 DEALER ADVANCE CATALOG

Lionel Catalogs and Paper Products

	VG	EX	LN	RARITY
1933 CONSUMER CATALOG: 52 pages, 11-1/4" x 8-3/8" horizontal format color catalog with color cover.	$100	$175		4
1934 CONSUMER CATALOG: 36 pages, 11-1/2" x 7-1/2" horizontal format color catalog with color cover.	100	175		4
1935 CONSUMER CATALOG: 44 pages, 11-1/4" x 8-3/8" horizontal format color catalog with color cover.	75	150		3
1936 ADVANCE CATALOG: 10" x 7-1/2" black and white horizontal format catalog.	175	250		7
1936 CONSUMER CATALOG: 48 pages, 11-1/4" x 8-3/8" horizontal format color catalog with color cover.	100	175		4

1936 CATALOG

Lionel Catalogs and Paper Products

1937 CONSUMER CATALOG

1937 MASTER CATALOG

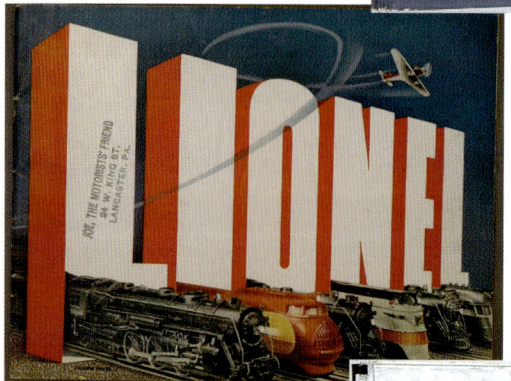
1938 CONSUMER CATALOG

1938 MASTER CATALOG

Lionel Catalogs and Paper Products

	VG	EX	LN	RARITY
1937 MASTER CATALOG: Spiral bound with stiff blue cover, intended for use by the Lionel sales force.	$300	$500		8
1937 ADVANCE CATALOG: 28 pages, 10-1/8" x 7-1/2" black-and-white horizontal format catalog.	175	250		7
1937 CONSUMER CATALOG (Type I): 48 pages, 11-1/4" x 8-3/8" horizontal format color catalog with color cover.	75	150		3
1937 CONSUMER CATALOG (Type II): 24 pages, 10-1/2" x 7-1/2" horizontal format black-and-white catalog with black-and-white cover.	20	40		3
1938 MASTER CATALOG: 58 pages spiral bound with stiff shiny silver cover, intended for use by the Lionel sales force.	400	700		8
1938 ADVANCE CATALOG: 20 pages, 8-1/2" x 10-7/8" black-and-white vertical format catalog.	175	250		7
1938 CONSUMER CATALOG (Type I): 52 pages, 11-1/2" x 8-1/2" horizontal format color catalog with color cover.	75	150		3
1938 CONSUMER CATALOG (Type II): 32 pages, 10-1/4" x 7-1/2" horizontal format black-and-white catalog with black-and-white cover.	20	40		3
1938 LIONEL SALES AIDS AND COMPLETE RETAIL PRICE LIST: 12 pages, 8-3/8" x 10-7/8" blue-and-white vertical format price list with blue-and-red cover.	50	100		6

Lionel Catalogs and Paper Products

1939 CONSUMER CATALOG

1940 CONSUMER CATALOG

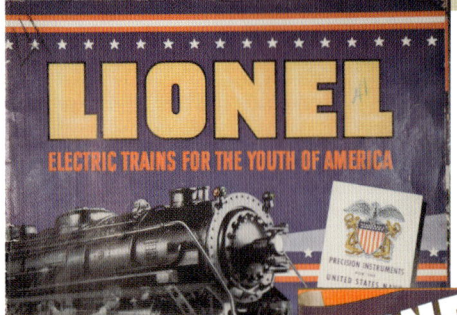

1941 CONSUMER CATALOG

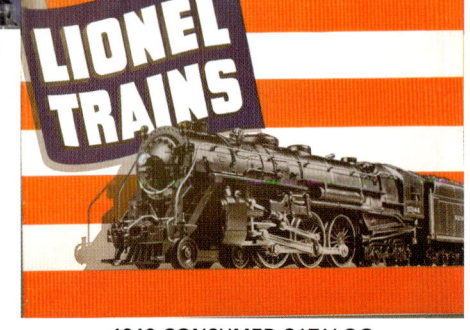

1942 CONSUMER CATALOG

Lionel Catalogs and Paper Products

	VG	EX	LN	RARITY
1939 MASTER CATALOG: 68 pages spiral bound with stiff bright red cover, intended for use by the Lionel sales force.	$300	$500		8
1939 CONSUMER CATALOG: 52 pages, 10-3/4" x 8-3/8" horizontal format color catalog with color cover.	60	125		3
1939 LIONEL ASSORTMENTS AND DEALER DISPLAYS PRICE LIST: Red cover.	250	400		8
1940 EXECUTIVE CATALOG: Spiral bound with cloth-covered cover, intended for use by the Lionel sales force.	300	500		8
1940 CONSUMER CATALOG: 64 pages, 11-1/4" x 8-1/8" horizontal format color catalog with color cover.	60	125		3
1941 CONSUMER CATALOG: 64 pages, 11-1/4" x 7-3/8" horizontal format color catalog with color cover.	60	125		3
1941 LIONEL DEALER DISPLAYS PRICE LIST (Type I): 16 pages, vertical format price list with red stripes on cover.	50	100		6
1941 LIONEL DEALER DISPLAYS PRICE LIST (Type II): 16 pages, vertical format price list with blue stripes on cover.	50	100		6
1941 REPLACEMENT PARTS FOR LIONEL TRAINS AND ACCESSORIES: Brown soft-cover binder.		Too rarely traded to establish accurate pricing.		
1942 ADVANCE CATALOG: 12 pages, 10" x 11" red and black on white catalog.	250	400		8
1942 CONSUMER CATALOG: 32 pages, 11" x 8-1/2" horizontal format color catalog with color cover.	60	125		6

APPENDIX 1
Awakening Sleeping Toys
How To Clean And Prepare Trains for Use After Long-Term Storage

In the instruction booklet Lionel furnished with its outfits, it recommended to customers that they keep all the original packaging materials to protect the trains during storage or travel. Oftentimes, however, that was not the case, and the boxes went outside or in the fireplace on Christmas morning.

In the passing years, trains were stored in attics, basements or closets, oftentimes in no box at all. Dust and dirt filtered into the working mechanisms of the trains as well as coating the shiny finish Lionel had carefully applied. With trains stored in hot attics, lubricants solidified into solid blocks. In damp basements, humidity allowed rust to work its evil on plated or blackened surfaces and on wheels once worn shiny from use.

The essential tools for repair of prewar Lionel trains are a screwdriver with various sizes and types of tips, and a wire stripping and crimping tool. Also handy would be a soldering iron and a side-cutting pliers.

Awakening Sleeping Toys

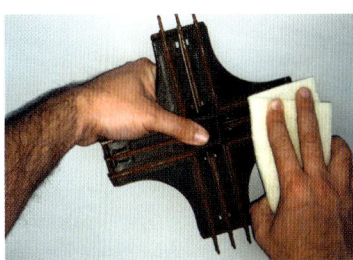

Dirty, rusty track is best cleaned by scouring with a Scotchbrite pad, as shown here. Do NOT use steel wool or sandpaper.

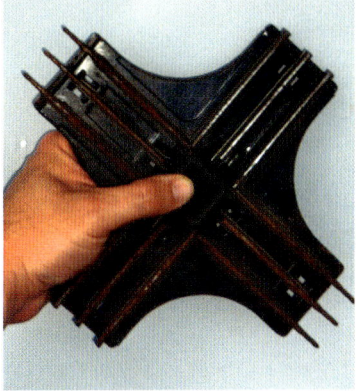

Only the tops of the rails, and the connecting pins, must be clean for good operation of the trains.

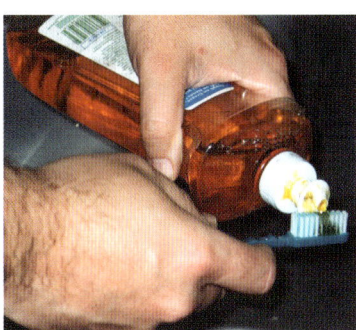

In the case of severe dirt and grime build-up on the bodies of the trains, cautious use of a mild detergent applied with a soft toothbrush or cotton swab sometimes produces excellent results. Be careful, however, as some markings are easily damaged by even the mildest of detergents.

Work slowly, and in a circular motion, for best results. Too vigorous scrubbing risks scratching the paint.

Rinse the train thoroughly, avoiding wetting the paper label (if present) on the bottom, and dry in a warm area before storing.

If it is your intention to sell your trains to a collector or dealer wholesale (see Chapter 2), then it is my recommendation that you do not attempt to clean the trains. The dealer or collector knows how to clean each piece without damage and can tell even in a dirty state how the item will clean up and what it will be worth. He will pay slightly less for a dirty piece to recoup his time. However, certain trains are easily damaged by inappropriate cleaning and, once the damage is done, the value is permanently diminished. Better that you allow the dealer do the cleanup than for you to take this risk.

If you are keeping the trains for yourself and want to clean them up, following are a few general tips.

The first thing that most people notice that needs cleaning is the track. Do NOT use steel wool or sandpaper to clean the track. Steel wool will deposit fine metal fibers that will cause short circuits and sandpaper will remove the tinplating that protects the track from further rust. Excellent results can be had with 3-M "Scotchbrite" pads available in auto parts stores. Various textures are available. These non-metallic pads make short work of dirt and light rust deposits, especially the courser textures. While the entire exposed surface of the connecting pins needs to be clean, only the tops of the rails require thorough cleaning.

A small piece of the Scotchbrite pad can be used to clean the contact surfaces of the locomotive's wheels as well as the center contact rollers. This will insure good electrical connection and prevent intermittent operation.

Lionel's trains are usually easily disassembled with a screwdriver. In many cases, the bodies of various items are assembled to the frames with sheet metal tabs, which are bent to secure the parts together. It is NOT recommended that you straighten these tabs. They are easily broken, which seriously affects the value of an item, as well as its functionality.

Items that are designed to come apart usually are held together with screws. Trucks are retained with screws, cotter pins or steel clips. If you feel like you have to force something apart–STOP. More than 99 percent of the items fit together easily. If force is required, that is usually a sign that you have not located and removed all the necessary screws or are not following the proper procedure.

If simple dusting does not clean the train, then cautiously use plain tap water. Be particularly careful around decals or lettering. Some collectors use a diluted mild liquid dishwashing detergent applied with a soft toothbrush or cotton swab to clean the surfaces, but beware that such techniques risk damaging the item, particularly markings. Rinse the body thoroughly in running water, making sure to keep the paper lubrication labels, if present, dry. Let the body air dry thoroughly. Incomplete rinsing will leave rings and spots on the body. If you are uncomfortable with this, find a shop that specializes in Lionel and have it clean that item for you.

Bare metal components and blued steel car frames can be wiped with a cloth moistened with a product such as WD-40 that will remove built-up dirt and leave a protective petroleum barrier against rust.

While the cars are dismantled, inspect the wiring on any operating cars

Awakening Sleeping Toys

A light oil and a light plastic-compatible grease, available at most hobby stores, are needed to lubricate your trains.

or whistling tenders. Check for wires that have broken loose or have cracking insulation. Replace them with similar sized, highly flexible wires. Use rosin core solder, not acid core. Do any soldering with the body removed (and preferably on another bench). It is amazing the number of otherwise beautiful collectable trains we see that have been bumped and ruined by a hot soldering iron.

The bodies of most locomotives are removed by first removing screws, although a few are held on by pins driven in place.

On spur gear-driven locomotives, the commutator can be seen. This is usually a three-segmented copper disk. Using a little cigarette lighter fluid on a cotton swab (with appropriate safety measures concerning flammable liquids), wipe this down. A little lighter fluid washed over the brushes will remove excess carbon deposits as well. After the lighter fluid has evaporated, apply a couple of

The locomotive, of course, with its abundance of moving parts, requires the most lubrication. A single drop of oil on the armature shaft, as well as the axle bearings, greatly improves the life and performance of the motor. The spur gears are best lubricated with a light grease.

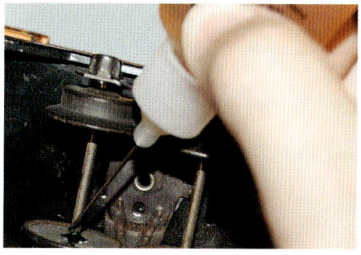

Lubricating the cars' axles and truck pivot points will quiet the train and reduce the load on the locomotive substantially.

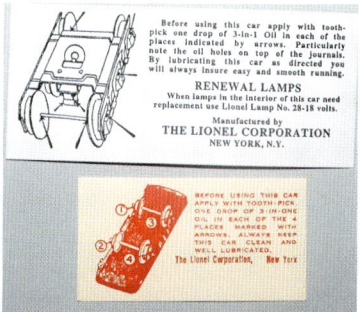

Some of Lionel's prewar cars had lubrication instructions pasted on their bottoms. These instructions are as valid today as they were when the cars were new.

drops of light, plastic-compatible grease to each end of the armature shaft, taking care not to get any lube on the brushes, brush holders or commutator. Some motors are equipped with felt oil wicks to lubricate the armature shaft. On these motors, saturate the wick with a light, plastic-compatible oil.

The 700E, 700K and 763E steam locomotives have internal gearboxes accessed by removing the boiler. These locomotive models are driven through a worm and wheel arrangement. Both the worm and gear should be lubricated with a light grease. Be advised that disassembly and proper reassembly of these locomotives is tedious and time consuming. Once exposed, the old lubricant should be scraped out and disposed of properly. Final clean up of the old lube is aided by the use of cigarette lighter fluid. The gearboxes should be refilled with light plastic-compatible grease, taking time to work it thoroughly into the gear train.

The driving axles of many locomotives turn in porous bronze bushings, which should be lightly lubricated with light oil. While you have your light oil out, it would be a good time to lubricate the junction of the wheels and axles on all your cars. You will be surprised what an improvement in performance this step will bring.

Reassemble your trains, taking care to put the screws back into their proper holes. None of Lionel's screws should require more than finger effort to install. If they do, make sure you have the proper screw and recheck your alignment. Use caution and do not overtighten any of the screws.

Your trains should now be ready to run.

SETTING UP YOUR TRAIN

APPENDIX 2
SETTING UP YOUR TRAIN

Lionel's trains were well-made, reliable toys. Often they will work as well today as the day they were made. However, there are some simple steps you should take to protect the trains and, more importantly you and your family, before plugging in the toys you just hauled down from the attic or home from a garage sale.

The instructions here serve two purposes. They will aid failing memories in the event the train's original instructions have been lost or discarded. They also contain some tips necessary due to the age of the trains. Remember, when Lionel wrote its instruction sheets, they were for use with new toys!

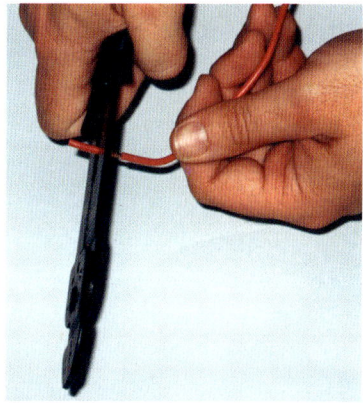

The power leads from the transformer are connected to the track by means of a lockon. Lockons were produced in multiple styles. Using a pair of wire strippers (shown in Appendix 1, figure 1), carefully remove a short section of the insulation from each end of the hook up wire.

First, and absolutely most importantly, examine the transformer (power pack). If it has been exposed to an obvious roof leak, or has a broken or cracked case, take it in to a qualified Lionel center before proceeding. Next, grasp the power cord and bend it 180 degrees, tightly. If the insulation cracks or breaks off, the transformer needs service. This is a common problem, and the transformer is the only area with much potential for injury. Do not be tempted to wrap the cord in electrical tape or to splice on a new wire. Lionel knotted its power cords inside the transformer case to act as a strain relief, and the insulation there will also be failing if the insulation you can see is.

Next, examine the visible wiring on the underside of illuminated or operating cars such as steam locomotive tenders, cabooses, passenger cars or unloading freight cars. Make sure that none of the tiny wire leads have broken loose, and that the insulation on those leads is still intact and pliable.

Unless the locomotive has been serviced recently, follow the procedure for doing so as outlined in Appendix 1.

Finally, examine the track. Make sure that all the connecting pins are in place (see the special note concerning switches before you begin installing replacements) as well as the insulation between the center rail and the crossties. If any insulation is missing, it must be replaced or that section should be discarded.

If the tops of the rails are dirty or rusty, follow the steps listed in Appendix 1 to clean them. Connect the sections of track into the configuration of your choice. Note that the track-to-track connections should be firm, the firmer the better. It may be necessary to tighten the open ends of the rails to ensure a tight fit. Specially-made track pliers are ideal for this, however conventional needle-nose pliers can be used as well with patience.

Should you choose to permanently attach your train's track to a board, don't do this until it has been test run and then use screws, not nails, to attach the truck. Nails work loose, and a misplaced hammer blow can permanently deform the rails. Even at this, based on the author's years of experience in the hobby shop industry, if the train is for a child, resist the urge to fasten the track to a sheet of plywood. This, in essence, is the same as gluing together Legos. The creativity, as well as the ability to expand the railroad, stops when the track is screwed down. From then on, the child is destined to only watch the train circle round a sheet of plywood, and hence will lose interest rapidly.

Once you have your track sections connected together, attach the wires to the end then the lockon to the track as shown in photos 1 through 4. After checking the condition of the transformer (Appendix

Setting Up Your Train

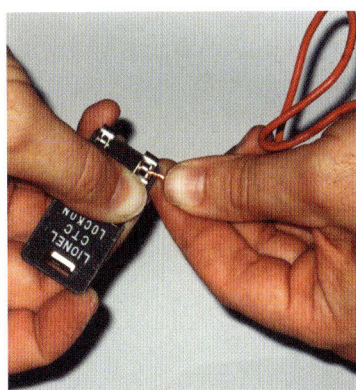

Depress the end of one fahnstock clip on the lockon and slip the end of the wire through the SMALL loop. Releasing the end of the clip locks it in place. Repeat the process with the second wire and the other fahnstock clip, ensuring that not even a single strand of wire touches between the two clips.

1), connect the other ends of the wires to the appropriate terminals on the transformer. Before placing the trains on the track, plug the transformer into a wall outlet. If your transformer is equipped with lights, the green one should now glow, and the red one, if so equipped, should be off. On transformers equipped with a red light, that lamp's illumination indicates that the circuit breaker has opened due to a short circuit. Advance the throttle again, watching for a change in any indicator lights. A dimming green light or glowing red light is a sign of a short circuit. If your transformer has no lights, it should emit a pleasant hum when plugged in; a clicking is a sign of a short circuit.

The UTC universal lockon can be used with either Standard Gauge or O-Gauge track.

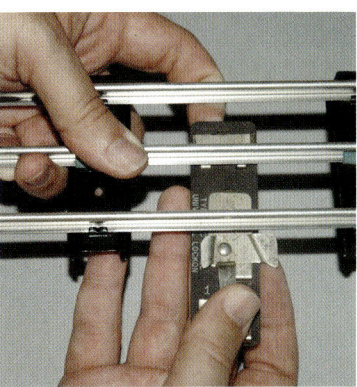

To attach the UTC to Standard Gauge track, hook the tangs furthest from the fahnstock clips over the flange at the bottom of the center rail, as shown here.

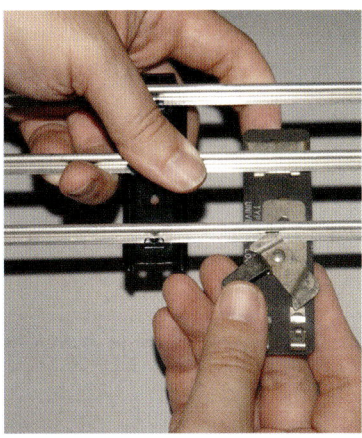

Using the attached lever, swing the short end of the lock plate over the flange of an outer rail, locking the lockon in place.

SHORT CIRCUITS, NO TRAIN

If the short circuit exists with the throttle closed, verify you have connected the leads to the track to the proper posts on the transformer. If they are properly connected, you should take the transformer in for service.

If, with the throttle closed, there is no short, yet there is with the throttle advanced, make sure the two wires are not touching each other at either the lockon or transformer binding posts. Make sure that there are no loose screws, nails or track pins lying on the track. Remove any debris from the track and try again. If the short persists, separate the section of track with the lockon affixed from the others, and begin adding sections one at a time. When a bad section is added, the short will return. Either repair or replace the defective section.

PLACE THE TRAINS ON THE TRACK

Put the cars on one at a time, coupling them to each other as you place them on the track. After each one is placed on the track, roll it back and forth to ensure that the wheels are properly in place. Turn the power on, again checking for potential short circuits. If a short exists, begin removing cars until the short goes away. When the short is corrected, the most recently removed car was at fault. Examine it for broken wires or low, loose hanging coupler components. If no shorts existed with all the cars on the track, place the locomotive on the track.

OPEN THE THROTTLE

Moving the throttle regulates the speed of the train by increasing and decreasing the track voltage. Voltage is normally somewhere between 6 and 18 volts, although some transformers go up to 24 volts.

REVERSING

Many Lionel locomotives are equipped with a remote reversing mechanism commonly referred to as an "E-unit." This mechanism is operated by current interruptions. These interruptions can be caused by operating the "direction" control on the transformer (if so equipped) or by closing and reopening the throttle. Some locomotives have only two-position E-units, shifting directly from forward to reverse. Many locomotives have a three-position E-unit, which sequences as follows: Forward-neutral-reverse-neutral-forward. The neutral position allows power to flow to the track without moving the train in order to operate special features such as log, coal and merchandise cars that unload.

The E-unit, or reversing mechanism, can be disconnected if so desired. Start the train moving in the desired direction at a low speed. Hold it

Setting Up Your Train

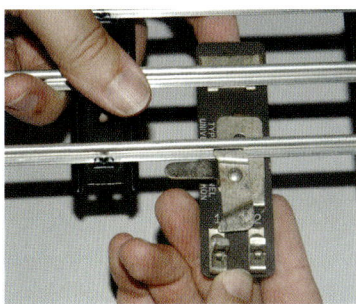

When properly installed, the UTC rigidly spans two rails (wires omitted here for clarity).

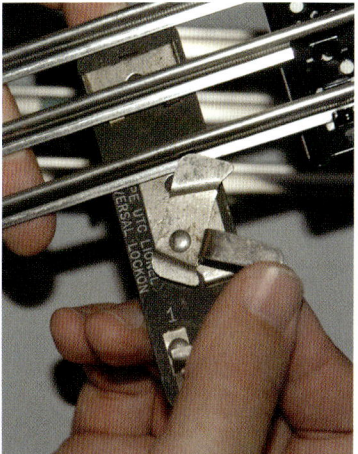

When a UTC lockon is used with O-Gauge track, the connection procedure is the same, except the long extension of the lock plate is swung over the rail flange.

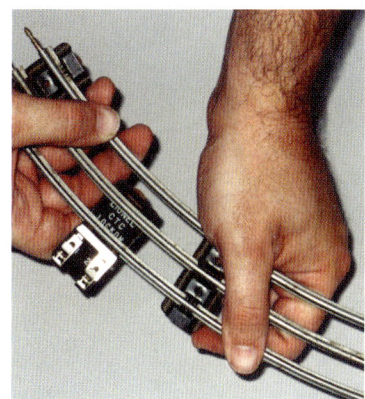

If you are using the more common, and currently produced, CTC lockon with O-Gauge track, place the bar beneath the word "LOCKON" over the lower flange of the outer rail. The tab above the word "LIONEL" will now snap over the opposite flange of the center rail. The lockon will now be securely in place. The lockon can be attached to any section of track, curved or straight.

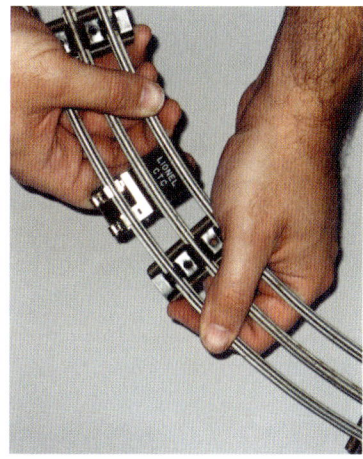

This is how NOT to attach a lockon. This is the number one mistake made in the initial set up. If it is hooked up like this, not only will the train not run, but if allowed to remain this way, serious damage to the transformer can occur.

still with your hand and move the E-unit control lever on the locomotive (NOT a transformer control) to the opposite position. The E-unit control is USUALLY a shiny lever protruding from the top of the locomotive, or in some instances from the bottom or rear of the locomotive.

BLOWING THE WHISTLE

Many of Lionel's steam locomotive replicas included a whistle. The whistle mechanism was actually housed inside the locomotive's tender. It was operated by slowly moving the appropriate control on the transformer. In some instances, it may be necessary to move the control (lever or button) only part way through its travel for best operation. Excessive slowing of the train is an indication that the whistle unit is in need of service.

OPERATING CARS

Electrically operated cars such as the 3652 gondola, 3651 log car or 3659 coal dump car are operated electrically. The current flows from the control rails of the uncoupling track section, through small rivets in the car's sliding shoes and to the car's mechanism, when the proper button is pushed on the controller. These cars reset themselves after use, although most must still be manually reloaded.

INSTALLING TURNOUTS (SWITCHES)

Switches, often referred to as turnouts to prevent confusing them with electrical off-on switches, add considerable play value to a miniature railroad. Lionel made turnouts in both manual and remote control versions. Left-hand turnouts, as the name implies, have the train exit (or enter) from the left side of the straight segment; right-hand turnouts are the opposite.

Manually operated turnouts are installed in the track just like any other piece of track. Remote control switches are only slightly more complicated. Later Lionel O-Gauge turnouts have a built in non-derailing feature that automatically aligns the moveable rails to prevent a train from running "against" them.

This non-derailing feature is the cause of Lionel's installation of fiber pins in two rails on these turnouts. These insulating pins are installed on the two-track end of the turnout. On left-hand 022 turnouts, the pins are in the ends of the left-most rails of both the straight and curved segment. On right-hand turnouts, they are in the ends of the right-most rails.

It is very important that these pins not be removed or replaced with steel pins. It will be necessary to either add or remove steel pins from the track sections that connect to the turnouts.

Removing crimped-in pins from Lionel track is easily done using side-cutting pliers. Grip the pin in the jaw of the pliers. Use the flange of the rail as a lever point and ease the pin out slowly. It may be necessary to reshape the rail if it was distorted by the removal of the pin.

Setting Up Your Train

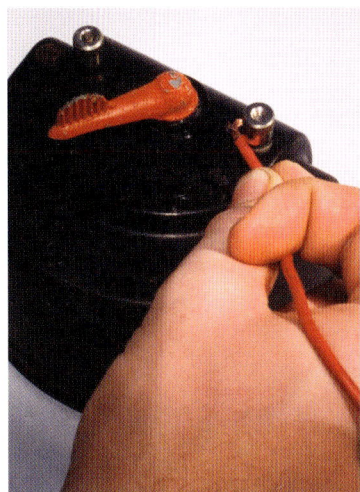

Many of Lionel's smaller transformers have only two binding posts for attaching the other ends of the track power wires. Once again, the end of each wire is stripped, the binding post nut loosened, the wire wrapped around it in a clockwise manner and the binding post nut retightened.

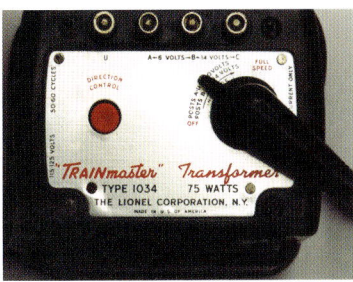

Lionel's larger transformers have multiple binding posts. Lionel solved the problem of remembering which to use by thoughtfully providing that information near the throttle. The letters, such as "A-U" shown here, correspond to the letters adjacent to the binding posts. Often two pairs of posts are indicated for an individual throttle, indicating that two different voltage ranges are available depending on which combination is used.

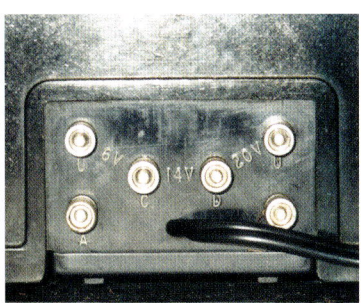

The binding posts are sometimes located on the back of the transformer near the 110-volt power cord. Additional combinations of posts, labeled appropriately, yield various fixed voltages for powering lights and accessories. It is usually considered that the outer rails are the "ground" and as such terminal 2 on the lockon is generally connected to the "U" post on the transformer, although the train will run with the connections reversed.

VOLTAGE DROP

The rails of the track are the path of the electrical current to the train. The steel rails have a much higher resistance to current flow than does copper wire. Therefore, on larger railroads, it is not unusual for the train to slow as it travels farther from the lockon.

The solution is not, as many people think, buying a larger transformer. The solution is buying more lockons and connecting them equidistant about the railroad. Then all the terminal 1 lockon connections are connected to the same transformer post, and all the terminal 2 lockon connections are connected to the other appropriate transformer post.

ENJOY YOUR TRAINS

Although sometimes mechanically complex, Lionel trains were intended to be primarily children's toys. As such, the connecting and operating of these items were kept deliberately simple. Oftentimes simply sitting down and getting started will bring back old memories of how each step is to be done. Much like riding a bicycle, it is not easily forgotten.

Lionel, through the years, produced detailed instruction sheets and booklets to accompany its train sets, locomotives, accessories and cars. There is no substitute for these original instructions. Fortunately, many of these have been reproduced and are available at hobby shops and train shows.

Glossary

AAR: Association of American Railroads, a full-sized railroad industry standards and lobbying group.

Bakelite: A brand of hard, brittle thermoset plastic. Heating Bakelite does not soften it, making it popular for electrical components. Lionel also used Bakelite occasionally for car bodies.

Cupola: The raised structure on the roof of a caboose that allowed a clear view of the sides of the train, making dragging equipment and "hot boxes" easily spotted regardless of the height of the remainder of the train.

Die-casting: A manufacturing process that involves forcing molten metal, usually a zinc alloy, into a mold, called a die, under high pressure. Rugged, detailed, precisely made parts can be mass-produced in this manner.

E-unit: This has two meanings. A) In Lionel trains, the electromechanical switch that selects motor contacts, and thus the motor's direction of rotation, is called an "E-unit." It is usually cycled by interrupting the current flow to the track. These come in two-position (forward-reverse) or three-position versions, as well as a manual version that is two-position, but requires hands-on operation by the operator. Three-position E-units are the most common, and their sequence of operation is forward-neutral-reverse-neutral-forward. B) In real railroading, E-unit is slang for a General Motors Electro-Motive Division E-series twin-engine diesel that rode on two A-1-A trucks. The two terms are not generally confused, as Lionel did not build a miniature E-unit locomotive during the prewar era.

Gauge: The distance between the tops of the rails. On most real U.S. railroads, this is 4', 8 1/2". For Lionel's most popular size of trains, this width is 1 1/4".

Heat stamping: A decorating process in which a heated die is used to transfer and adhere colored decoration to the subject piece. When used on plastics, heat stamping often leaves an impression, the depth of which varies with the temperature of the tool and the duration of contact. When used on painted sheet-metal components, the underlying paint is occasionally softened, and thus the stamping can sometimes be felt.

Hot box: Early railroad wheel bearings were lubricated with oil-soaked cotton called "waste." These bearings, or journals, as well as the "waste," were housed in journal boxes. If the lubrication ran dry, the bearing would overheat, setting fire to the waste. If the train continued to operate, the bearing would fail, derailing the train.

Glossary

House car: This standard railroad industry term is used for enclosed freight cars such as box, stock, refrigerator and poultry cars. These cars are used for lading requiring protection from weather, and the construction of these cars rather resembled that of a house.

Journal box: The enclosure at the junction of the axle and truck sideframe, which housed the axle bearing, or journal, and the cotton waste that acted as a lubricant reservoir.

Lithography: A printing process often used on metal surfaces. Part of the surface is treated to retain ink while other areas are treated to repel ink. This process allows elaborate and colorful decorations to be applied.

Rubber-stamping: A decorating process that uses an engraved rubber block, which is inked then pressed to the subject. Rubber-stamping tends to not be as bold, or as permanent, as heat stamping. However, rubber-stamping can be used on irregular surfaces which heat-stamping cannot, and the set-up cost is considerably less.

Scale: A numeric ratio describing the relative size of a miniature to an original.

Silk screening: A labor-intensive decorating process. A piece of sheer fabric (originally silk, now polyester) is stretched tight. A thin sheet of plastic, with holes cut out to reveal where ink is to appear on the work piece, is placed over the screen. The screen is pressed to the work piece ink, then forced through the openings in the plastic, and through the screen onto the work surface. Multi-color designs require multiple screens, and the inks are applied sequentially starting with the lightest color and moving up to the darkest.

Sintered Iron: Sintering is a metallurgical process in which powdered metal is poured into a mold and subjected to heat and pressure, thus forming it into a single part.

Tack board: Wooden panels on an otherwise steel door provided a place to attach various notes.

Truck: The structure consisting of paired wheels with axles, side frame, bolster and suspension system beneath railroad cars. This is referred to as a "bogie" in Europe.

STOUT AUCTIONS

Many of the photos in this volume were provided by Stout Auctions, one of the nation's premier toy train auctioneers. Located in both Williamsport, Indiana and West Middlesex, Pennsylvania, Stout specializes in liquidating collections of premium quality trains, including the previous owner of Lionel and other high profile individuals. Stout currently has many record auction items including one of the most important toy trains ever sold- the brass Lionel 700E scale Hudson that sat in Joshua Lionel Cowen's office. Consigned items are offered for both on-site and internet bidding. For more information call 765-764-6901, or visit www.stoutauctions.com

NATIONAL TRAIN MUSEUM

National Train Museum
Headquarters for the Train Collectors Association

Many of the trains shown in this volume are from the collection of the National Toy Train Museum, headquarters for The Train Collectors Association. The TCA is an international organization of men and women dedicated to collecting and preserving toy trains.

The Train Collectors Association, was born from a 1954 meeting in the Yardley, Pennsylvania barn of Ed Alexander. The TCA has grown to nearly 32,000 members today. A national office, along with a museum, was built in Strasburg, Pennsylvania to accommodate the growing needs. The building has undergone 3 expansions since that time.

Toy trains are presented in a colorful and exciting turn-of-the-century setting. The Museum's vast collection of floor toys, electric trains and train-related accessories includes those from the mid-1800s through the present. See Lionel, American Flyer, Marx, Marklin, LGB and many, many others.

The National Toy Train Museum offers five operating layouts: Standard, "O", "S", "G" and HO gauges. The Standard gauge layout highlights tinplate trains from the 1920s and 1930s. The "O" gauge layout presents trains from the 1940s through current production items. The "S" gauge layout highlights American Flyer trains manufactured during the 1950s. The "G" gauge layout shows what one can do with large, durable modern trains which are made for indoor or outdoor use. The HO gauge layout was professionally built by Carstens Publications, Inc. for a series of articles published in its Railroad Model Craftsman magazine.

A continuously running video show in The Museum's Theater area features cartoons and comedy films about toy trains. The Museum Gift Shop offers a wide and unusual selection of toy train-related gifts. Also

NATIONAL TRAIN MUSEUM

housed in the Museum is an extensive Toy Train Reference Library, which is open to the public. On file are catalogs, magazines and books devoted to toy trains from 1900 to the present.

Come to Strasburg and visit the National Toy Train Museum where we have 5 different gauge layouts operating and displays of trains dating from 1840 until the present. If you are a person with a few trains or a house full, come join us.

OPEN:
- Weekends in April, November and December
- Daily — May through October
- 10:00 a.m. - 5:00 p.m.

visit their website at
www.traincollectors.org
for additional information.

BUILD A CITY AROUND THE TRACKS OF YOUR RAILROAD

No. 911 Illuminated Country Estate—A beautiful and realistic addition to a model railroad. The house is sturdily built of steel and colorfully enamelled. It is 7¼ inches long, 5 inches wide, 5¼ inches high. The roof is removable so that bulb can be renewed. Around the house are grouped colorful naturalistic shrubbery, hedges and trees. The base is covered with green imitation grass. Base, 16 inches long, 8 inches deep. **Price $4.50**

No. 910 Grove of Trees—These extremely natural trees were modeled by a scenic artist. They are made by a special process and colored in a beautiful leaf green. The base is covered with imitation grass. Trees may be removed from base and placed in any desired spot, or the assemblage as shown can be used as a unit. Base is 16 inches long, 8 inches deep. **Price $2.00**

No. 914 Park Landscape—A colorful centerpiece that can be used together with other scenic effects shown on this page. Consists of two grass plots with small cedars and flowering bushes. In the center is a garden vase with flowering foliage. The sturdy base represents a concrete walk. Base measures 16 inches long, 8 inches deep. **Price $1.50**

No. 922 Illuminated Lamp Terrace—A copy of those seen in the center of boulevards and in parks. Includes the attractive No. 56 Lamp Post. Around the post are flowering shrubs and bright green grass. 12 inches long, 3½ inches deep. **Price $2.75**

No. 913 Illuminated Landscaped Bungalow—A cozy country bungalow surrounded by flowering shrubbery and green bushes. The bungalow is made of steel and has an interior light. It is 4¾ inches long, 4 inches high, 2¾ inches wide. The roof is removable. Base is 16 inches long, 8 inches deep. **Price $3.50**

No. 912 Illuminated Suburban Home—The illuminated house is built of steel, enamelled in bright colors. The roof is removable so that bulb can be renewed. House is 5½ inches long, 5 inches wide, 5½ inches high. Base is covered with grass. It is 16 inches long, 8 inches deep. **Price $4.50**

All the charm and beauty of a natural hillside have been built into this beautiful Lionel mountain. Nestled on a knoll is a little red-roofed house. At the foot of the mountain, stately trees and shrubs surround a country home.

Made of strong felt composition mounted on a sturdy base. Hand painted and colorfully decorated.

No. 917—34 inches long, 9½ inches high, 15 inches wide. **Price $4.00**

No. 918—30 inches long, 9½ inches high, 10 inches wide. **Price $3.00**

No. 917
No. 918

No. 919 Lionel Park Grass—You can create beautiful effects around your railroad by means of this bright green grass. You can spread it around the tracks. To make a permanent effect cover the ground with shellac or glue and sprinkle the grass over it. When dry, shake off or blow away the excess. 8 oz. to a bag. **Price $.30**

GIRDER STEEL BRIDGE SPANS AND THE FAMOUS "HELL GATE"

No. 280

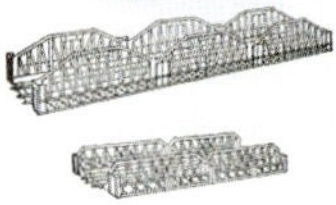

No. 280 Single Span for "Standard" Gauge
Built of steel to represent modern heavy girder construction. Footpaths and portals on each side. Handsomely enamelled by Lionel's exclusive process. Single spans can be attached to each other, as shown in sketch, to make a bridge as long as you desire. Complete with one section of track. 14 inches. **Price $2.75**

No. 270 Bridge Span for "O" Gauge
Because this type of bridge has proved highly satisfactory for railroad construction, it is one that you will find on nearly every road. Made of steel embossed and beautifully enamelled. Single spans can be attached to each other, as shown in sketch, to make a bridge as long as you desire. Complete with one section of track. 10½ inches long. **Price $1.75**

No. 270

No. 300 Hell Gate Bridge for Standard Gauge or "O" Gauge Track
In New York City there is a famous bridge that spans the East River. The section where it is located is called "Hell Gate" and that is the name of the bridge. Lionel No. 300 is an exact copy of the real one. The two archways at each end are embossed and enamelled to represent limestone. The train passes through the bridge at regular track level, thus avoiding the necessity of grade approaches. You will be proud to watch your train speed through a bridge that is so majestic. 28¾ inches long, 11 inches high, 10⅜ inches wide. **Price $16.50**

No. 1023 "O" Gauge Tunnel—On nearly every railroad in the country there is at least one mountain tunnel, so there ought to be one in your railroad system. This model is constructed of strong felt composition, hand-painted in beautiful colors. Will accommodate all Lionel Junior and "O" Gauge Trains. 13 inches long, 10 inches wide, 8 inches high. Tunnel opening, 4½ inches wide, 5½ inches high. **Price $1.00**

No. 916

No. 916 Curved Tunnel—For all "O" Gauge Outfits except No. 240E—Constructed of strong felt composition with a durable base. Decorated with metal houses, trees and shrubbery. 29¼ inches long. 13½ inches high, 24 inches wide. Portals 4¼ inches wide, 5½ inches high. **Price $5.50**

No. 923 Curved Tunnel—For all "O" Gauge and "Standard" Gauge outfits—Similar to No. 916. 40 inches long, 16½ inches high, 23 inches wide. Portals 7 inches wide, 8 inches high. **Price $9.50**

No. 123 Curved Tunnel—For all "O" Gauge Outfits except Nos. 239E, 240E and 241E—Similar to No. 916. 18½ inches long, 16¼ inches wide, 10 inches high. Portals 4 inches wide, 5 inches high. **Price $3.50**

No. 915 Curved Tunnel—65 inches long, 23½ inches high. Portals 6¼ inches wide, 7¼ inches high. **Price $15.00**

No. 120L Illuminated Tunnel—Constructed of steel and hand painted. A red roofed bungalow is nestled on each side with footpath leading to the bridge under which flows a waterfall. Interior is illuminated. For use with large size Lionel Trains. 17 inches long, 12 inches wide, 9¼ inches high. Openings are 8¼ inches high, 6½ inches wide. **Price $5.50**

No. 119 Tunnel—Similar in construction to No. 120L but without bungalow and illumination. For use with all "O" Gauge trains and medium size "Standard" Gauge trains. 12 inches long, 9½ inches wide, 9¼ inches high. Tunnel openings are 6½ inches high, 5 inches wide. **Price $3.50**

More Must-Have Guides for Keeping Collections on Track

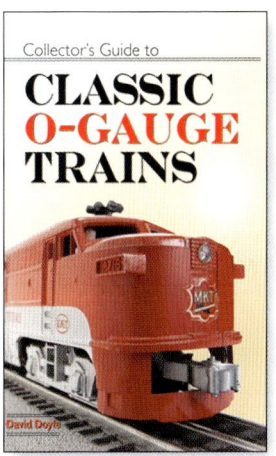

Collector's Guide to Classic O Gauge Trains
by David Doyle

This fact-packed toy train guide provides you with critical and expertly gathered classic O Gauge train data, plus more than 900 stunning color photos of the most highly collectible trains in North America. The essence of some of the best O Gauge trains in the hobby is captured in this handy and concise guide that's perfect to use while scouring shows and shops.

Among the companies included:
Lionel: Prewar and Postwar • American Flyer • Marx AMT • Hoge • Kusan • Unique • Ives

5 x 8 • 272 pages
900+ color photos
Item# Z0724 • $19.99

Standard Catalog of® Lionel Trains 1945-1969
2nd Edition
by David Doyle

Everything you need for successful Lionel Train collecting is in this book; including 1,450 vibrant color photos, current collector pricing, rarity ratings and tips for maintaining and repairing trains.

Softcover • 8-1/4 x 10-7/8 • 400 pages
1,450 color photos
Item# Z0096 • $32.99

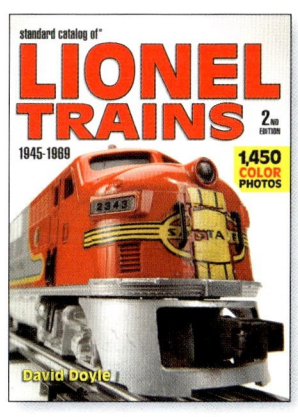

O'Brien's Collecting Toy Trains
Identification and Value Guide
6th Edition
Edited by David Doyle

Explore more than 6,000 train listings for companies including Marx, Lionel, American Flyer and more, plus 1,200 spectacular color photos for accurate identification.

Softcover • 8-1/4 x 10-7/8 • 400 pages
1,200 color photos
Item# CTT6 • $29.99

krause publications
An Imprint of F+W Publications

700 East State Street • Iola, WI 54990-0001
715-445-2214 • 888-457-2873

To Order Call **800-258-0929** Offer TYA7
Order online at **www.krausebooks.com**
Also available from booksellers nationwide

Gain *Expert* Insight and Exclusive Marketplace News

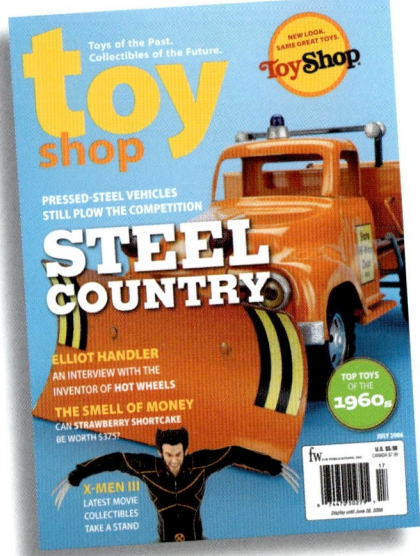

Toy Shop delivers the up-to-date and detailed toy collecting news you need in an easy-to-use format.

A complete marketplace for buyers and sellers of toys, action figures, Barbie, Hot Wheels, character toys, and more, each issue contains thousands of categorized classified ads, display ads and editorial content covering trends, auction outcomes, and show calander

Features entertaining and informative columns including:

- Shop Talk by Mark Rich
- Leave It To Karen by Karen O'Brien
- Take 10 by Rick Kelsey
- Vintage Toy Box by Mark Rich
- Movers and Shakers by Sharon Verbeten
- Retro Rockets by Anthony Taylor
- Figurative Language by Mark Bellomo

Visit www.toyshopmag.com
to subscribe